The Spatial Dynamics of U.S. Urban-Industrial Growth, 1800-1914:
Interpretive and Theoretical Essays

THE REGIONAL SCIENCE STUDIES SERIES
edited by Walter Isard

1 *Location and Space-Economy*
   WALTER ISARD

2 *The Location of the Synthetic-Fiber Industry*
   JOSEPH AIROV

3 *Industrial Complex Analysis and Regional Development*
   WALTER ISARD, EUGENE W. SCHOOLER, AND THOMAS VIETORISZ

4 *Methods of Regional Analysis*
   WALTER ISARD

5 *Domestic Airline Efficiency*
   RONALD E. MILLER

6 *The Spatial Dynamics of U.S. Urban-Industrial Growth: 1800–1914*
   ALLAN R. PRED

The Spatial Dynamics of U.S. Urban-Industrial Growth, 1800-1914:
Interpretive and Theoretical Essays

ALLAN R. PRED

THE M.I.T. PRESS
*Massachusetts Institute of Technology
Cambridge, Massachusetts, and London, England*

LIBRARY
FLORIDA STATE UNIVERSITY
TALLAHASSEE, FLORIDA

Copyright © 1966 by
The Massachusetts Institute of Technology
Designed by Spencer Qualls
set in Times Roman
and printed in the United States of America by
The Heffernan Press

All rights reserved. This book may not be
reproduced, in whole or in part, in any form
(except by reviewers for the public press),
without written permission from the publishers.

Library of Congress catalog card number: 66-26016

Foreword

Dr. Pred's volume is the sixth in the Regional Science Studies Series. It represents an approach which scholars may well claim has been insufficiently developed in the fields of history, geography, regional science, economics, urban planning, and others; but it is an approach that is as essential as any other. It is for this reason that I welcome his investigation in our multidisciplinary Regional Science Studies Series.

Dr. Pred's approach combines the analytic with the descriptive in the study of a basic historical-spatial process — the emergence of an urban pattern and structure in the United States. He boldly sets forth hypotheses such as *circular and cumulative causation.* He unhesitatingly assigns a major role to the spatial framework within which invention takes place and innovation diffuses. He portrays the parallel processes of industrialization and urbanization as spatial interaction phenomena. He does this, exhibiting considerable acumen and skill in the interweaving of diverse empirical materials, unhesitatingly drawing upon the diverse social sciences.

Without question Dr. Pred's interpretations will be seriously questioned. His hypotheses will provoke much critical comment. But all this is to the good for a subject area that has been sadly neglected from the standpoint of analysis. Even the strong statements in his Introduction about the relationship of economic location theory to geographic location theory will generate much disagreement. But in any case his statements, and more important his work itself, will help those of us in the several fields of economics, regional science, geography, urban planning, and human ecology, and in related areas, to sharpen our own concepts of location theory and its relationship to the processes of urbanization and industrialization, and spatial evolution.

WALTER ISARD

Acknowledgments

The acknowledgments presented in an academic work usually assault the reader with a cannonade of familiar, half-familiar and totally unfamiliar names. Rather than get bloodied, the experienced reader generally relents after a paragraph or two, or proceeds directly to the book's substantive matter.

With this in mind, and hoping that personally delivered thanks will suffice for the many helpful and cooperative individuals who contributed to the evolution of this book, I confine my public and especially deepfelt thanks to the following:

To Allan L. Rodgers, of the Department of Geography, The Pennsylvania State University, for convincing me long ago that geographical research should be phrased in problem-oriented terms and that scholarly matter should be read with a rigorously critical eye; to Torsten Hägerstrand, of the Department of Geography, Lund University, because his standards of empirical scholarship and original thinking on spatial processes have, unknown to him, proved an indirect source of inspiration; and to James E. Vance, Jr., my departmental colleague at Berkeley, for the stimulation provided in our innumerable informal discussions.

To Robert Elgie and Richard Peet, for the kind of criticism and encouragement that can be provided only by intelligent and dedicated graduate students.

To the editors of the *Geographical Review, Annals of the Association of American Geographers,* and *East Lakes Geographer* for allowing me to reproduce excerpts from articles written prior to the final shaping of the ideas and research contained in this book.

And last, but not least, to my wife Hjördis, for her understanding and patience while I have devoted long hours to this work.

Berkeley, California ALLAN R. PRED
May, 1966

Contents

Foreword   v

Acknowledgments   vii

1 Introduction   1

2 American Metropolitan Growth: 1860–1914, Industrialization, Initial Advantage   12

    Underlying Theoretical Themes   13
    American Urbanization and Industrialization, 1860–1914   16
    A Model of Urban-Size Growth for Periods of Rapid Industrialization   24
    Components of the Model   29
    Additional Stimulants to Urban-Size Growth   41
    Selective Growth of Cities during Periods of Rapid Industrialization   46
    Concluding Remarks   83

3 Industrial Inventions, Industrial Innovations: Some Locational Relationships with Urban Growth   86

    A Distinction Between Invention and Innovation   88
    The Urban Concentration of Inventive Activity   90
    The Urban Concentration of Industrial Innovations   98
    The Location of U.S. Urban-Industrial Inventions and Innovations: 1860–1900   105
    The Diffusion of Industrial Innovations: Suggestions for a Typology   134
    Concluding Remarks   141

4 The American Mercantile City: 1800–1840, Manufacturing, Growth, and Structure 143

The Economic Functions of the Mercantile City 146
Restraints on Early Nineteenth-Century
    Urban Manufacturing 152
The Manufactures of the Mercantile City 167
A Model of Urban-Size Growth for the American
    Mercantile City: 1800–1840 177
The Selective Growth of American Mercantile Cities 186
The Intraurban Location of Manufacturing 196
Conclusions and Reservations 213

Index 217

The Spatial Dynamics of U.S. Urban-Industrial Growth, 1800-1914:
Interpretive and Theoretical Essays

1

Introduction

Within the urban corpus and its contiguous surroundings the vast majority of contemporary Americans enact their daily income-earning routines, play hide-and-seek with their dreams, delusions, and anxieties, and occasionally encounter the frustrating nightmare of suspended public services. The metropolitan orientation of our frighteningly fecund population has intensified previously existing problems of local transportation networks, race relations, air pollution, water supply, public welfare, and uncoordinated metropolitan government. The telescoped maturation of these problems has of necessity shunted a swelling stream of academic and professional energy into the realm of urban studies. The pressing character of the problems has forced most concerned economists, sociologists, political scientists, geographers, regional scientists, and atmospheric and hydrologic specialists to use the present as a cornerstone in the formulation of future projections, ameliorations, and solutions. Although foresight requires hindsight, lay and scholarly preoccupation with quick answers to pragmatic questions has tended to obscure the need for a more profound comprehension of the past processes of U.S. urban evolution.

If the urban heritage of the United States has not received the scholarly attention it merits, it has by no means been ignored. Commencing with Adna Weber's turn-of-the-century masterpiece,[1] significant works on individual cities, such as those of Albion,[2] Hoyt,[3] and Hand-

---

[1] Adna Ferrin Weber, *The Growth of Cities in the Nineteenth Century* (New York: Columbia University Studies in History, Economics and Public Law, Vol. 11, 1899). Weber's book dealt with European as well as U.S. developments within the context of the then newly born social sciences.

[2] Robert Greenhalgh Albion, *The Rise of New York Port 1815–1860* (New York: Charles Scribner's Sons, 1939).

[3] Homer Hoyt, *One Hundred Years of Land Values in Chicago: The Relation-*

lin,[4] have appeared spasmodically, with more general period studies, such as those of Bridenbaugh[5] and Schlesinger,[6] coming out at even more irregular intervals. In recent years historians have continued to produce urban biographies and period studies of the traditional type,[7] with increasing emphasis placed on the antecedents of today's racial problems.[8] At the same time, the application of modern social science methods and concepts to the interpretation of previous American urban development has begun to gather momentum. Following somewhat less than a decade of almost deafening silence after Lampard's groundbreaking statement,[9] economists interested in economic history have turned some of their inquiries toward the relationships between past economic growth and city expansion in the United States.[10] Concur-

---

ship of the Growth of Chicago to the Rise of its Land Values, 1830–1933 (Chicago: University of Chicago Press, 1933).

[4] Oscar Handlin, *Boston's Immigrants, 1790–1865* (Cambridge: Harvard University Press, 1941).

[5] Carl Bridenbaugh, *Cities in the Wilderness: The First Century of Urban Life in America, 1625–1742* (New York: The Ronald Press, 1938); and *idem, Cities in Revolt: Urban Life in America, 1743–1776* (New York: Alfred A. Knopf, Inc. 1955).

[6] Arthur Meier Schlesinger, *The Rise of the City, 1878–1898* (New York: The Macmillan Company, 1933).

[7] For example, see Constance M. Green, *Washington* (2 vols.; Princeton: Princeton University Press, 1962–1963); and Blake McKelvey, *The Urbanization of America, 1860–1915* (New Brunswick: Rutgers University Press, 1963). Also note the review of the literature by Charles N. Glaab, "The Historian and the American City: A Bibliographic Survey," in Philip M. Hauser and Leo F. Schnore, eds., *The Study of Urbanization* (New York: John Wiley & Sons, Inc., 1965).

[8] See Richard C. Wade, *Slavery in the Cities: The South 1800–1860* (New York: Oxford University Press, Inc., 1964); and Gilbert Osofsky, *Harlem: The Making of a Ghetto — Negro New York, 1890–1930* (New York: Harper & Row, Publishers, 1966).

[9] Eric E. Lampard, "The History of Cities in the Economically Advanced Areas," *Economic Development and Cultural Change*, Vol. 3 (1954–1955), pp. 81–136.

[10] See the collection of papers entitled "The City in Technological Innovation and Economic Development," in Oscar Handlin and John Burchard, eds., *The Historian and the City* (Cambridge: The M.I.T. Press and Harvard University Press, 1963); Eugene Smolensky and Donald Ratajczak, "The Conception of Cities," *Explorations in Entrepreneurial History*, Second Series, Vol. 2 (Winter, 1965), pp. 90–131; Jeffrey G. Williamson, "Antebellum Urbanization in the American Northeast," *Journal of Economic History*, Vol. 25 (1965), pp. 592–608; and other relevant references cited throughout this book. A considerable literature, not considered here, has also developed, in which sociological and economic growth theories have been directly or indirectly applied to the urban dynamics of non-Western societies.

rently, there have been efforts to employ communications theory in dissecting and analyzing specific aspects of urban history.[11]

Despite the growing number of attempts to gain insight into the urban past from a vantage point near the advancing forefront of the social sciences, there have been few contributions that have succeeded in even partially rectifying what Lampard suggested to be the primary shortcoming of U.S. urban historical studies — the inability to view the growth of cities as a *process*. Even in Warner's book, which is emphatically subtitled "The Process of Growth in Boston, 1870–1900,"[12] the result has been long on description and short on concepts relating to the city as a constantly evolving system. With this persistent shortcoming in mind, the three essays contained in this book are intended to form supporting piers for an as yet unconstructed bridge over the gap of ignorance that separates the already existing state of knowledge in the social sciences from a thorough comprehension of nineteenth- and early twentieth-century urban growth processes. The emphasis here is on spatial processes, i.e., on the historical dimension of the two primary themes that permeate both the traditional and modern schools of urban geography, and on the interacting spatial dynamics of urbanization and industrialization. In seeking an understanding of spatial dynamics it is also hoped that some contribution will be made toward the formulation of a geographic, rather than an economic, location theory.

For the uninitiated, it should be pointed out that urban geographers approach the city either as a point in space — a unit influencing functional hinterlands of a variety of sizes, a unit interacting and competing with other units in a system of cities — or as an integral area whose spatial structure and organization (morphology) and functions are to be analyzed.[13] Once the historical dimension is introduced, it is difficult

---

[11] See Richard L. Meier, *A Communications Theory of Urban Growth* (Cambridge: The M.I.T. Press, 1962); and Seymour J. Mandelbaum, *Boss Tweed's New York* (New York: John Wiley & Sons, Inc., 1965). The former work is general in its approach and only indirectly concerned with the history of U.S. urban growth.

[12] Sam B. Warner, Jr., *Streetcar Suburbs: The Process of Growth in Boston, 1870–1900* (Cambridge: Harvard University Press and The M.I.T. Press, 1962).

[13] The most significant portions of the pre-1947 urban geographic literature were synthesized in Robert E. Dickinson, *City Region and Regionalism* (London: Routledge & Kegan Paul, Ltd., 1947). A more recent treatment of the literature of the traditional school of urban geographers is Harold M. Mayer's "A Survey of Urban Geography," in *The Study of Urbanization, op. cit.*, pp. 81–113. The main body of the modern school, which has been preoccupied with statistical

to keep the approaches mutually exclusive, for it is quite plain that as cities grow in population, acquiring new functions and expanding old activities, their interurban and hinterland relationships become altered, while their physical extent and internal arrangement undergo transformation and metamorphosis.

The initiated as well as the uninitiated may well wonder what the author means by his distinction between geographic location theory and economic location theory. Economic location theory, and industrial location theory in particular, has traditionally focused on the firm and individual establishments, and therefore has been prepossessed with optimizing locational behavior, with minimizing transportation costs, with maximizing profits. The output of economists (and economists qua regional scientists) working with these pecuniary and utilitarian objectives is well suited to the contemporary entrepreneur or the city and regional planner who seeks ideal or normative solutions; however, to the economic or urban geographer, whose legitimate realm is interpreting and analyzing the economic landscape and the spatial structure of the economy as it exists, the abstractions and constructs of existing location theory provide only partial insights, for the "real" spatial organization of economic activities is, at any time, the product of both economic *and noneconomic* forces and is comprised of establishments whose locations either permit varying degrees of profit taking, or prohibit the earning of long-run profits, but very rarely allow profit maximization. Thus, there is a need for a geographic location theory (series of descriptive and mathematical models) that would aid in deciphering

---

tests of existing theories and concepts, and which on occasion has confused quantitative analyses with the creation of theory, has had its work reviewed in Brian J. L. Berry's "Research Frontiers in Urban Geography," *ibid.,* pp. 403–430. The bulk of the firepower of the modernists has been directly or indirectly aimed at central place theory, a subject that has been overworked almost to distraction, and a more complete coverage of this aspect of the literature is to be found in Brian J. L. Berry and Allan Pred, *Central Place Studies: A Bibliography of Theory and Applications* (including supplement through 1964 by H. G. Barnum, R. Kasperson, and S. Kiuchi) (Philadelphia: Regional Science Research Institute, 1965). For a well-rounded view of the current interests of urban geographers see the collection of 36 papers in Knut Norborg, ed., *Proceedings of the IGU Symposium in Urban Geography Lund 1960 (Lund Studies in Geography,* Series B, Human Geography, No. 24, 1962). Finally, it should be made clear that the urban geographer's interest in the internal spatial patterns of cities is not a monopoly, but is shared by economists, regional scientists, and "human ecologists," e.g., see works cited in Leo F. Schnore, "On the Spatial Structure of Cities in the Two Americas," in *The Study of Urbanization, op. cit.,* pp. 347–401.

specific spatial manifestations of the economy. Such a body of theory would embellish existing (economic) location theory by taking into account irrational behavior, imperfect knowledge, other psychological variables, socially dictated constraints, and the impact of existing patterns on subsequent patterns (processes). Geographers have taken a few steps in this direction, and those of Torsten Hägerstrand on migration and the diffusion of agricultural innovations are most notable.[14] But the tripartite core of existing location theory — agricultural location theory, industrial location theory, and central place theory — has not really been enlarged upon according to the above formula.[15]

One alternative route toward the formulation of a geographic location theory originates with the consideration of urbanization and industrialization (the cumulative implementation of industrial location decisions) as interacting spatial processes. This joint consideration is justified as a working foundation by the obviously parallel timing of the emergence of concentrated large-scale manufacturing and the meteoric growth of multifunctional metropolises in the developed economies of Europe, North America, and Japan during the last 100 to 200 years.

---

[14] Torsten Hägerstrand, *Innovationsförloppet ur Korologisk Synpunkt* (Lund: Meddelanden från Lunds Universitets Geografiska Institution, Avhandlingar No. 25, 1953), see also *Innovation Diffusion as a Spatial Process,* a translation by Allan Pred, with postscript (Chicago: University of Chicago Press, 1967); and Hägerstrand, "Migration and Area," *Lund Studies in Geography,* Series B, Human Geography, No. 13 (1957), pp. 27–158. Also note Richard L. Morrill, "Migration and the Spread and Growth of Urban Settlement," *ibid.,* No. 26 (1965).

[15] However, an enviable attempt has very recently been made to develop a theoretical framework for interpreting existing industrial location patterns (see D. M. Smith, "A Theoretical Framework for Geographical Studies of Industrial Location," *Economic Geography,* Vol. 42 (1966), pp. 95–113). While this article introduces behavioral variables to a limited extent, and also theoretically considers the locational ramifications of price changes and cost fluctuations (while avoiding any real treatment of spatial competition), it fails to satisfy this author's basic requirement for a geographic location theory; i.e., it fails to identify processes or the impact of patterns prevailing during one time interval on those in the subsequent time interval.

In addition, there have been attempts to put certain aspects of central place theory within an evolutionary stochastic framework (see Morrill, *ibid.;* and *idem,* "Simulation of Central Place Patterns over Time," in *The IGU Symposium on Urban Geography Lund 1960, op. cit.,* pp. 109–120), and, in a not unrelated manner, to apply modified Löschian logic to the intraurban locational dynamics of tertiary activities (James E. Vance, Jr., "Emerging Patterns of Commercial Structure in American Cities," *ibid.,* pp. 485–518). Morrill's ambitious but disappointing monograph is primarily concerned with simulating the end products of processes, rather than dissecting their inner workings, and is only indirectly behavioristic.

It also permits geographic interpretations of industrial concentration, urban-size growth, systems of cities, and the intraurban location of manufacturing to be emancipated from the fetters of the optimalizing assumptions of Alfred Weber's original industrial location theory and its modern revisions.[16] Thus visually freed from narrow horizons, urban and economic geographic questions can be answered, as in this book, not only by invoking traditional location theory, but also by employing such concepts as the principle of circular and cumulative causation, the adaptive versus adoptive dichotomy of locational behavior, the converging and dovetailing character of manufacturing inventions and innovations, and the stage of transportation.[17]

This optional approach and its corollary concepts, which are elaborated upon in a skeletal fashion in the three essays that follow, represents but one example among many alternative ways of thinking. One need not, for example, confine himself to depicting industrialization and urbanization as interacting spatial processes. One might instead consider all the geographic reflections of economic growth as interacting spatial processes.[18] By so doing, changing agricultural land-use and production patterns can be incorporated into the scheme of generalizations.[19] Such a broad approach would also be somewhat akin to the present inclination of some "human ecologists" to view the "ecological complex" affecting human spatial distributions as being comprised of

[16] Alfred Weber, *Theory of the Location of Industries* (translated, with an introduction and notes by Carl J. Friedrich, Chicago: University of Chicago Press, 1929). Walter Isard has put Weber in an equilibrium context and generally made the most significant modifications of the theory in *Location and Space-Economy* (New York: John Wiley & Sons, Inc., and The M.I.T. Press, 1956).

[17] The treatment of urbanization and industrialization as interacting spatial processes also facilitates the construction of projection-oriented economic models of urban growth. See John H. Neidercorn and John F. Kain, "An Econometric Model of Metropolitan Development," *Papers and Proceedings of the Regional Science Association*, Vol. 11 (1963), pp. 123–143; and Stanislaw Czamanski, "A Model of Urban Growth," *ibid.*, Vol. 13 (1964), pp. 177–200.

[18] The possibility of theoretically intertwining locational and economic growth processes has been suggested by, among others, Bert F. Hoselitz in his call for "a theory in which the development of a given system of cities is related to processes of economic growth." "Generative and Parasitic Cities," *Economic Development and Cultural Change*, Vol. 3 (1954–1955), p. 293.

[19] For a tentative attempt to interrelate theoretically the spatial patterns of urban growth and agricultural production during the initial-rapid-industrialization phase of economic growth see Allan Pred, *The External Relations of Cities during 'Industrial Revolution'* (Chicago: University of Chicago, Department of Geography, Research Paper No. 76, 1962), pp. 44–56.

interacting environmental, technological, demographic, and organizational variables,[20] and therefore would promise the fruits of closely parallel research. However, regardless of the alternative chosen, the problem of developing geographic location theory remains one of being more precise and explicit in interpreting previous and ongoing empirical observations and field studies, and of synthesizing and conceptually embellishing these observations so as to identify those spatial processes that yield an ever-dynamic, ever-fluid, geographic organization of economic activity.

This emphasis on process may justifiably cause some to clamor that the geographic location theory sought, if at all attainable, is in reality an attempt to transmute economic location theory into a retrospective, *evolutionary* location theory. At best, such accusations can only degenerate into a fruitless debate on subtle semantic questions that have no absolute answers. It may be equally well contended, either that any geographic location theory must definitionally be evolutionary, insofar as all spatial patterns are to varying degrees dependent on past events; or that any evolutionary location theory must definitionally be geographic, insofar as it seeks to identify and systematize the dynamic regularities of economic-geographic phenomena.

This book then is an overture, a prelude to more detailed studies to be carried out in the future. Its three integrated themes are condensations of as yet unscored, longer, and more specific orchestral works dealing with the spatial dynamics of U.S. urban-industrial growth during the nineteenth and early twentieth centuries; its over-all structure, its component tempos, rhythms, timbres, and key shifts, is governed by the anticipated but far-off construction of a geographic location theory relating spatial processes to economic growth processes.

The first theme (essay) centers on the interval of time between the Civil War and World War I, a period when the bonds between the growth of inordinately large concentrations of manufacturing and metropolitan expansion were more closely knit than in any prior or subsequent era of U.S. history. An attempt is made to answer two questions: How and why do cities expand precipitately during periods of rapid industrialization? Why do some cities grow more rapidly than, and at the expense of, other cities? The theme is spun out, and the questions respectively answered, first by erecting a descriptive model that envisions urban-size growth as a circular and cumulative process, and

---

[20] See Schnore, *loc. cit.*

second by introducing a number of ambivalent forces that simultaneously slowed the process in some units in the evolving system of cities and precipitated the emergence of multimillion metropolises in others by accelerating the operation of that same circular and cumulative chain of events. Of necessity, throughout most of this essay the city is treated as a point in space, although the appearance of electric traction is treated as an agency that permitted certain cities to continue to grow at the expense of others by facilitating important changes in their internal structure and physical extent.

The theme of the second essay derives directly from the first. With full recognition of the initial essay's incomplete emphasis on the late nineteenth-century American city's increasing propensity for invention and innovation (a propensity that supposedly devolved from an increasingly more complex network of interpersonal communications and confrontations in an expanding urban population), and while acknowledging the resurgent concern of economists with the interplay between technological progress and economic growth, an exploration is undertaken of the locational relationships between industrial inventions, industrial innovations, and urban growth. Once again, two questions are posed: To what degree, and why, are manufacturing inventions and innovations a function of the size and rate of growth of cities during that period (the post-Civil War decades in the United States) when the foundations of an economy complete their metamorphosis from the commercial-mercantile to the industrial-capitalistic? How, at any period of time, and especially in the era prior to the institutionalization of industrial-technological development, do (did) the spatial patterns of innovation diffusion for different broad categories of urban-industrial activity theoretically behave and vary from one another?[21] Almost ineluctably, a large portion of this essay consists of a synthesis of the invention and innovation literature and an endeavor to give it an until now nonexistent spatial dimension. In much of the remaining segment, which uses manufacturing patent statistics as a springboard, the city is alternately considered as a growing unit competing with other points in space, and as an integral area whose internal geographic organization has a profound influence on the circulation of information and on in-

[21] Much of the inspiration for this essay, and the specific questions propounded within it, can be traced to the opening chapter of Abbot Payson Usher's *A History of Mechanical Inventions* (revised edition; Cambridge: Harvard University Press, 1954).

dividual exposure to stimuli crucial to industrial invention and innovation in a pre-mass-communications environment.

The final essay reverts to an earlier period (1800–1840) when the economy of the country's major cities was predominantly commercial and had not as yet fully entered the transition to an industrial, multifunctional base. No fewer than four questions are set forth regarding the process of urban growth and role of industry in the American mercantile city during these formative decades: What factors militated against the location of additional manufacturing activities in the larger commercial cities? Why were existing industries located in New York, Boston, Philadelphia, and Baltimore? In the absence of a primary stimulus from manufacturing, how did the urban growth process function, and how did selective urban growth occur within a rudimentary system of cities? What forces operated in shaping the intraurban locational patterns of specific industries? The answers to the first two questions serve both as a means of explaining why the circular and cumulative process of urban-size growth did not function as it did in the post-Civil War era, and as a foundation for replying to the third question. The key to the third two-pronged query again is found in a descriptive model of circular and cumulative causation, with a number of ambivalent forces eventually inserted to account for different expansion patterns and the growth of some cities at the expense of others. So as to avoid falling into the trap of depicting urban growth as something that occurs in discrete stages rather than as a continuous process, the 1800–1840 model is developed in such a way as to be self-converting; i.e., it can be extended to cover the 1840–1860 transition period, and it can metamorphose itself into the post-1860 model. The last question returns to the city's spatial structure and is partially designed to demonstrate that at this relatively early date, just as in the future when U.S. cities were no longer extremely compact, the intraurban permutations of industrial location were influenced by transportation technology, real estate costs, and the need of some firms to realize "communication economies" or to take advantage of interindustry linkages.

The focus and detailed treatment of the final question will undoubtedly impress some as an abrupt detour from the course followed in the remainder of the book. This is so, and it is intentionally so. Because the very nature of all three essays demands that the internal geography of the city take a back seat to the city as a point in space, the last question is in part intended as no more than an aside, as an indicator of the wealth of materials that are largely untapped and whose exploitation promises a deeper comprehension of the configuration of our present-day central cities.

Answers to the questions in each of the essays require inescapable excursions into economics, economic history, and, to a lesser degree, the behavioral sciences. No apology need be proffered for these wanderings from the path of traditional academic geography; for in the contemporary world of scholarship the peripheral areas between all social and behavioral disciplines have grown increasingly hazy, while their cores have become more identifiable by the problems they single out for study rather than by the methods and concepts they employ.[22] In other words, the orientation of this book is geographical, its question-posing format is largely a device to emphasize the author's geographical perspective, but, without defensive trepidation, its themes are followed into alien territory whenever they lead there. The book's geographical approach is underscored by its concern with areas and points in space that are integral from both a functional and developmental point of view, a concern that stands in contrast to the statistically convenient groups of states that are often validly used, but also frequently misused, by economists and others.[23]

If no excuses are attempted for straying occasionally into a no man's land where several disciplines overlap and intersect, some qualifying clarifications must be made in other terms. First, the interpretations and models presented are not conceived of as reproductions of reality, but as means for gaining insight into that reality, into some of the past

---

[22] Note Rollo Hardy and Paul Kurtz, *A Current Appraisal of the Behavioral Sciences* (Great Barrington, Mass.: Behavioral Research Council, 1963); and the comments of a young geographer on this examination in Peter Gould, "Joshua's Trumpet: The Crumbling Walls of the Social and Behavioral Sciences," *Geographical Review*, Vol. 55 (1965), pp. 599–602.

[23] See, for example, the "regional" groups of states used in analyzing certain aspects of U.S. economic growth in Harvey S. Perloff and others, *Regions, Resources and Economic Growth* (Baltimore: The Johns Hopkins Press, 1960); and Simon Kuznets and others, "Population Redistribution and Economic Growth: United States, 1870–1950," *Memoirs of the American Philosophical Society,* Vols. 45, 51, 61 (1957, 1960, 1961). Among the more questionable features of these groupings is the repeated treatment of the six New England states as a viable economic whole. The results of such a treatment can often be undermined by the fact that southwestern Connecticut and much of the Connecticut River Valley have historically had, and at present still have, stronger economic ties with the New York Metropolitan Region than with the remainder of New England.

and, by extension, present geographical expressions of economic growth in the United States. Many of the hypotheses introduced beg further testing (based on primary source materials), modification, and, in some instances, rejection and reformulation. At the very least, there would seem to be a need for a probing of the 1840–1860 transition period, a refinement of the model for that same era, an empirical investigation of specific nineteenth-century industrial innovation diffusions, an exploration of the questions raised at the end of the second essay, and depth applications of the models to individual cities.

Second, although a number of previously untapped source materials are called into play, such as the locational information contained in late nineteenth-century Patent Office publications (second essay) and early nineteenth-century New York City directories (third essay), the intent is to synthesize, reinterpret, and formalize the rapidly growing mass of published concepts, facts and statistics[24] relating to the American economic and geographic past, rather than to compile new materials. This methodology is justified by the sweeping scope of the questions posed, the parallel effort to work toward a geographic location theory, and the volume of relevant material already in print. Finally, it must be reiterated that this volume is a start, a preliminary to more detailed and elaborate empirical and theoretical studies to be carried out by the author and, hopefully, by other geographers.[25] One aim beyond penetrative illumination, therefore, has been to provoke rather than to provide proofs that pretend to unimpregnability. And certainly the points of possible controversy are plentiful. Hopefully, more problems are suggested than questions answered. Only if this is the case is there any promise of ultimately contriving a meaningful simulator of urban-industrial geographic patterns.

[24] Some of the more significant, recently published, data collections and analyses include Kuznets and others, *ibid.; Trends in the American Economy in the Nineteenth Century* (A Report of the National Bureau of Economic Research; Princeton: Princeton University Press, 1960); and several other reports of the National Bureau of Economic Research.

[25] One such study has already been completed by one of the author's students, Robert Elgie, *The Development of Manufacturing in San Francisco in the Period from 1848 to 1880: An Analysis of Regional Locational Factors and Urban Spatial Structure* (Berkeley: University of California, Berkeley, Department of Geography, unpublished M.A. thesis, 1966).

American Metropolitan Growth: 1860-1914

Industrialization, Initial Advantage

The spatial, as well as the economic and social, processes of nineteenth- and twentieth-century urbanization and industrialization are not independent. The phenomena that led to the concurrent emergence of the modern American metropolis and large-scale manufacturing are dynamically involuted and nearly always inseparable.[1] Urbanization, as in the case of Miami or Washington, D. C., is not inexorably associated with industrial growth;[2] yet, conversely, the multiplication of factories, product output, and markets since 1860 is virtually synonymous with city development. That the largest urban concentrations have played a monumental role in American industrial expansion is underscored by the fact that, in 1962, 38.3 per cent of the nation's value added by manufacture was accounted for by eleven metropolises, which in turn contained 27.3 per cent of the total 1960 population.[3]

---

[1] Some of the more durable cogent statements concerning the interrelationships between urbanization and industrialization are contained in Eric E. Lampard, "The History of Cities in the Economically Advanced Areas," *Economic Development and Cultural Change*, Vol. 3 (1954–1955), pp. 81–136; and in R. D. McKenzie, "The Rise of Metropolitan Communities," in *Recent Social Trends in the United States: Report of the President's Research Committee on Social Trends* (New York: McGraw-Hill, Inc., 1933), Vol. 1, pp. 443–496.

[2] The bonds between urban and manufacturing expansion are obviously less pronounced in non-Western traditional societies. For statistical comparisons see Thomas O. Wilkinson, "Urban Structure and Industrialization," *American Sociological Review*, Vol. 25 (1960), pp. 356–363.

[3] Based on U.S. Bureau of the Census, *1962 Annual Survey of Manufactures* (Washington, D. C.: 1963, 1964); and *Census of Population: 1960* (Washington, D. C.: 1961), Vol. 1, Part A, p. 1-66 [Table 28]. The Bureau of the Census statistics for both population and value added by manufacturing fail to do full

The complex reciprocals of urbanization and industrialization are crucial girders in the superstructure of economic growth. Perhaps because capital formation, investment, and technological progress are viewed as this entity's most significant components, economists and others have logically and legitimately emphasized their part in the growth process, and have conducted only limited theoretical inquiries into the spatial interaction of urban and manufacturing growth.[4] Within this context, the concentration of much of American manufacturing and population in eleven metropolises leads one to pose at least two questions basic to the dynamics of urban-economic geography: How and why do cities expand precipitately during periods of rapid industrialization? Why do some cities grow more rapidly than, and at the expense of, other cities? No fewer than three traditional frameworks of locational thinking provide theoretical ammunition with which to assault these two questions.

Underlying Theoretical Themes

Superficially, intellectual derivations from Weberian and Marshallian agglomeration and scale economies provide the most potentially fruit-

---

justice to the importance of the country's eleven largest metropolises (SMSAs). In each of the multimillion metropolises there is a high degree of spatial and economic interaction between the "central city" and an area within a radius of approximately 50 miles from that core. However, because of inconsistencies in delimitation, in individual cases the correspondence between SMSA population and the functionally integrated population within a 50-mile radius varies from close association (e.g., the 1960 50-mile radius figures for Los Angeles exceed the SMSA datum by 300,000) to considerable discrepancy (e.g., the 5,089,380 population within a 50-mile radius of Boston is almost twice the total given for the SMSA). In every instance the 50-mile radius statistics are larger, see *U.S. Bureau of the Census Geographic Reports,* GE-10, No. 1 (April, 1963), and it is reasonable to assume that if comparable value-added statistics were available they would be similarly augmented.

[4] This is not to imply that the spatial aspects of economic growth have been totally ignored. For some of the efforts in this area see Walter Isard, "Transportation Development and Building Cycles," *Quarterly Journal of Economics,* Vol. 57 (Nov., 1942), pp. 90–112; Lampard, *loc. cit.;* Wolfgang Stolper, "Spatial Order and the Economic Growth of Cities," *Economic Development and Cultural Change,* Vol. 3 (1954–1955), pp. 137–146; John R. P. Friedmann, "Locational Aspects of Economic Development," *Land Economics,* Vol. 32 (1956), pp. 213–227; Walter Isard, *Location and Space-Economy* (New York: John Wiley & Sons, Inc., 1956), pp. 1–23; Benjamin Chinitz, "The Effect of Transportation Forms on Regional Economic Growth," *Traffic Quarterly,* Vol. 14 (1960), pp. 129–142; and Eugene Smolensky and Donald Ratajczak, "The Conception of Cities," *Explorations in Entrepreneurial History,* Second Series, Vol. 2 (Winter, 1965), pp. 90–131.

ful source of theoretical concepts. The unique array of scale, localization, and urbanization economies available at urban industrial sites is frequently employed to explain the industrial growth and specialization of metropolitan centers. The city's internal and external manufacturing economies were presumably of particular importance during the late nineteenth century. At that time individual firms were in a position both to minimize the internalization or absorption of external diseconomies and to maximize the reduction of per unit input costs "through acquisitions, combinations, or mergers with closely interdependent economic activities."[5] While these and other related observations are helpful in contributing to an understanding of why manufacturing grows in cities, they are an inadequate means with which to achieve a comprehension of the precise dynamics of city-size growth, despite the fact that agglomeration economies imply that manufacturing on a grand scale must be limited to a few cities. Even if these observations were of more explicit assistance, it should be pointed out that "the concept of external economies is at best only one among a number of possible keys to the understanding of modern city development."[6]

The possible interrelationships between central-place theory and the urbanization-industrialization syndrome are somewhat less obvious, especially in view of the criticism that has been leveled at Christaller's theory for its failure to deal with the location of manufacturing activities. Attempts to apply central place theory to dynamic problems of urban growth have admittedly exaggerated the role of business and service activities and generally emphasized small urban places at the expense of the multimillion metropolis.[7] However, these shortcomings aside, central-place theory may be combined with Löschian market area hypotheses to provide two basic avenues of approach to the questions under investigation. One is the threshold concept, from which it can be inferred that industries "oriented" toward local or regional markets will not appear in cities until their local or regional thresholds are attained.

---

[5] Albert O. Hirschman, *The Strategy of Economic Development* (New Haven: Yale Studies in Economics, No. 10, 1958), p. 58.

[6] Alexander Gerschenkron, "City Economies — Then and Now," in Oscar Handlin and John Burchard, eds., *The Historian and the City* (Cambridge: The M.I.T. Press and Harvard University Press, 1963), p. 58.

[7] See, for example, H. Carter, "The Urban Hierarchy and Historical Geography: A Consideration with Reference to North-east Wales," *Geographical Studies*, Vol. 3 (1956), pp. 85–101; and Richard L. Morrill, "The Development of Spatial Distributions of Towns in Sweden: An Historical-Predictive Approach," *Annals of the Association of American Geographers*, Vol. 53 (1963), pp. 1–14.

Second, if the schema of a hierarchy of market areas is extended to include manufacturing activities, the largest or most nodal cities will logically have the greatest variety of manufacturing functions. Although both the detailed implications of, and the supporting evidence for, this elementary translation of central-place theory from tertiary to secondary activities remain to be spelled out, such a translation cannot in itself provide complete insight into the interlocking spatial processes of urbanization and industrialization.

Of the several other ingredients to be added to this theoretical amalgamation, the concept of initial advantage is probably most important. Initial advantage is here employed as an umbrella to cover three overlapping ideas: that existing locations are usually characterized by tremendous inertia and a temporal compounding of advantages; that existing locations often exert considerable influence on subsequent plant location decisions; and that once concentration is initiated it has a self-perpetuating momentum.[8] These three ideas contribute substantially to one of the major themes of this essay, namely that some centers, through the medium of rapid industrialization, generate their own conditions for growth into multimillion metropolises, and that such centers are usually those possessing relative initial advantages. A rationale for viewing urban and industrial growth as an interrelated process, with each stage of development being a function of previous stages, is contained within Gunnar Myrdal's succinctly stated "principle of circular and cumulative causation." Myrdal contends that "In the normal case a change does not call forth contradicting forces but, instead, supporting changes, which move the system in the same direction but much further. Because of such circular causation a social process tends to become cumulative and often to gather speed at an accelerated rate."[9]

---

[8] See Edward L. Ullman, "Regional Development and the Geography of Concentration," *Papers and Proceedings, Regional Science Association,* Vol. 4 (4th Annual Meeting, 1957), Philadelphia, 1958, pp. 179–198.

[9] Gunnar Myrdal, *Rich Lands and Poor* (New York: Harper Brothers, World Perspectives, Vol. 16, 1957), p. 13. For related statements on cumulative growth and initial advantage see Bertil Ohlin, *Interregional and International Trade* (Cambridge: Harvard Economic Studies, Vol. 39, 1933), pp. 235–236; Hirschman, *op. cit.,* p. 5; Harvey S. Perloff and others, *Regions, Resources and Economic Growth* (Baltimore: The Johns Hopkins Press, 1960), p. 82; Joseph A. Schumpeter, *The Theory of Economic Development* (translated by Redvers Opie; new printing; New York: Oxford University Press, 1961), pp. 9 and 64; and Wilbur R. Thompson, *A Preface to Urban Economics* (Baltimore: The Johns Hopkins Press, 1965), pp. 17–18.

Of course, all cities would grow indefinitely if urban-industrial growth were merely an uninterrupted process of circular and cumulative causation. Therefore it is imperative to elaborate explicitly the means by which initial advantages favor some cities at the expense of others.

American Urbanization and Industrialization, 1860–1914

If it is contended that the emergence of inordinately large concentrations of manufacturing in the United States' greatest metropolises is a function of agglomeration economies, the fulfillment of successive market thresholds, and initial advantage, then, prior to the spelling out of a growth model, the period when these forces were most operative should be identified and outlined; for there comes a time when tertiary activities supplant manufacturing as the principal component, if not the determinant, of urban-size growth.[10]

If the late 1840's and 1850's constituted the first youthful burst of American industrialization outside of the textile industries, then the 1860's may be regarded as the onset of adulthood within the continuum of U.S. urban and manufacturing growth. The share of manufacturing in the nation's total commodity output rose from 32 per cent in 1860 to 53 per cent in 1900,[11] and in the ensuing ten years manufacturing production burgeoned almost as much as it had in the previous thirty-year span (Table 2.1). "In 1860 the product of our manufacturing industries was valued at less than $2,000,000,000 and our factories and work shops employed about 1,300,000 wage earners. In 1914, the last year for which we have a comparable dollar, the product had multiplied by more than twelve and exceeded $24,000,000,000, while the number of wage earners had increased over fivefold, to slightly above 7,000,000."[12] In short, in the decades after 1860 the economy completed its transition from an agricultural and commercial-mercantilistic

---

[10] The importance of manufacturing is merely subordinated, not completely replaced, once business, service, and professional activities have become the principal element of metropolitan-size growth. Although significant, the mechanisms through which tertiary activities induce the growth of some cities and not others are not treated at length in this essay. Presumably, tertiary activities play an important role even when the industrial sector dominates the urban growth process.

[11] Robert E. Gallman, "Commodity Output, 1839–1899," in *Trends in the American Economy in the Nineteenth Century* (A Report of the National Bureau of Economic Research; Princeton: Princeton University Press, 1960), p. 26.

[12] Victor S. Clark, *History of Manufactures in the United States* (New York: McGraw-Hill, Inc., 1929), Vol. 3, p. 351.

TABLE 2.1 The Urbanization and Industrialization of the United States, 1860–1910

		1860	1870	1880	1890	1900	1910	% increase 1860–1910
A.	Total U.S. Population (1000's)	31,513	39,905	50,262	63,056	76,094	92,407	193.2
B.	Total Urban Population (1000's)	6,217	9,902	14,130	22,106	30,160	41,999	575.6
C.	Population in Cities > 100,000 (1000's)	2,639	4,130	6,211	9,698	14,208	20,302	669.3
	B/A	19.7	24.8	28.1	35.1	39.6	45.5	—
	C/A	8.4	10.3	12.4	15.4	18.7	22.0	—
	Cities 10,000–100,000/A	6.4	8.5	9.1	12.3	13.0	15.0	—
	Cities 2,500–10,000/A	5.0	6.0	6.6	7.4	8.0	8.6	—
	Miles of Railroad Operated[a]	30,626	52,922	93,262	166,703	206,631	266,185	769.1
	Rails Produced (1000's of long tons)	183	554	1,305	1,885	2,386	3,636	—
	Pig Iron Production (1000's of long tons)	821	1,665	3,835	9,203	13,789	27,304	—
	Steel Ingots and Castings Produced (1000's of long tons)	11.8	68.8	1,247	4,277	10,188	26,095	—
	Index of Manufacturing Production (1899 = 100)	16	25	42	71	100	172	975.0

SOURCES: U.S. Bureau of the Census, *Historical Statistics of the United States, Colonial Times to 1957* (Washington, D. C.: 1960), pp. 14, 427, 429; and Edwin Frickey, *Production in the United States 1860–1914* (Cambridge: Harvard University Press, 1947), pp. 10–11, 54.

[a] Not including yard tracks and sidings.

base to an industrial-capitalistic one.[13] Concomitantly, the top of the urban hierarchy became characterized more and more by industrial, multifunctional cities, and less and less by cities dominated by mercantilistic wholesaling and trading functions.

"By the 'fifties the more far-sighted leaders of midwestern communities had realized that potential growth was limited so long as it was based exclusively on commerce. The editor of the Cleveland *Leader* declared: '. . . no thinking man with capital will stop here when we leave only commerce to sustain us. A manufacturing town gives a man full scope for his ambitions.' "[14] This emerging attitude combined with the demands and opportunities created by the Civil War[15] to provide a considerable stimulus to previously initiated industrialization, and to the momentum of urban growth throughout the country[16] (e.g., in Philadelphia alone, between 1862 and 1864 the city's industrial facilities had an annual increment of about 60 factories).[17] Before this crucial period, and before the nation's railroad network was fully articulated, markets for locally manufactured goods were not a primary concern of urban business interests. But by 1865 the attention of the financial solons of Boston, New York, and other mercantile cities was "no longer focused primarily upon foreign commerce," and had instead "turned to manu-

---

[13] Noteworthily, the decade 1860–1870 was the first in U.S. history during which the absolute increase in urban population exceeded the absolute increase in rural population.

[14] Lampard, *op. cit.*, p. 121.

[15] For example, it is frequently pointed out that the war hastened the maturation of the agricultural machinery industry (by creating a farm-labor shortage), and the sewing machine and standardized clothing industries (by requiring quick delivery of large military uniform consignments).

[16] There has been some questioning of the positive impact of the Civil War upon American manufacturing development. Stephen Salsbury's "The Effect of the Civil War on American Industrial Development," and Thomas C. Cochran's "Did the Civil War Retard Industrialization: A Re-Examination," (*Mississippi Valley Historical Review*, Vol. 48 [Sept., 1961], pp. 197–210), are respectively the strongest pro and con statements. Both are available in Ralph Andreano, ed., *The Economic Impact of the American Civil War* (Cambridge, Mass.: Schenkman Publishing Co., 1962), pp. 148–168. There is little inclination to be detoured by this dispute, especially since Frickey's index of manufacturing production shows an increase of over 50 per cent between 1860 and 1870 (Table 2.1), and since Cochran himself confesses, "Two indirect effects of the war aided industrial growth to degrees that cannot accurately be measured. These were, first, a more satisfactory money market, and secondly, more security for entrepreneurial activity than in the prewar period."

[17] Victor S. Clark, "Manufacturing Development During the Civil War," in Andreano, *ibid.*, p. 47 (article originally published in *Military Historian and Economist*, Vol. 3 [1918], pp. 92–100).

facturing and the distribution of its products to domestic markets."[18] Contemporary entrepreneurs had been won over to the sentiment that " 'The encouragement of the manufacturing industries is the most direct and most lucrative method of increasing the wealth of a community.' "[19]

By 1910 evolving systems of mass production had been made economical by the development of mass domestic markets, despite periodic interruptions by inflation, protracted deflation, and depression (even in the seventies, when prices were tumbling and commerce was slumping, manufacturing output grew at a high rate). Within a span of fifty years, much of which Rostow would be inclined to label "the drive to maturity,"[20] the United States relinquished its status as a secondary industrial nation and attained a position of manufactural pre-eminence.[21] Clark went so far as to state that the experience of these years constituted "a greater quantitative expansion of industry than [that] in all the previous history of the race."[22]

Clearly, then, by 1910 the modern industrialization of the United States was an accomplished fact, and its major metropolises, with their newly integrated suburban dependencies, were more than commercial entrepôts. Within this context it is not surprising to find the contention that before 1910 "industry rather than commerce was the chief source of urban growth."[23] This position is most vividly borne out by the changes in employment composition and worker productivity that occurred in some of the country's most important cities between 1860 and 1890 (Table 2.2. Similar alterations in the following score of years

---

[18] Edward Chase Kirkland, *Men, Cities, and Transportation: A Study in New England History 1820–1900* (Cambridge: Harvard University Press, 1948), Vol. 2, p. 268.

[19] Cited in *idem, Industry Comes of Age* (New York: Holt, Rinehart & Winston, 1962), p. 163.

[20] W. W. Rostow, *The Stages of Economic Growth* (Cambridge, England: Cambridge University Press, 1960), p. 59.

[21] "It has been estimated that in 1860 the value of manufactured goods in each of the three leading countries, the United Kingdom, France, and Germany, was greater than in the United States. By 1890 the United States had not only moved into first place, but the value of its manufactures nearly equaled the combined output of the three former leaders." L. C. A. Knowles, *Economic Development in the Nineteenth Century* (London: London School of Economics and Political Science Monographs: Studies in Economics and Political Science, No. 109, 1932), p. 201. See also George Rogers Taylor and Irene D. Neu, *The American Railroad Network 1861–1890* (Cambridge: Harvard University Press, 1956), p. 1.

[22] Clark, *History of Manufactures in the United States, op. cit.*, Vol. 2, p. 6.

[23] Blake McKelvey, *The Urbanization of America, 1860–1915* (New Brunswick: Rutgers University Press, 1963), p. 45.

TABLE 2.2 *Growth of Manufacturing Employment and Value Added in Ten U.S. Cities: 1860–1890*

	Employment in manufacturing		% of population in manufacturing	
	1860	1890	1860	1890
New York	106,216[a]	477,186	9.0	19.0
Philadelphia	98,983	260,264	17.5	24.9
Chicago	5,360	210,366	4.8	19.1
St. Louis	9,352	94,051	5.8	20.8
Boston	19,283	90,805	10.8	20.2
Baltimore	17,054	83,745	8.0	19.3
Pittsburgh	8,837	56,438	18.0	23.7
San Francisco	1,503	48,446	2.6	16.2
Cleveland	3,462	50,674	8.0	19.4
Detroit	2,350	38,178	5.2	18.5

	Value added in 1879 prices[b] (thousands)		% of national value added	
	1860	1890	1860	1890
New York	$91,537.1[a]	$611,804.1	10.2	13.6
Philadelphia	69,738.5	297,459.3	7.8	6.6
Chicago	5,027.2[c]	283,443.9	.6	6.4
St. Louis	9,434.7[c]	119,773.7	1.1	2.7
Boston	17,921.1	117,974.1	2.0	2.6
Baltimore	8,881.7	76,107.9	1.0	1.7
Pittsburgh	6,368.0[c]	63,702.8	.7	1.4
San Francisco	1,501.4[d]	63,805.6	.2	1.4
Cleveland	2,331.8[c]	53,305.8	.3	1.2
Detroit	1,611.3[c]	40,310.5	.2	.9
Total			24.1[e]	38.5[e]

	Value added per worker in 1879 prices[b]			1860	1890
	1860	1890			
New York	$ 861.8	$1,386.9	Baltimore	$520.8	$908.8
Philadelphia	704.5	1,142.9	Pittsburgh	720.6	1,128.7
Chicago	937.9	1,347.4	San Francisco	998.9	1,317.0
St. Louis	1,008.8	1,267.4	Cleveland	673.6	1,051.9
Boston	929.4	1,299.2	Detroit	685.7	1,055.9

SOURCES: 8th Census of the U.S., 1860, *Statistics of the United States* (Washington, D. C.: 1866), p. xviii; idem, *Manufactures of the United States in 1860* (Washington, D. C.: 1865); 11th Census of the U.S., 1890, *Report of Manufacturing Industries in the United States* (Washington, D. C.: 1895), Parts I, II; Gallman (see footnote 11), p. 43; Clarence D. Long, *Wages and Earnings in the United States 1860–1890* (A Study by the National Bureau of Economic Research; Princeton: Princeton University Press, 1960), p. 84; and *Census of Population: 1960* (see footnote 3), p. 1–66.

[a] "New York and its boroughs as constituted under the act of consolidation in 1898." *Census of Population: 1960, op. cit.,* p. 1–67.

ᵇ Derived from Gallman's national price index for value added by manufacturing.

ᶜ Estimated from value of production figures for each city, and respective county value added data (value of production minus cost of raw materials). In all five cases the city's share of county value of production was so high that the magnitude of error for the value-added estimates is presumably quite small.

ᵈ In order to compensate for extreme inflation in San Francisco, the city's value added was reduced on the basis of regional wage differentials presented by Long.

ᵉ Los Angeles, whose growth did not really gain momentum until some time after 1890, is not included in this table because of the absence of adequate 1860 statistics.

are obscured by the elimination of "neighborhood and hand" industries from the manufacturing census, by an increased ratio of administrative personnel to factory hands, and by the suburbanization of large producing units).[24] Although the observed relationship between industrialization and the expansion of cities is elementary, recognition of this relationship is crucial to acceptance of the urban-size growth model to be presented here. That this relationship has weakened, and that urban-size growth since World War I has been perpetuated more by tertiary activities than by manufacturing, is most clearly reflected by the fact that the percentage of population gainfully employed in the latter sector has been decreasing at the expense of the former.[25] Because manufacturing apparently continued to be the prime inducer of urban expansion for a few years beyond 1910, it was not until the appearance of the 1930 census that it became apparent "that the factors involved in metropolitan growth . . . were primarily commercial and institutional, with industry playing a relatively smaller role."[26] Economists usually attribute this shift in sectoral employment to the different income elasticities of demand for the goods and services of industrial and tertiary activities, and to simultaneous increases of real product per man-hour in manufacturing greater than those in other sectors of the economy.[27]

[24] McKelvey apparently had these last-named considerations in mind when, although he argued that manufacturing was the principal urban growth stimulus until a date beyond the turn of the century, he also pointed out that after 1890 most large industrial cities began "to show a more rapid increase in tradesmen and white-collar workers than in factory hands." *Ibid.,* pp. 50–51.

[25] See, for example, the collection of data in H. Dewey Anderson and Percy E. Davidson, *Occupational Trends in the United States* (Stanford University Press, 1940).

[26] McKenzie, *op. cit.,* p. 493. McLaughlin noted that the rate of manufacturing growth in most industrial metropolises had slumped by 1919. Glenn E. McLaughlin, *Growth of American Manufacturing Areas* (Pittsburgh: University of Pittsburgh, Bureau of Business Research Monographs, No. 7, 1938), pp. 203–204.

[27] Stigler has attested to the relevancy of this well-known thesis (originally put forth by Colin Clark) to twentieth-century U.S. employment trends. George

The impetus manufacturing provided to urban growth between 1860 and 1910 is crudely manifested by Table 2.1, which reveals that manufacturing output increased at a pace surpassing the growth rates of national population, urban population, and population in large cities. Manufacturing also outstripped the development of railroad facilities vital to its raw-material assembly and finished-product distribution. However, the extension of markets and the alterations in average scale of production, which were the outward expressions of rapid industrial growth, can be seen in their proper perspective only in relation to certain railroad developments: intensification of trunk lines, spread of feeder lines, and integration of fragmented operating units; technical improvement of motive drawing power, rails, roadbeds, terminal facilities, and freight-car carrying capacity (up to 50 tons in the larger cars); financing innovations adopted by industrial enterprises; precipitation of an enormous demand for steel rails, steam engines, and rolling stock; and elaboration of consumer demand through wages paid to line employees and construction workers.[28]

A generous part of post-Civil War urban growth occurred in those cities and suburbs that now comprise the country's eleven most important industrial metropolises, and which contained almost 41 per

---

J. Stigler, *Trends in Employment in the Service Industries* (A Study of the National Bureau of Economic Research; Princeton: Princeton University Press, 1960), p. 165. Fuchs has tentatively concluded that "Between 1929 and 1961 the rate of growth of output per man in the goods sector was 1.7 per cent per annum more rapid than in the service sector." Victor R. Fuchs, *Productivity Trends in the Goods and Service Sectors, 1929–1961: A Preliminary Survey* (New York: National Bureau of Economic Research, Occasional Paper 89, 1964), p. 39.

[28] Although the role of the railroad as an initiator of economic growth has recently been a subject of contention, even the skeptics are willing to grant that the part it played was most dramatic in the era immediately following the Civil War. Fishlow has convincingly maintained that "By the turn of the century, railroad operating expenses *alone* come to about 6 percent of gross (national) product." Albert Fishlow, *American Railroads and the Transformation of the Ante-Bellum Economy* (Cambridge: Harvard University Press, 1965), p. 103. For various sides of the railroad debate also see Paul H. Cootner, "The Role of the Railroads in United States Economic Growth," *Journal of Economic History,* Vol. 23 (1963), pp. 477–521; Leland H. Jenks, "Railroads as an Economic Force in American Development," *ibid.,* Vol. 4 (1944), pp. 1–20; Taylor and Neu, *op. cit.;* Robert W. Fogel, "A Quantitative Approach to the Study of Railroads in American Economic Growth: A Report of Some Preliminary Findings," *Journal of Economic History,* Vol. 22 (1962), pp. 163–197; and idem, *Railroads and American Economic Growth: Essays in Econometric History* (Baltimore: The Johns Hopkins Press, 1964).

cent of U.S. urban population in 1910 (Table 2.3). The absolute gains registered between 1860 and 1910 by ten of these cities were the largest in the country, and the magnitude of population increase in the remaining center (Los Angeles) ranked thirteenth in the nation.[29] Relative

TABLE 2.3 *Population Growth in Eleven U.S. Cities: 1860–1910*

	Population 1860	Population 1910[a]	Metropolitan district population 1910[b]
New York	1,174,779[c]	4,766,883	6,474,568
Chicago	112,172	2,185,283	2,446,921
Philadelphia	565,529	1,549,008	1,972,342
Boston	177,840	670,585	1,520,470
Pittsburgh	49,221	533,905	1,044,743
St. Louis	160,773	687,029	828,733
San Francisco	56,802	416,912	686,873[d]
Baltimore	212,418	558,485	658,715
Cleveland	43,417	560,663	613,270
Detroit	45,619	465,766	500,982
Los Angeles	4,385	319,198	438,226

SOURCES: 13th Census of the U.S., 1910, *Population 1910* (Washington, D. C.: 1913), Vol. 1, p. 74; and *Census of Population: 1960* (see footnote 3), p. 1–66.

[a] This column, unlike the next, understates metropolitan growth, as it includes only the population within the municipal boundaries of each city. In 1860 transport facilities permitted a negligible degree of development beyond the central city; but by 1910 there were justifiable grounds for combining the populations of politically independent urban units, for, although suburbanization was still in its initial stages, there was considerable integration between central cities and the areas contiguous to their boundaries. Central city population figures do particular injustice to Boston and Pittsburgh, both of which had long possessed a number of factories and mills in their essentially rural surroundings.

[b] The metropolitan districts for which statistics are presented . . . include not only the area within the corporate limits but also parts of the surrounding territory [all civil divisions of urban character lying within 10 miles of the city limits] which may in a general way be regarded as closely associated with the development of the city. . . . Although these districts were not defined on an industrial basis, it is believed that they include most of the important factories which are intimately connected with the growth of the central cities. 13th Census of the U.S., 1910, *Manufactures: Reports for Principal Industries* (Washington, D. C.: 1913), Vol. 10, p. 903.

[c] "New York and its boroughs as constituted under the act of consolidation in 1898." *Census of Population: 1960, op. cit.*, p. 1-67.

[d] "San Francisco–Oakland."

[29] Buffalo and Milwaukee, which respectively had the eleventh and twelfth largest urban population increases during the 1860–1910 period, were arbitrarily excluded from the tables in this introductory section because their present-day size and role in the national economy is somewhat smaller than that of the listed centers. However, the urban-size growth model presented on the following pages is presumably equally applicable to these two Great Lakes industrial nucleii, as

gains of an equally striking character were also recorded in most of the emerging metropolises, with Chicago's better than 18-fold multiplication (central city only) and Los Angeles' 100-fold expansion the most imposing of the lot. Except for Los Angeles, these cities were, to one degree or another, established commercial centers, and in the capacity of financial and transport nodes they served as logical foci for industrial development. However, commercial supremacy in 1860 was obviously not completely prophetic of future urban-industrial significance. New Orleans, Cincinnati, Albany, and Louisville, among the eleven largest cities of 1860, are not among today's eleven most important urban-industrial concentrations.

A Model of Urban-Size Growth for Periods of Rapid Industrialization

It is commonly acknowledged that "there are close relations between urban growth and changes in the structure of urban activities";[30] or, more precisely, that "Since . . . the functions being performed in the city change radically as the city grows, . . . the stage of development reached by any city should be evident in the industrial and occupational distribution of the labor force."[31] Through the use of a simple descriptive model, such growth relationships can be tersely expressed for major American cities from 1860 to about 1910 or shortly thereafter.[32]

Imagine a mercantile city, with some minor industrial functions,[33]

---

well as to lesser cities that underwent rapid manufacturing expansion in the late nineteenth century.

[30] Brian J. L. Berry and William L. Garrison, "A Note on Central Place Theory and the Range of a Good," *Economic Geography,* Vol. 34 (1958), p. 311.

[31] Smolensky and Ratajczak, *op. cit.,* p. 92.

[32] Although this essay makes no detailed attempt to consider the relevance of the model to patterns of urban-size growth during periods of rapid industrialization (past and present) outside of the United States, recent findings would seem to imply that its geographic manifestations would prove valid wherever urban-industrial expansion occurred (occurs) within a context of western capitalistic institutions. For example, see Leslie J. King, "Urbanization in an Agriculturally Dependent Society, Some Implications in New Zealand," *Tijdschrift voor Economische en Sociale Geografie,* Vol. 56 (Jan.-Feb., 1965), pp. 12–21.

[33] It is quite apparent from Table 2.2 that in 1860 industrial functions were already of considerable importance in Pittsburgh (due to then unique raw-material advantages) and Philadelphia (largely because of the incorporation of its textile-industry suburbs in 1854). These facts should not be interpreted as invalidations of the model but merely as indicators of slight variations in the timing of the growth process and as a confirmation of the uniqueness of cities. Other lesser urban

that is indiscriminately located in space and unengaged in market-area competition with other cities (although it does export some goods and import others that are not produced locally). Assumption of these essentially aspatial and monopolistic conditions permits concentration on the growth process itself and defers inquiry into the interplay of initial advantages and the growth of some cities at the expense of others.

Further imagine the introduction into this city of one or more large-scale factories (in one or more manufacturing categories), whose location may have been determined either rationally or randomly. Sooner or later this event evokes two circular chains of reaction (Figure 2.1).

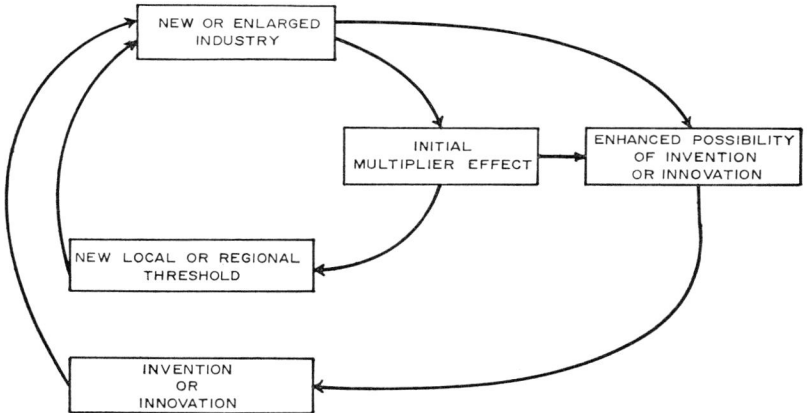

FIGURE 2.1 The circular and cumulative process of industrialization and urban-size growth.

New manufacturing functions, *whether or not they primarily serve local markets,* will have an initial multiplier effect; that is, new local demands created both by the factories themselves and by the purchasing power of their labor force will call into being a host of new business, service, trade, construction (of housing, streets, street railways, sewers and water mains, schools and other public buildings, and stores and other business establishments), transportation, local government, pro-

---

centers, such as Denver, Omaha, and Kansas City, Missouri (each of which had less than 10 per cent of its 1890 population employed in manufacturing), while acquiring relatively large populations in the late nineteenth century, did not enter the industrial growth phase until some time after 1890 (i.e., their post-1860 growth in size proceeded in much the same manner as that of major Atlantic Coast ports in the early nineteenth century — see the model presented in this book's final essay).

fessional, and miscellaneous white-collar jobs. Large doses of new manufacturing may also be expected to amplify the initial multiplier by encouraging the local appearance of linked industries that either provide inputs for the recently arrived factories ("backward linkages") or utilize the semifinished outputs of these same growth leaders ("forward linkages").[34] The combined effect of new industrial employment and an initial multiplier effect will be an alteration of the city's occupational structure (with a more even balance struck between the industrial sector and the wholesaling-trading complex), an increase in population, or growth in urban size, and the probable attainment of one or more new local or regional industrial thresholds. These higher thresholds (larger markets) will support new manufacturing functions as well as additional plants or capacity in existing industrial categories. Once production facilities have been constructed in accordance with the new thresholds, a second round of growth is initiated, and eventually still higher thresholds are achieved. Plant construction in response to these thresholds again generates an initial multiplier effect and higher thresholds, and the process continues (at an irregular pace) in a circular and cumulative manner until interrupted or impeded by diseconomies (or, if the conditions of isolation are relaxed, by new competitive advantages gained by other concomitantly growing centers).[35]

The movement of this first cycle of events will also be propelled by the secondary multiplier effects deriving from the nonindustrial jobs brought into existence by new or enlarged manufacturing. In particular, the satisfaction of new local or regional threshold levels will be hastened by the sizable independent multiplier associated with new housing construction activity (Figure 2.2). (Economic historians have repeatedly underlined the enormous part played by building construction in U.S. capital formation, and thereby in U.S. economic growth. However, inasmuch as Isard has demonstrated that nineteenth-century U.S. building construction followed "the natural . . . concentration of industry and population" brought about by transportation innovations,

---

[34] See Hirschman, *op. cit.,* pp. 98–104.

[35] For specific related statements on the cumulative effect of new manufacturing on regional rather than urban growth see Myrdal, *op. cit.,* pp. 23–26; and Perloff and others, *op. cit.,* pp. 94–96. Note also Hans Carol, "Die Entwicklung der Stadt Zürich zur Metropole der Schweiz," *Geographische Rundschau,* Vol. 5 (1953), pp. 304–307; Isard, "Transportation Development and Building Cycles," *op. cit.,* p. 93; and observations on the effect of industrial growth "on the size of local industrial populations" in E. A. Wrigley, *Industrial Growth and Population Change* (Cambridge, England: Cambridge University Press, 1961).

i.e., inasmuch as local building cycles were propagated when urgent demands were created by suddenly telescoped manufacturing increments,[36] there seems to be no justification for assigning primacy to the role of the construction sector in the urban-size growth process during periods of rapid industrialization.) The construction multiplier not only

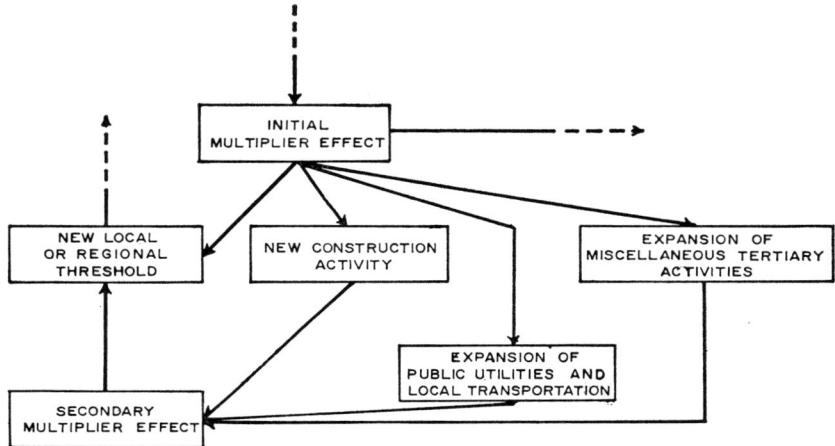

FIGURE 2.2 A more detailed view of the sequence from an initial multiplier effect to the fulfillment of a new local or regional threshold. This sequence is not included in Figure 2.1 in order to ease comparison of that figure with Figure 4.1 of the final essay.

subsumes the business, service, and local government functions required to serve painters, carpenters, plumbers, plasterers, masons, and real estate speculators but also carries backward to the local production of bricks, glass, and other construction materials.[37] In like fashion, the construction, operation, and maintenance of capital-intensive street railways and public utilities will of itself procreate higher employment (urban-size growth) in the city's tertiary and local government sectors. Also, tertiary activities, which increase in functional variety as the city reaches a larger and larger size and as a succession of central-place

---

[36] Isard, op. cit., p. 93. With respect to Chicago, Isard concluded "that she has experienced building cycles [including those from 1862 to 1878, and from 1878 to 1900] of approximately the same order and timing as those in the cities of the United States as a whole; and that similarly these building cycles are attributable to the development of the several transport innovations" [pp. 110–111].

[37] "Since the costs of transportation increased rapidly with the distance such heavy materials were carried, nearly every [late nineteenth-century] city was rimmed with clay pits from which its buildings had been dug." Kirkland, op. cit., p. 256.

thresholds are fulfilled, will have a secondary multiplier effect, because they will to some degree perpetuate one another through "taking in each other's washing."

A second circular sequence of reactions occurs at the same time and compounds and reinforces the effects of the first (Figure 2.1). This chain stems from the continually more complex network of interpersonal communications and confrontations that derives from an expanding population. The multiplication of interactions among the growing number of individuals engaged in the manufacturing and tertiary sectors enhances the possibilities of technological improvements and inventions (*in nonthreshold as well as threshold industries*), enlarges the likelihood of the adoption of more efficient managerial and financial institutions, increases the speed with which locally originating ideas are disseminated, and eases the diffusion of skills and knowledge brought in by migrants from other areas.[38] Although, as Schumpeter[39] would have it, inventions and ideas are not immediately implemented but await an imaginative or aggressive entrepreneur to exploit them, once implementation has occurred, that is, once new factories have been erected or old ones enlarged, employment and population increase, the web of interpersonal communications is again extended and densened, the chances for invention and innovation are further enhanced, and the circular process continues, perhaps even at an accelerated pace, until diverted or hindered.

The three principal components of this descriptive model obviously possess important systematic interrelationships. In addition to the explicit dependence of both the occurrence of invention or innovation and the satisfaction of new local or regional thresholds upon the multiplier effect, at least two other less frequent interactional permutations may be identified. (1) When the fulfillment of a higher threshold is

---

[38] For a discussion of urban growth and the flow of ideas see Richard L. Meier, *A Communications Theory of Urban Growth* (Cambridge, Mass.: The M.I.T. Press, 1962). See also Torsten Hägerstrand, "The Propagation of Innovation Waves," *Lund Studies in Geography,* Series B, Human Geography, No. 4 (1952); Gunnar Olsson, *Distance and Human Interaction* (Philadelphia: Regional Science Research Institute, 1965); and the review of the diffusion literature in Everett M. Rogers, *Diffusion of Innovations* (New York: The Free Press of Glencoe, 1962); as well as the exposition and sources cited in the next essay. The mechanisms by which innovations are spread must have operated with particular efficiency in late nineteenth-century American urban environments, which were still characterized to a great degree by relatively small and cohesive built-up areas and a close relationship between place-of-work and place-of-residence.

[39] Schumpeter, *loc. cit.*

brought about by independent exogenous forces, e.g., by transportation improvements or rural population increases that permit accessibility to larger market areas (export hinterlands), then the multiplier and invention-innovation cycles proceed *forward from, rather than toward,* threshold attainment. Under such circumstances the velocity of the entire growth process is stepped up, because, by definition, the model would continue reiterating itself without the aid of an external stimulus. (2) Technological innovations that not only foster expansion within a single industrial category but also dictate the establishment of linked industries, result in a *locally concentrated, rather than a geographically dispersed,* multiplier and a quickened achievement of higher thresholds and more new industrial injections.[40]

Components of the Model

As thus far explained, this descriptive model suffers from glaring omissions and imprecisions, as well as from the other shortcomings commonly associated with high-order generalizations. However, only in rare circumstances can models pertaining to the past be very explicit, and therefore "the insight furnished by the simplest of models makes the effort involved in . . . more complicated theories economically unsound."[41] Hence, further expansion of this capsuled theory is limited to examination of the single components presented, identification of additional impetuses to the circular and cumulative process, and, most important, introduction of the ambivalent forces that influence the selective growth of cities.

The Multiplier Effect

In order to avoid unnecessary rigidities in our hypothesized process of urban-size growth, the initial multiplier has been defined rather vaguely. Little controversy can result from an assertion that the multiplier is not a constant, that it varies from industry to industry (depending on wage levels and on the extent and variety of linkages involved), and from place to place and time to time within a single industry.[42]

---

[40] This does not constitute a duplication of the earlier reference to linked industries, since the previous allusion pertained to all "backward" and "forward" linkages and not to specifically technological linkages.

[41] Cootner, *op. cit.*, p. 478.

[42] "The time element is important because technology and organization influencing activity interaction within any given industry is subject to change. . . ."

However, any implication that *all* new or expanded manufacturing activities generated some initial multiplier in the era from 1860 to 1914 is open to immediate contention by some, and therefore demands justification.

The original expositions on the multiplier per se restricted their emphasis to the effect of investment in the capital-goods industries upon employment in other sectors of the economy, and, conversely, to the effect of investment outside of the capital-goods industries upon employment in that sector.[43] Geographers and city planners independently developed an essentially modified and broadened version, the economic base or basic/nonbasic ratio,[44] and eventually maintained that export ("basic" or "city-forming") industries were the primary determinants of regional and urban growth.[45] If this is the case, how can the association of an initial multiplier effect with all new manufacturing be rationalized?

For one thing, "There is no reason to believe that exports are the sole or even the most important autonomous variable determining regional [or urban] income."[46] On the contrary, Leven has suggested

---

Perloff and others, *op. cit.*, p. 94. See also Walter Isard, *Methods of Regional Analysis* (New York: John Wiley & Sons, Inc., 1960), p. 227.

[43] John M. Keynes, *The General Theory of Employment, Interest and Money* (New York: Harcourt, Brace & World, Inc., 1936), pp. 113–131; and Richard F. Kahn, "The Relation of Home Investment to Unemployment," *Economic Journal*, Vol. 41 (1931), pp. 173–198.

[44] The earliest known descriptions of this concept appeared in M. Aurousseau, "The Distribution of Population: A Constructive Problem," *Geographical Review*, Vol. 11 (1921), p. 574; and in Robert Murray Haig, *Major Economic Factors in Metropolitan Growth and Arrangement* (New York: Regional Plan of New York and Its Environs, 1927), pp. 42–43. For a history of the economic base literature see Richard B. Andrews, "Mechanics of the Urban Economic Base: Historical Development of the Base Concept," *Land Economics*, Vol. 29 (1953), pp. 161–167; or John A. Alexander, "The Basic-Nonbasic Concept of Urban Economic Functions," *Economic Geography*, Vol. 30 (1954), pp. 246–261.

[45] For relatively recent contentions of this sort see Douglass C. North, "Location Theory and Regional Economic Growth," *Journal of Political Economy*, Vol. 63 (1955), pp. 243–258; Gunnar Alexandersson, *The Industrial Structure of American Cities* (Lincoln: University of Nebraska Press, 1956), pp. 15–17; and Smolensky and Ratajczak, *op. cit.*, p. 93.

[46] Charles M. Tiebout, "Exports and Regional Economic Growth," *Journal of Political Economy*, Vol. 64 (1956), p. 161. Artle echoed the same sentiment when he wrote: "Indeed, it is a tremendous simplification to maintain that the export base is *the* determinant of employment or income in a metropolitan area. A city may very well continue to grow even if its exports do not increase." Roland Artle, *The Structure of the Stockholm Economy* (Ithaca: Cornell University Press, 1965), p. 3.

that the magnitude of a multiplier effect is not conditioned by whether it originates from a local-market or export industry.[47] Because, in addition to wages and local inputs, retailing and/or other "forward linkages" are associated with the initiation of a local-market factory, its initial multiplier effect may very well exceed that of an exporting plant. An increase in productivity on the part of already existing local-market manufactures can also promote urban growth by amplifying local income.[48] Each of these points gains stature from the fact that it has been demonstrated (through the use of a national-income-like model) that local-market industries, by perpetuating income circulation within the city, further generate income (and jobs) and hence development.[49]

Further support for dispensing with the basic/nonbasic distinction, and for conceding some multiplier effect to virtually all new or expanded manufacturing, may be gained from other sources. For example, a multiplier effect restricted to export industries would often suppress the development-instigating qualities of local industries that provide inputs for the exporters. (The inducement to development would be particularly strong where the output of the local input-providing industry lowered the marginal production costs of the export industry.) Or factories might shift from producing exclusively for local consumption to serving a more extensive market area.[50] One might also invoke the common argument that the importance of exports dwindles as the economic unit (metropolis) grows in area and population; in other words, the degree to which multiplier effects are localized, or "leakages" to other areas reduced, is a function of city size.[51] Finally, one may point to the somewhat mercantilistic observation that "a city

---

[47] Charles L. Leven, *Theory and Method of Income and Product Accounts for Metropolitan Areas, including the Elgin-Dundee Area as a Case Study* (2nd edition; Pittsburgh: Center for Regional Economic Studies, University of Pittsburgh, 1963), p. 17.

[48] Compare with Charles M. Tiebout, *The Community Economic Base Study* (New York: Committee for Economic Development, 1962), p. 75; and Artle, *loc. cit.*

[49] Ralph W. Pfouts, "An Empirical Testing of the Economic Base Theory," *Journal of the American Institute of Planners*, Vol. 23 (1957), pp. 64–69. As a case in point, Los Angeles' manufacturing growth before World War I was almost wholly confined to industries producing for a virtually local market.

[50] Industries catering to purely local or nonlocal markets are exceptional. For further comments and a review of the literature concerning the conceptual and technical difficulties of the economic base as a multiplier see Isard, *op. cit.*, pp. 194–205. Also note Leven, *op. cit.*, pp. 13–15.

[51] Charles M. Tiebout, "Community Income Multipliers: A Population Growth Model," *Journal of Regional Science*, Vol. 2 (Spring, 1960), pp. 75–84.

may also grow by purchasing something locally that it has previously imported."[52] The qualitative effect of these growth-stimulating local purchases is the same, whether they assume the form of formerly imported production inputs, or of formerly imported consumer goods. In both instances, capital flows within the urban economy are increased rather than decreased.

If the preceding paragraphs justify the implication that all new or expanded manufacturing activities generated some initial multiplier, then, when modified, they also support the contention that the varying secondary multiplier effects of local-market nonindustrial functions contributed to urban-size growth. Certainly the construction, public utilities, local government, and miscellaneous tertiary activity sectors of the urban economy, just as local-market manufacturing, increase aggregate local income through salaries and wages, propagate additional income increases (jobs) by adding to endogenous income flows, and prevent capital outflows by providing previously imported goods and services. Moreover, if empirical studies indicate that the tertiary sector is a primary source of size growth in modern U.S. cities,[53] then there seems to be no ground for questioning the secondary role of that sector in late nineteenth-century urban population expansion.

The foregoing views should not be misinterpreted. They attempt to balance rather than to overweigh or exaggerate. The assignment of a place in the urban-size growth process to establishments serving local market areas is not synonymous with denying the significance of export functions. After all, Vining has shown that nonbasic employment tends to be directly related to basic employment,[54] and most of the large-scale urban manufactures that materialized in the post-1860 decades were basic to some extent; i.e., at least a portion of their individual sales were of a nonlocal character. The real problem in dealing with late nineteenth-century urban multipliers is not the question of imports versus exports but, as Lampard has pointed out, the near impossibility of reconstructing the local income data necessary to assess their precise composition.[55]

[52] Robert L. Steiner, "Urban and Inter-Urban Economic Equilibrium," *Papers and Proceedings, Regional Science Association,* Vol. 1 (1st Annual Meeting, 1954), Philadelphia, 1955, p. C8.

[53] For example, see Pfouts, *loc. cit.*

[54] Rutledge Vining, "Location of Industry and Regional Patterns of Business-Cycle Behavior," *Econometrica,* Vol. 14 (1946), pp. 37–68.

[55] Lampard, *op. cit.,* p. 123.

Thresholds and the Urban Hierarchy

As employed here, the threshold concept may be interpreted as an economic phenomenon. A threshold is the minimum population or volume of sales required to support a new optimum-scale factory or an economical addition to existing facilities; and, under normal circumstances, until the city attains this demand level, it must import the industry's product from a more complex center. Rigid connotations should not be attached to this definition, for, at the urban as well as the national level, it is unrealistic to assume that "investments will necessarily and always be undertaken as soon as the threshold is passed."[56] In fact, as Hoover suggested long ago, a single plant could appear when a local market area failed to create demands sufficient for operation at a technically optimal scale (but the materialization of others would be unlikely since decreasing costs would apply).[57] However, "The important point remains that investment decisions are made much easier once this [threshold fulfillment] is the case."[58] For these reasons, plus those to be introduced in a subsequent discussion of variations in entrepreneurial behavior, it is best to assume that the materialization of new industrial functions will not necessarily coincide with threshold achievement, but will occur within an "entry zone" overlapping both sides of that optimal entry level.[59]

Thresholds may also be placed in a sociological context; that is, new industrial capacity is created through a sequence of events determined by a locality's "dominant value system" and initiated "when elements in the population express a dissatisfaction with industrial productivity."[60] Regardless of the framework chosen, it is obvious that ease of entry into the market varies enormously from industry to industry. Both the economic and sociological modes of thinking, until modified by the introduction of the question of selective urban growth, are consistent with Weber's assumption that small production units will agglomerate

---

[56] Hirschman, *op. cit.*, pp. 115–116.

[57] Edgar M. Hoover, *Location Theory and the Shoe and Leather Industries* (Cambridge: Harvard University Press, 1937), p. 110.

[58] Hirschman, *op. cit.*, p. 116.

[59] Note the observations and findings regarding tertiary threshold levels and tertiary "entry zones" in P. Haggett and K. A. Gunawardena, "Determination of Population Thresholds for Settlement Functions by the Reed-Muench Method," *The Professional Geographer*, Vol. 16 (July, 1964), pp. 6–9.

[60] Neil J. Smelser, *Social Change in the Industrial Revolution* (Chicago: University of Chicago Press, 1954), pp. 3, 32–33 ff.

(concentrate) whenever the minimum requirements for a larger scale of production are satisfied.[61]

It might legitimately be asked what evidence supports the theoretical interconnection (implied in the model and logically derived from the "nested" hierarchical system of market areas formulated by Lösch and Christaller) between city size and the fulfillment of a succession of manufacturing thresholds. It is one thing to demonstrate theoretically that the conflict between the cost of overcoming distance and the cost savings of specialization and concentration should resolve itself in an urban-centered hierarchy; it is quite another thing to produce substantiation. Nonetheless, the contemporary available evidence, though far from definitive, is not inconsiderable. Based on 1954 data for individual states, rather than for metropolitan units, a correlation coefficient of .936 has been found between U.S. manufacturing employment and population.[62] At a more concrete level, the measurement in American cities of minimum requirements, or k values (the minimum percentage of economic activity in a particular industry in all cities of a given size), has revealed that manufacturing categories infrequently encountered "in small cities become more or less ubiquitous in large cities";[63] i.e., it is likely that the larger the city, the larger the number of industrial specialities supported. Studies of k values have specifically indicated that the minimum percentage in durable manufactures increases more rapidly with city size than corresponding increases in nondurable manufactures; and this too is consistent with the threshold concept, since individual producers of durable goods generally operate at larger scales and require larger markets. In a similar manner, Rodgers' diversification index demonstrates that the diversity of manufacturing in metropolitan areas is to some degree a function of population[64] and of regional market ac-

---

[61] Alfred Weber, *Theory of the Location of Industries: Translated with an Introduction and Notes by Carl J. Friedrich* (Chicago: The University of Chicago Press, 1929), p. 140. The employment of the threshold and multiplier concepts in the urban-size growth model is also in harmony with the following remark by Weber: ". . . each particle of industrial production which moves to a certain place under the influence of locational factors creates a new distribution of consumption on account of the labor which it employs at the new location, and this may become the basis of further locational regrouping" [p. 213].

[62] Perloff and others, *op. cit.,* pp. 315, 393–398.

[63] Irving Morrissett, "The Economic Structure of American Cities," *Papers and Proceedings of the Regional Science Association,* Vol. 4 (4th Annual Meeting, 1957), p. 246. Similar findings are reported in Edward L. Ullman and Michael F. Dacey, "The Minimum Requirements Approach to the Urban Economic Base," *ibid.,* Vol. 6 (6th Annual Meeting, 1959), 1960, pp. 175–194.

[64] Allan Rodgers, "Some Aspects of Industrial Diversification in the United

cessibility (potential). Although Rodgers himself did not make the latter point, it is apparent from his data that the most anomalous smaller metropolitan centers,[65] places having industrial structures unexpectedly comparable to those of the largest urban centers, were all located in Megalopolis, the area with the highest market accessibility in the country. In addition, Beckmann[66] has shown the rank-size concept to be compatible with the idea of an urban-centered hierarchy of market areas; and, on the grossest of scales, broad similarities exist in the industrial structure of countries with corresponding populations (and levels of technology).[67]

If coarse present-day proofs are admissible as testimony to the existence of an urban-industrial hierarchy prior to World War I, they at best imply that such an hierarchy was evolving at the time and therefore demand the presentation of historical support. Because, with the exception of a few categories, the pertinent manufacturing censuses are incompatible and inconsistent with one another, and because detailed statistics are wanting for cities with a population below 50,000, it is difficult to reconstruct evidence supporting the emergence of an urban-centered manufacturing hierarchy between 1860 and some date shortly after 1910. In spite of these obstacles, a few relevant indicators can be extracted from the statistical morass. Most importantly, there are clear indications that, by 1910, the number of manufacturing functions (categories enumerated in the census) present in cities with a population in excess of 50,000 was a function of their size (Figure 2.3). The character of this association is weakened by the inevitable inclusion of non-threshold categories and *its failure to indicate the manifold duplication of low-level thresholds in the larger cities.* Still, the association might even have appeared stronger if it were not somewhat undermined by the fact that neither threshold-fulfilling markets, nor threshold-localized urban manufactures need be entirely located within the arbitrary confines of municipal boundaries.[68]

States," *Economic Geography,* Vol. 33 (1957), pp. 21–22. See also Otis Dudley Duncan and others: *Metropolis and Region* (Baltimore: The Johns Hopkins Press, 1960), pp. 15, 65, 69.

[65] Trenton, Springfield-Holyoke, York, and New Haven.

[66] Martin J. Beckmann, "City Hierarchies and the Distribution of City Size," *Economic Development and Cultural Change,* Vol. 6 (1957–1958), pp. 243–248.

[67] Alfred Maizels, *Industrial Growth and World Trade* (Cambridge, England: The University Press, 1963), pp. 9–13.

[68] The 1910 Census manufacturing statistics for "metropolitan districts," unlike those for politically integrated urban units, did not include the identification of all functional categories.

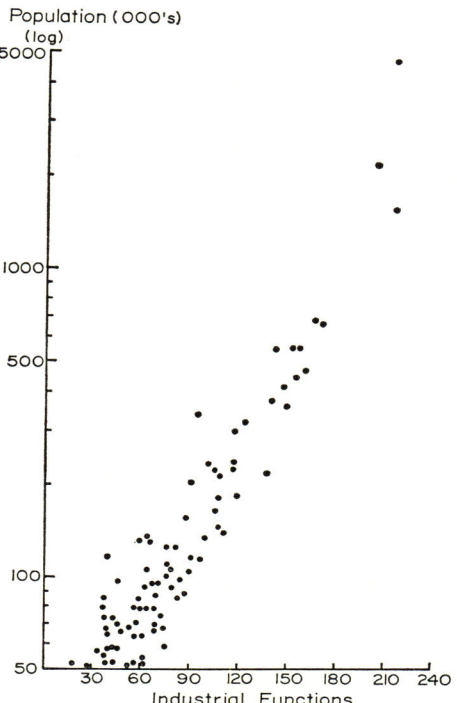

FIGURE 2.3 Number of industrial functions in U.S. cities with a population in excess of 50,000, 1910. Source: 13th Census of the U.S., 1910, *Manufactures: Reports by States with Statistics for Principal Cities* (see footnote 71). Washington, D. C., and cities that were part of larger "metropolitan districts" are excluded. This figure does not mean to imply that individual manufacturing categories as a whole, or in individual cities, are comparable with one another in terms of value added, employment, or any other characteristic. Notice New Orleans' aberrant position (population 339,000).

The applicability of the threshold concept to post-1860 conditions is also suggested by the distribution of specific industries. The 1910 factory production of boots and shoes was ubiquitously important in cities with a population of 350,000 or more; was only occasionally found on a large scale in cities in the 100,000-350,000 category; and, except for two, old, specialized centers (Manchester, New Hampshire, and Brockton, Massachusetts), was either totally absent or of little significance in centers whose population was between 50,000 and 100,000.[69] Similarly, the aggregate output of "malt liquors" and other

---

[69] Not irrelevantly, Hoover concluded that "During the last decades of the nineteenth century the westward movement of shoe production could be accounted for in large part by the movement of population." Hoover, *op. cit.*, p. 270.

food products in 1910 increased with city size.[70] The repetition of this phenomenon in other consumer goods industries was probably in part attributable to converging tastes and emerging similarities in the daily pattern of urban existence. In the producers' goods sector, and in the electrical machinery industry in particular, there was an even more pronounced tendency for production units to be thinly scattered in smaller cities, but ubiquitous to "metropolitan districts."[71]

All this is not tantamount to saying that industries are (or were) only market oriented; nor does it follow that similar-sized metropolises (past or present) will have nearly identical manufacturing structures, for no two centers are likely to possess equivalent initial advantages for the same industries, or are likely to contain an identical mix of raw-material-oriented industries and other nonthreshold manufactures.[72]

Invention and Innovation

The number of patents granted by the U.S. Patent Office stood at less than 27,000 in 1860, but this total skyrocketed to almost one million by 1910,[73] and most of the increment was associated with applications of urban origin. Although this simple fact grossly substantiates the role of inventiveness in encouraging urban-industrial growth, further and more rigorous steps should be taken (a few ideas are here outlined, but a more thorough inquiry into the locational relationships between industrial inventions, industrial innovations, and urban growth is postponed until the next essay).

Because the model implies that a multiplication of personal contacts and the importation of nonlocal skills and knowledge were fundamental to urban-size growth, and since a good part of American urban growth from 1860 to 1910 was the consequence of a great influx of European migrants[74] and an "urban implosion" of the domestic rural population

---

[70] This generalization must be modified for most Southern cities, where, because of subcultural differences in consumption patterns, beer production was rarely important.

[71] References to the boot and shoe, "malt liquor," and electrical machinery industries are based on the 13th Census of the U.S., 1910, *Manufactures: Reports by States with Statistics for Principal Cities* (Washington, D. C.: 1912).

[72] Differences in manufacturing structure between cities in the same size group are further commented upon at later points in this essay. See also Stolper, *op. cit.*, especially p. 140.

[73] U.S. Bureau of the Census, *Historical Statistics of the United States: Colonial Times to 1957* (Washington, D. C.: 1961), pp. 607–608.

[74] In 1870, the first date for which data are available, 30 per cent of the U.S. urban population was comprised of foreign-born whites, and 40 years later

(brought about by agricultural surpluses, the downfall of rural manufactures, and "the lure of the city"), it is worth while, perhaps critical, to take a momentary detour in order to gain a fuller appreciation of the migration process and its connection with inventions and innovations.

In the late nineteenth century, and particularly after 1890, the ease of acquiring fertile land declined, agricultural opportunities for immigrants diminished, and the ultimate destination of the stream of migrants arriving from Europe became increasingly urban-oriented. "In practically all works on [post-Civil War] emigration to America it has been shown that the emigrants usually had considerably more contacts and better information about the opportunities in the United States than in other parts of their own country."[75] Transatlantic contacts between friends and relatives and job information diffused through the mails were so influential that the U.S. Industrial Commission was forced to conclude in 1898 that letters were "the principal means by which, . . . , employers desiring to import laborers secure their immigration. They simply speak to their friends, advising them of the opportunities for employment, and the latter attend to the correspondence . . . necessary to bring the foreigners to these shores."[76] The role of previous migrations in determining subsequent movements is also reflected by the fact that in the early years of the twentieth century approximately one-third of the migrants disembarking in the United States had their passage paid by relatives who had arrived earlier.[77] The importance of job opportunities to the migration process is underscored by repeated demonstrations of the correlation between U.S. business cycles (high and low opportunity periods) and the volume of emigration from European agricultural areas.[78] Moreover, studies made in other con-

---

the corresponding figure was still as high as 22.6 per cent. More impressively, foreign-white "stock," or foreign-born whites and their offspring, accounted for 53.6 per cent of the U.S. urban population in 1890, and 51.6 of that same total in 1910. In New York City, the foreign-white "stock" constituted no less than 80.5 per cent of the population in 1890, and 78.6 per cent of the population in 1910. See Hope T. Eldridge and Dorothy Swaine Thomas, *Demographic Analyses and Interrelations* ("Population Redistribution and Economic Growth: United States, 1870–1950," Vol. 3), *Memoirs of the American Philosophical Society*, Vol. 61 (1964), pp. 206–208.

[75] Olsson, *op. cit.*, p. 24.

[76] Cited in Charlotte Erickson, *American Industry and the European Immigrant: 1860–1885* (Cambridge: Harvard University Press, 1957), p. 86. Also see pp. 78 and 227–228 of Erickson's work.

[77] Harry Jerome, *Migration and Business Cycles* (New York: National Bureau of Economic Research, 1926), p. 77.

[78] See *ibid.*, pp. 88, 121, 208; Brinley Thomas, *Migration and Economic*

texts suggest that late nineteenth-century, rural-to-urban migrations in the United States were also governed by informational contacts and opportunity awareness.[79]

The preceding digression merely emphasizes the specific historical applicability of the general principle that knowledge of the labor market and destinations of previous migrants are two of the most important determinants of individual migration decisions.[80] *It follows logically that new or enlarged urban industries and their multiplier effects created the employment opportunities that successively attracted "active" and "passive" migrants*[81] *to the infant metropolises, and eventually led to additional manufacturing growth by directly or indirectly enhancing the possibility of invention and innovation,* as well as through the attainment of new market thresholds. Opportunities for the semiskilled or untrained urban arrival multiplied as industry became progressively more mechanized; and, by 1910, 43.4 per cent of the country's gainfully occupied foreign-born whites were employed in "manufacturing and mechanical industries."[82] In addition, migrants, such as Pittsburgh's British and Dutch glassmakers and St. Louis' German brewers, often introduced new industries or production techniques to the larger cities;

Growth (Cambridge, England: Cambridge University Press, 1954), pp. 83–122; and Dorothy S. Thomas, *Social and Economic Aspects of Swedish Population Movements: 1750–1933* (New York: The Macmillan Company, 1941), pp. 88–92.

[79] Note John F. Hart, "Migration from a Southern Appalachian Community," *Land Economics,* Vol. 34 (1958), pp. 44–53; and Torsten Hägerstrand, "Migration and Area," *Lund Studies in Geography,* Series B, Human Geography, No. 13 (1957), pp. 27–158, especially pp. 127–132.

[80] See Esse Lövgren, "The Geographical Mobility of Labour," *Geografiska Annaler,* Vol. 38 (1956), p. 352; and Morrill, *op. cit.,* p. 13, for references to this principle. For an analysis of the voluminous literature relating industrialization, cityward migration, and migration theory, see Allan Pred, *The External Relations of Cities during 'Industrial Revolution'* (Chicago: University of Chicago, Department of Geography, Research Paper No. 76, 1962), pp. 57–68. Important literature reviews are also contained in Olsson, *op. cit.,* pp. 23–42; and Richard L. Morrill, "Migration and the Spread and Growth of Urban Settlement," *Lund Studies in Geography,* Series B, Human Geography, No. 26 (1965), pp. 33–43.

[81] The distinction between "active" and "passive" migrants is a corollary to the described process of late nineteenth-century migration. According to Hägerstrand's definition: "The active migrant seeks methodically for a suitable destination guaranteeing future prosperity (according to his lights). The passive migrant follows impulses emanating from persons of his acquaintance, perhaps principally from those who have themselves made 'fortunate' moves." Hägerstrand, *op. cit.,* p. 132.

[82] Jerome, *op. cit.,* p. 46.

and not infrequently the most fertile germinating grounds for industrial innovation and experimentation proved to be the larger and longer established industrial centers.[83]

Within the expanding urban agglomerations the increasing complexity of the network of interpersonal communications did more than merely induce invention and innovation within specialized industrial activities, because innovations and inventions usually constituted an addition to the existing repertory of know-how in each city. Put in slightly different terms, the communication-invention cycle of the model is validated by the fact that industrialization during the period under discussion "was characterized by the introduction of a relatively small number of broadly similar production processes to a large number of industries."[84] Many production techniques could be converted with little or no adjustment from the manufacture of one commodity to that of another. The chain of linked innovations is vividly illustrated by "the Leland, Faulconer and Norton Company (later the Cadillac Automobile Company) of Detroit, which was founded in 1890 as a producer of machine tools and special machinery, introduced machinery for producing bicycle gears during the brief heyday of the bicycle, switched to building gasoline engines for motor boats when the bicycle industry began to decline, and by 1902 had undertaken the production of automobile engines."[85]

This last point also casts light on the anchoring of so-called "footloose" industries in existing manufacturing complexes, and the further reinforcement of the hypothesized circular and cumulative process of urban-size growth. Theoretically, the cost structure of footloose manufactures permits them to locate as economically in one area or city as in another. Since such industries generally serve a market area of vast or national dimensions, the fulfillment of local or regional thresholds is immaterial to economical operation. Therefore the manufacture of special machinery, light chemicals, machine tools, and other products of high value per unit of weight is likely to flourish at the place of invention or initial innovation, regardless of its size or geographical situation, though an already industrialized city is the most likely location of new technological conceptions. This line of reasoning regarding the adapt-

[83] See Edgar M. Hoover, *The Location of Economic Activity* (New York: McGraw-Hill, Inc., 1948), pp. 175–176.

[84] Nathan Rosenberg, "Technological Change in the Machine Tool Industry, 1840–1910," *Journal of Economic History,* Vol. 23 (1963), p. 422.

[85] *Ibid.,* pp. 442–443.

ability of techniques and footloose industries is consistent with the more traditional argument that additional opportunities for industrial specialization are associated with every increment in manufactural differentiation,[86] particularly insofar as opportunities for specialization may be compounded by the multiplier effects of footloose industries. It should be added that the random inception of footloose manufactures is a major cause of dissimilar industrial structures among metropolises of similar size.

Finally, it is not to be inferred from the model that invention on the part of the laborer or the entrepreneur inevitably met with success and another round of job and investment opportunities. Innovators were constantly confronted with "the appearance of equally good alternative solutions," and few "were fortunate to withstand the rigors of competition, substitution, technological obsolescence, and senescence."[87] However, the model is not invalidated by these conditions, for its soundness rests on the successful materialization of *some* inventions and newly introduced skills and ideas.

Additional Stimulants to Urban-Size Growth

A number of factors other than those already introduced provided momentum to the circular and cumulative process of industrialization and urban-size growth. Although it is not feasible to catalogue them exhaustively, identification of the most important is almost mandatory.

Natural population increase of urban "natives" is perhaps the most obvious omission. Although it is generally conceded that migrants and their progeny dominated metropolitan population growth in the late nineteenth century, it is undeniable that *endogenous natural increases also contributed to the aggregate demand of the metropolis and the*

---

[86] See Allyn Young, "Increasing Returns and Economic Progress," *Economic Journal*, Vol. 38 (1928), pp. 527–542. Lampard's much later work on urban growth is largely based on a variation on this theme, which he summarizes as follows: "We argued at the beginning of this study that the history of economic progress was in a large part the history of increasing specialization: that the integration of differentiated functions tended toward the spatial concentration of factors in urban localities; and that the concentration of differentiated functions made for further specialization." Lampard, *op. cit.*, p. 127. Also see subsequent comments in this essay on vertical disintegration and linkages, and Simon Kuznets, "Retardation of Industrial Growth," *Journal of Economic and Business History*, Vol. 1 (1929), pp. 534–560, especially p. 548.

[87] Richard L. Meier, "The Organization of Technological Innovation," in *The Historian and the City, op. cit.*, p. 76.

realization of higher thresholds. Admittedly, the high mortality rates of major U.S. cities considerably reduced their respective scales of natural increase, but, as the nineteenth century progressed, these sometimes alarming rates decreased remarkably, e.g., deaths per 1,000 capita in New York City steadily fell from a level of 32.19 for the period 1856–1865, to 26.32 for 1876–1885, to 21.52 for 1896.[88] In any case, barring emigration from the city, natural increase, of whatever magnitude, in itself would have generated some enlargement of food processing and other essential local industries.

Average annual wages per manufacturing employee in the United States rose from $378 in 1869 to $512 in 1909 (data in current dollars).[89] Since 1869 was an inflationary year, these figures are not as telling as those that reveal that daily manufacturing wages advanced roughly 50 per cent between 1860 and 1890,[90] and that "the real earnings of manufacturing workers rose 37 percent from 1890 to 1914."[91] Furthermore, throughout this period, the real per capita consumption of manufactured items in cities was in all probability expanding as a consequence of the fall in manufacturing prices vis-à-vis agricultural and construction prices.[92] *The absolute increase of wages and real buying power meant that with the passage of time the multiplier effect of many manufacturing increments became more extensive, and thereby the speed of absolute urban-size growth was accelerated.* Higher average levels of per capita consumption were particularly stimulating to the expansion of industries whose products had a high income elasticity of

[88] Adna Ferrin Weber, *The Growth of Cities in the Nineteenth Century* (New York: Columbia University Studies in History, Economics and Public Law, Vol. 11, 1899), p. 356. There are also indications, based on the study of late nineteenth-century Massachusetts cities, that the highest birth rates occurred in the largest urban concentrations. *Ibid.*, pp. 333–334.

[89] Simon Kuznets, Ann Ratner Miller, and Richard A. Easterlin, *Analyses of Economic Change* ("Population Redistribution and Economic Growth: United States, 1870–1950," Vol. 2), *Memoirs of the American Philosophical Society,* Vol. 51 (1960), p. 129.

[90] Clarence D. Long, *Wages and Earnings in the United States, 1860–1890* (A Study by the National Bureau of Economic Research; Princeton: Princeton University Press, 1960), pp. 13–15. Long's book contains a detailed breakdown of wage increases by industry and state. Also note the findings of Stanley Lebergott's "Wage Trends 1800–1900," in *Trends in the American Economy in the Nineteenth Century, op. cit.,* pp. 462, 476–489.

[91] Albert Rees, *Real Wages in Manufacturing, 1890–1914* (A Study of the National Bureau of Economic Research; Princeton: Princeton University Press, 1961), p. 5.

[92] Gallman, *op. cit.,* p. 41.

demand. The ramifications of higher average earnings were compounded by the fact that total family incomes were also being increased through the more widespread employment of women; that is, the female working force was increasing more rapidly than total employment.[93]

The growth process may also be interpreted as having accelerated because all "urban qualities which can be construed as providing external economies would seem in some measure to increase with size."[94] In other words, the locational attraction exerted by external agglomeration economies (or localization and urbanization economies) increases functionally rather than arithmetically. Furthermore, since agglomeration diseconomies also mount and eventually become oppressive, external economies were of "unique importance" to the urban concentration of manufacturing prior to World War I, and especially during the 1860–1890 period, when land costs and other factors had not as yet begun to drive large production units to the uncongested suburbs.[95] The multiplication of external economies at that time amounted to more than the benefits usually associated with more efficient interfirm communication and the sharing of facilities and urban "social overhead capital." Urban linkages and concentration were also the consequence of an increasing vertical disintegration of production and concomitant decreases in the locational influence of coal and other primary raw materials. As technology progressed, there was a greater specialization of manufacturing functions that often dictated locational proximity of successive stages of production and/or by-product industries ("backward" and "forward" linkages as in the metal fabricating and meat packing industries), although some forms of technological progress

---

[93] Between 1870 and 1910 the percentage of gainfully occupied U.S. males of 16 years old and over increased 2.4 points, from 88.7 to 91.1 per cent. During that identical period the percentage of gainfully occupied U.S. females of 16 years old and over jumped 10.8 points, from 14.7 to 25.5 per cent. See data in Everett S. Lee and others, *Methodological Considerations and Reference Tables* ("Population Redistribution and Economic Growth: United States, 1870–1950," Vol. 1), *Memoirs of the American Philosophical Society,* Vol. 45 (1957), pp. 588, 599.

[94] Aaron Fleisher, "The Economics of Urbanization," in *The Historian and the City, op. cit.,* p. 72. This contention is supported by Lösch's logic regarding the coincidence of market networks in regional metropolises. August Lösch, *The Economics of Location* (translated from the 2nd revised edition by William H. Woglom with the assistance of Wolfgang F. Stolper; New Haven: Yale University Press, 1954), p. 77.

[95] Compare with Shigeto Tsuru, "The Economic Significance of Cities," in *The Historian and the City, op. cit.,* p. 49.

required single-plant integration of geographically independent production facilities (as in the iron and steel industry).[96] This increasing interdependence was characterized by a mounting complexity of inputs both of raw materials and semifinished products, a reduction in importance "of any one material in the locational calculus"[97] (a condition in itself theoretically encouraging market-oriented or urban location), and, definitionally, by a growing tendency for the multiplier effects of large manufacturing units to be localized rather than geographically diffuse. The advantages of urbanization economies and market accessibility were further enhanced by the establishment of higher freight rates on manufactured goods than on raw materials, and by the introduction in the late 1890's and early 1900's of cheap, easily transmitted electrical energy, improved hydroelectric motors, and larger and more efficient hydroelectric and thermoelectric plants.[98] (The consumption of electrically generated power in manufacturing mushroomed from 182,562 horsepower in 1899, to 3,897,248 horsepower in 1914).[99] If all these observations are considered simultaneously, it may be argued that the growing stockpile of agglomeration economies in the urban environment had the net effect of increasing the locational attraction

[96] See Lampard, *op. cit.*, pp. 90–91; George J. Stigler, "The Division of Labor Is Limited by the Extent of the Market," *Journal of Political Economy,* Vol. 59 (1951), p. 192; and Alfred Weber, *op. cit.*, pp. 194–196.

[97] Raymond Vernon, "Production and Distribution in the Large Metropolis," *Annals, American Academy of Political and Social Science,* Vol. 314 (1957), p. 20. See also comments by Friedmann, *op. cit.*, pp. 222–227; and Norton Ginsburg, "Natural Resources and Economic Development," *Annals of the Association of American Geographers,* Vol. 47 (1957), pp. 197–212.

[98] "Electric power's greatest advantage over other forms of power transmission existed where long distances were involved. By 1900, this fact was universally recognized. In factories, where the transmission distances were relatively short, the advantages of electric power were not so striking but nevertheless of importance. The first advantage . . . was the elimination of countershafting and belting. The gains from this elimination were numerous. The expense of shafting was saved, the power lost in transmission was reduced, working conditions were better, and maintenance expenses were less. Furthermore, there was much greater flexibility in production planning and control. The machines no longer had to be arranged in straight lines or in the same building, the buildings did not have to conform to a cubical shape, and speed control of individual machines was much easier. The clearance of overhead areas permitted the use of large cranes for the handling of materials inside the shops. This substitution of mechanical power for human power resulted in substantial cost reductions." Harold C. Passer, *The Electrical Manufacturers, 1875–1900* (Cambridge: Harvard University Press, 1953), p. 344.

[99] William L. Thorp, *The Integration of Industrial Operation* (Washington, D. C.: Bureau of the Census Monographs III, 1924), pp. 33, 45.

exerted by cities per se in such a manner as to make the threshold concept applicable to a greater and greater number of manufacturing categories.

Finally, introduction of an adaptive-adoptive dichotomy of locational processes provides additional insight into the size growth of cities. Two polar viewpoints exist: one affirms that economic activities rationally adapt themselves to the conditions of the society in which they exist (firms rationally locate in cities because of the size of the local market or the availability of localization and urbanization economies); the other asserts that activities react to their environment in relative ignorance, with the "lucky ones" adopted by the system (successful or profit-making operation, and thereby spatial survival, "does not require proper motivation but may rather be the result of fortuitous circumstances").[100] Put in slightly different terms, the adaptive-adoptive dichotomy represents a conflict between purely random and economically rational forces. Theoretically, at any point in time, geographical distributions stemming from the behavioral patterns of a given category of locational decision-makers do not solely reflect either of the adaptive-adoptive extremes but instead manifest various permutations of rational and irrational action; that is, during the late nineteenth and early twentieth centuries, among the adaptors, or those making spatial choices based on large and accurate quantities of knowledge, there were those who came to viable conclusions (successful adaptors), and those who, through faulty reasoning and improper employment of information, selected unprofitable, short-lived sites (unsuccessful adaptors); and similarly, among the adopters, or those making spatial choices based on small and highly imperfect quantities of knowledge, there were those who chose profitable locations by "chance" (successful adopters), and those who unwittingly selected locales not conducive to long-term survival (unsuccessful adopters). (The validity of this interpretive scheme is suggested by empirical findings showing that some geographical distributions, while "more regular than random," contain elements that in the terminology of mathematical statistics are the product of "random" processes, or processes of pure chance where each event has an equal

[100] Armen A. Alchian, "Uncertainty, Evolution, and Economic Theory," *Journal of Political Economy*, Vol. 58 (1950), pp. 211–221; and Charles M. Tiebout, "Location Theory, Empirical Evidence, and Economic Evolution," *Papers and Proceedings of the Regional Science Association*, Vol. 3 (3rd Annual Meeting, 1956), Philadelphia, 1957, pp. 74–86. Also see Julian Wolpert's concept of the "spatial satisficer" in "The Decision Process in Spatial Context," *Annals of the Association of American Geographers*, Vol. 54 (1964), pp. 533–558.

probability of occurrence.)[101] To come to the point, *acknowledgment of the concurrent operation of adaptive and adoptive processes and their permutations permits the addition of new urban productive capacity, with attendant multiplier effects and perpetuation of the circular and cumulative growth process, even before higher thresholds are attained or new innovations become economically sound.*

By extension, the long-term adaptation or survival of some firms that, because of incomplete and imperfect knowledge have thus located purely by chance or in an effort to minimize their uncertainty (risk of input shortages is minimized in large metropolitan areas) is also a key to disparate industrial structures in metropolises of nearly equal size. The composition of manufacturing activity in comparably sized urban units also tends toward asymmetry because adaptive behavior, which so often assumes the form of imitating observed patterns of success, permits, if not governs, the accumulation of "footloose" industries in specialized locations — a phenomenon exemplified by the concentration of automobile production in Detroit shortly after the turn of the century.[102]

Selective Growth of Cities during Periods of Rapid Industrialization

If the circular and cumulative process of urban growth during rapid industrialization functioned flawlessly, and if all cities were isolated units not in market-area competition with one another, then every city would expand indefinitely, or at least as long as available natural resources permitted, and those urban concentrations that were initially similar in population would presumably progress in stride alongside one another into categories of larger sizes. However, between 1860 and 1910 some cities in the United States grew more rapidly and at the expense of others. Only a few attained supremacy in the urban hierarchy, others grew moderately, some stultified and declined significantly in rank (Table 2.4). In 1860, Albany, Charleston (South Carolina), New Haven, Troy, and Richmond were in the same size category as Pitts-

---

[101] Michael F. Dacey, "Modified Poisson Probability Law for Point Pattern More Regular than Random," *Annals of the Association of American Geographers,* Vol. 54 (1964), pp. 559–565. Other spatial distributions may be described as more concentrated than random; yet others, as more dispersed than random.

[102] The roles of uncertainty, imitation, and other entrepreneurial-behavior variables in the post-Civil War pattern of urban-industrial growth are further pursued in the next essay.

TABLE 2.4 *Change in Rank of U.S. Cities with an 1860 Population of 25,000 or More, 1860–1910*

	Rank in 1860[a]	Rank in 1910[b]	Net change in rank
New York	1	1	0
Philadelphia	2	3	− 1
Baltimore	3	7	− 4
Boston	4	5	− 1
New Orleans	5	14	− 9
Cincinnati	6	13	− 7
St. Louis	7	4	+ 3
Chicago	8	2	+ 6
Buffalo	9	10	− 1
Louisville	10	22	−11
Albany	11	44	−33
Washington, D. C.	12	16	− 4
San Francisco	13	11	+ 2
Providence	14	21	− 7
Pittsburgh	15	8	+ 7
Rochester	16	23	− 7
Detroit	17	9	+ 8
Milwaukee	18	12	+ 6
Cleveland	19	6	+13
Charleston, S.C.	20	77	−57
New Haven	21	31	−10
Troy	22	63	−41
Richmond	23	35	−12
Lowell	24	41	−17
Mobile	25	90	−65
Syracuse	26	30	− 4
Hartford	27	46	−19
Portland, Maine	28	78	−50

SOURCES: 8th Census of the U.S., 1860, *Statistics of the United States, op. cit.*, pp. xviii–xix; 13th Census of the U.S., 1910, *Population* (Washington, D. C.: 1913), Vol. 1, pp. 82-87; and *Census of Population: 1960* (see footnote 3), pp. 1-66, 1-67.

[a] In the 1860 rankings Brooklyn, then an independent municipality large enough to rank third on its own, is subsumed under New York, and the following places are disregarded because their fortunes were subsequently bound to larger metropolitan units: Newark, Jersey City, Cambridge, Allegheny (annexed by Pittsburgh in 1907), Roxbury (annexed by Boston in 1868), and Charlestown (annexed by Boston in 1874).

[b] Because of their geographical association with larger metropolitan configurations, the following cities are eliminated from the 1910 rankings: Newark, Jersey City, St. Paul, Oakland, Kansas City (Kansas), Paterson, Camden, Elizabeth, Hoboken, Bayonne, Passaic, Yonkers, East St. Louis, and Covington.

burgh, San Francisco, Cleveland, and Detroit; but, by 1910, the largest city in the former group (New Haven) had less than one-third of the population to be found within the corporate limits of the smallest city in the latter group (San Francisco). (Tables 2.3 and 2.5.) Most im-

48 AMERICAN METROPOLITAN GROWTH

TABLE 2.5 *Population Growth in U.S. Cities with High Losses in Rank, 1860–1910*

	Population 1860	Population 1910
New Orleans	168,675	339,075
Louisville	68,033	223,928
Albany	62,367	100,253
Charleston, S.C.	40,522	58,833
New Haven	39,267	133,605
Troy	39,235	76,813
Richmond	37,910	127,628
Lowell	36,827	106,294
Mobile	29,258	51,521
Hartford	26,917	98,915
Portland, Maine	26,341	58,571

SOURCE: *Census of Population: 1960* (see footnote 3), pp. 1-66, 1-67, 21-11, 23-9, 34-12.

portantly, after the relatively radical shuffling of urban ranks, today's eleven leading industrial centers had already been singled out by 1910 (Table 2.3), and although their individual importance has varied with westward population shifts, as a group they continue to dominate the urban hierarchy.[103]

Clearly then, within an interacting system of cities in an expanding space economy, the circular and cumulative growth process does not unravel itself in an identical manner for all places. In those cities registering gains that were relatively small for their respective 1860 size categories (or those cities falling down the ranks of the urban hierarchy), the process may be viewed as having had a relative rather than an absolute insufficiency of momentum.[104] In some instances, most

[103] See related remarks by Carl H. Madden in his "On Some Indications of Stability in the Growth of Cities in the United States," *Economic Development and Cultural Change,* Vol. 4 (1955–1956), pp. 236–252, and "Some Spatial Aspects of Urban Growth in the United States," *ibid.,* pp. 371–387; and by McLaughlin, *op. cit.,* pp. 193–251.

[104] The persistence of some growth momentum in all major urban places during the post-Civil War decades confirms Thompson's suggestion that "Perhaps some critical size exists, short of which growth is not inevitable and even the very existence of the place is not assured, but beyond which absolute contraction is highly unlikely even though the growth rate may slacken at times to zero. In sum, at a certain range of urban scale, set by the degree of isolation of the urban place, the nature of its hinterland, *the level of industrial development of the country* [underlining added], and various cultural factors, some growth mech-

INDUSTRIALIZATION AND SELECTIVE GROWTH   49

notably New Orleans, Mobile, and Charleston, this may be due in part to the perseverance of a form of circular and cumulative growth in size more typical of American cities earlier in the nineteenth century (see the model in the final essay of this book). But, for the urban system as a whole, growth discrepancies arose largely because a number of ambivalent forces simultaneously acted as a brake on cumulative expansion in some instances and precipitated the emergence of multimillion metropolises in others. It is to these forces, the most conspicuous of which may be construed as geographical expressions of initial advantages, that we now turn.

Transport Improvements

Railroad developments probably had the most profound influence on the growth of some centers at the expense of others. Reductions in the price of transport inputs, and expansion and intensification of the railroad net, both brought many repercussions for the relative importance and absolute size of American cities.

Late nineteenth-century innovations in motive power, carrying capacity, and operating procedure reduced average railroad freight charges to a revolutionary degree. On a representative line, the New York Central and Hudson River Railroad, average freight tariffs per ton-mile fell from 3.31 cents in 1865 to 0.70 cent in 1892.[105] Over a somewhat shorter time span, 1865–1884, the average ton-mile rates levied by a smaller railroad, the Boston and Albany, were diminished from 3.90 cents to 1.09 cents.[106] For U.S. railroads as a whole, rates dropped 41 per cent between 1882 and 1900, from 1.236 cents per ton-mile to 0.729 cent per ton-mile.[107]

---

anism, similar to a ratchet, comes into being, locking in past growth and preventing contraction." For an expansion on the "urban ratchet" concept see Thompson, *op. cit.*, pp. 22–23.

[105] Edward Atkinson, "Productive Industry," in Nathaniel Southgate Shaler (ed.), *The United States of America* (New York: Appleton and Company, 1894), Vol. 2, p. 712.

[106] Shelby M. Cullom, *Report of the Senate Select Committee on Interstate Commerce* (Washington, D. C.: Report No. 46, 49th Congress, First Session, 1886), Part 1, p. 71. Evidence brought before this same committee revealed that of 12 railroads "maintaining an average freight charge of from 1.85 to 3.168 cents per ton-mile, respectively, in 1868, the only ones maintaining for the year 1880 an average freight rate charge of [over] .88 of a cent per ton-mile were those having no water-route competition" [p. 203].

[107] Ralph L. Nelson, *Merger Movements in American Industry, 1895–1956*

The materialization of cheaper transport inputs "meant a spreading out of critical isodapanes, and an opportunity to realize previously untapped scale economies—even in the absence of advances in production technology."[108] This extension and enlargement of the firm's market area increased the feasibility of agglomeration and large-scale production (a tendency compounded by concurrent innovations in production technology), created the possibility of still further divisions of labor and mass-production economies, and increased the practicability of satisfying national and regional demands from a limited number of cities. In more formal terminology, then, *the spatial lengthening of production raised the threshold of some industries by increasing their minimum optimal scales of operation, and this, by extension, favored the growth of already efficiently producing centers* (places with successful adaptors and adopters) *over inefficient and nonproducing cities* (places with unsuccessful adaptors and adopters, and places with no risk-taking entrepreneurs).

The occurrence of this phenomenon is crudely mirrored by an increase in the average length of railroad hauls from less than 110 miles per ton in 1882 to about 250 miles per ton in 1910[109] and by even more impressive increments in the total volume of U.S. railroad freight traffic (from 76.2 billion ton-miles in 1890, to 255.0 billion ton-miles in 1910),[110] which Barger attributes at least in part to the substitution of long-distance railroad hauls by new large-scale manufacturers for shorter drayage (nonrailroad) hauls by previous small-scale producers.[111] Other more tenuous manifestations of this phenomenon are

---

(A Study by the National Bureau of Economic Research; Princeton: Princeton University Press, 1959), p. 80.

[108] Pred, *op. cit.*, p. 31. As employed here, "critical isodapanes" for any production site, or agglomeration point, refer to the locus encompassing all alternative production points at which the transport advantages, in terms of inputs and costs, are equal to, or less than, agglomeration or labor economies at the production site (or city). This use of the term is a liberalized and practical inversion of the traditional Weberian definition, where "critical isodapanes" only engulf points of minimum transport costs and, in each case, refer to the locus at which transport *dis*advantages are equal to or less than potential agglomeration or labor economies at a new production site.

[109] Atkinson, *op. cit.*, p. 708; *Historical Statistics of the United States, Colonial Times to 1957, op. cit.*, p. 431.

[110] *Historical Statistics of the United States, Colonial Times to 1957*, ibid.

[111] Harold Barger, *The Transportation Industries, 1889–1946; A Study of Output, Employment, and Productivity* (A Study by the National Bureau of Economic Research; Princeton: Princeton University Press, 1951), p. 48

indicated by the finding that 57 per cent of 2,546 studied, 1882 to 1900, firm disappearances occurred in manufactures where transportation costs were important,[112] and by the fact that some industries have historically not responded as quickly as others to regional redistributions of population and income (i.e., inertia, partly in the form of rising thresholds, reduced the locational mobility of some industries).[113] Also relevant are specific, firmly based speculations that the late nineteenth-century development of the manufacturing sector in certain small cities, such as San Diego, was inhibited by the expanded market possibilities (and therefore the scale and localization economy possibilities) that the railroads provided for producers in larger cities, such as San Francisco.[114]

The last observation implies that cheaper transport inputs presumably also worked to the advantage of cities with plants already having large market areas, as opposed to those having factories with small market areas. Diminished transport rates normally favor growth, with attendant multiplier effects, of the firm "which already has a larger market area because of its lower marginal cost of production," because "the firm with a larger market area, and therefore more transport inputs, has its total costs reduced more by a lowering of transport rates than any of its competitors."[115] Under more exceptional circumstances, where neither large nor small cities in a specific region possessed a population sizable enough to merit the presence of a given manufacturing activity, the cheapening of transportation presumably benefited the larger city (cities) by expanding their market area(s) to threshold level.[116]

Efficient factories (cities) tended to be favored also by the expansion of the railroad net, and particularly by the spread of feeder lines, the shortening of physical distances, and, in some areas, overconstruction. Feeder-line construction, like cheaper transport inputs, embellished the

---

[112] Nelson, *op. cit.*, p. 83. Nelson hesitates to draw any cause and effect relationships between reduced transport costs and the elimination of inefficiently located, transport-sensitive firms.

[113] Kuznets, Miller, and Easterlin, *op. cit.*, pp. 110–115.

[114] Smolensky and Ratajczak, *op. cit.*, p. 124.

[115] Pred, *op. cit.*, p. 38.

[116] Hagen has made a similar contention. To wit: "With distribution costs reduced, the profitable operation of a large-scale plant is easier than otherwise, and there must be cases in which this change is just sufficient to induce someone to make the attempt and causes it to be successful." Everett E. Hagen, *On the Theory of Social Change: How Economic Growth Begins* (Homewood, Ill.: The Dorsey Press, Inc., 1962), p. 44.

market area of the producer, usually increased returns through scale economies, and restricted the growth of nonproducing cities by raising the threshold. The completion of the transcontinental railroad in 1869, and the linking up of lines that were previously fragmented or had dissimilar gauges, frequently had the effect of shortening physical (and economic) distances by removing the necessity of using longer ocean or inland waterway routes. In the extreme case, the distance from New York to San Francisco was diminished from 6,100 to 3,400 miles. In turn, the distance reductions again favored firms that already had larger market areas by yielding them greater absolute mileage (cost) savings. Overconstruction, or, more accurately, the presence of parallel and alternative rail routes, concurrently led to abnormally low rates for riverine and coastal termini where major competing lines converged and to inordinately high rates for intermediate points serviced by a single freight carrier.

As transport improvements turned out to be more and more conducive to large-scale manufacturing, specialized production in a limited number of cities became to some extent self-generating. Large-scale production brought ton-mile or freight-volume economies to a firm, enabled still greater extension of its market area, and continued the accretion of initial advantages. Because ton-mile costs on railroads are usually a function of the total traffic per unit distance of track, freight-volume economies also accrued to cities as integral units, and in particular to rapidly expanding cities whose burgeoning traffic was not only comprised of incoming raw materials and outgoing manufactures but also of food supplies and goods in transit (domestically produced goods to be wholesaled and redistributed, plus, in the case of ports, import and export commodities). Thus, *the availability of lower freight tariffs in a relatively few cities on the major trunk lines,* the consequence of both rate competition and freight-volume economies, *acted as an urbanization* (agglomeration) *economy,* capable of attracting new manufacturing establishments and stimulating the expansion of existing production capacity, *and thereby diminished the importance of less favored points.* The traffic volume radiating in and out of some cities grew so rapidly that as early as the eighties much railroad construction was in response to existing, rather than to anticipated demand,[117] and by the

---

[117] Jenks, *op. cit.,* p. 15. According to Fishlow's recent persuasive findings, this was by no means the first instance when U.S. railroad construction followed demand. Fishlow, *op. cit.,* pp. 163–204.

last great surge of railroad building (1898–1914) this demand sequence was even more clearly enunciated.[118]

Large-scale production and specialized manufacturing agglomerations, and hence the growth of some cities at the expense of others, also gained impetus as it became apparent that railroad terminal and transshipment costs could be spread out by dividing them over increased distances. Realization of this cost relationship normally tended to promote a decrease in freight rates "for long hauls in comparison with short hauls" and encouraged the "movement of materials and products over longer distances."[119] Costly terminal and transfer charges also contributed to the polarization of manufacturing activity around trunkline terminals and major rail intersections by inspiring both the locational adjacency of successive stages of fabrication and the elimination of multiple transshipments of product mixes.[120]

An expanded railroad net, decreasing freight tariffs, and lower volume rates also strengthened the initial advantages of efficient producers and added to their scale and external economies by broadening the extent

[118] Figures for freight traffic on U.S. railroads in 1893 and 1897 are comparable, but between the latter date and 1913 ton-mileage increased from 95.1 billion to 301.7 billion (the 1870 total was only 13.0 billion), and between 1899, the earliest date for which statistics are available, and 1913 the quantity of revenue tons originating soared from .50 billion tons to 1.18 billion tons. See *Historical Statistics of the United States, Colonial Times to 1957*, loc. cit.; and Arthur F. Burns, *Production Trends in the United States since 1870* (New York: National Bureau of Economic Research Publications, 1934), pp. 302–303.

[119] William Henry Dean, Jr., *The Theory of the Geographic Location of Economic Activities* (selections from a Harvard doctoral dissertation; Ann Arbor: Edwards Brothers, Inc., 1938), p. 32. As the statistics given here clearly demonstrate, by the middle of the 1880's it was a well-established practice to assess ton-mile freight charges which fell off quite markedly, but not uniformly, with increases in the length of haul. The data were collected in 1884 for four different Michigan stations on each of the listed railroads. See Cullom, *op. cit.*, Appendix 39.

Railroad	Average haul (miles)	Revenue per ton-mile (cents)
Chicago and Grand Trunk	73.60	2.23
Detroit, Lansing and Northern	75.39	2.24
Detroit, Grand Haven, and Milwaukee	78.17	2.09
Flint and Père Marquette	100.34	1.69
Chicago and West Michigan	103.33	1.15
Michigan Central	111.95	1.72
Grand Rapids and Indiana	166.83	1.50
Lake Shore and Michigan Southern	202.90	0.887

[120] The standardization of railroad gauges was critical in facilitating the elimination of previously mandatory transshipments.

of possible supply areas, providing access to superior raw materials or semifinished goods, and allowing the combination of new resources. In effect, transport improvements permitted large producers or agglomerations with low marginal outlays per unit of product partially or totally to usurp the potential raw-material consumption of nonproducing urban centers and firms (cities) with higher production costs. In general, this ultimately resulted in a still larger scale of output, some multiplier effect, and additional growth of the favored city.

The paramount importance of initial rail and terminal facility advantages to urban-industrial growth is best exemplified by Chicago. In 1860 Chicago was a city of moderate size (Table 2.3), with less than 5,400 workers employed in printing, carpentering and cabinetmaking, boot and shoe production, baking, coopering, tailoring, brickmaking, and other small-scale industries that catered primarily to local markets.[121] Even the city's 16 foundries and machine shops, with almost 600 laborers, were occupied largely with fulfilling special local orders; and not one manufacturing establishment in the young metropolis had a working force in excess of 200.[122] Within fifty years industrial employment in the physically expanded metropolis had grown to more than 325,000, many of them in categories whose firms frequently served distant markets (e.g., the machinery and foundry product industry had 41,492 employees; the slaughtering and meat packing industry had 27,083 employees; and the iron and steel industry, 16,730 employees).[123] Chicago's phenomenal rise was foreshown by 1860, when the city had emerged as the nation's most important railroad center, a terminus for 11 trunk roads and 20 branch and feeder lines. The advantages inherent to these facilities were first compounded by the spread of the Granger railroads in Iowa, Kansas, and Nebraska during the late sixties, and later by the continued expansion of the U.S. rail network as a whole. (Between 1870 and 1890 "the mileage of railroads entering Chicago had increased 370 per cent; their tonnage 490 per

---

[121] 8th Census of the U.S., 1860, *Manufactures* (Washington, D. C.: 1865), pp. 86–87.

[122] *Ibid.*, p. 86. In 1860 Cyrus McCormick's agricultural machinery plant had exactly 200 workers. For a descriptive account of the early phases of Chicago's industrial ascent see Elmer A. Riley, *The Development of Chicago and Vicinity as a Manufacturing Center Prior to 1880* (Chicago: University of Chicago, Department of History, 1911).

[123] 13th Census of the U.S., 1910, *Manufactures: Reports for Principal Industries, op. cit.*, pp. 916–917.

cent.")[124] Most strikingly, when the number of industrial employees in Chicago doubled from 105,000 to 210,000 during the 1884–1890 boom period, "there was a rush of manufacturing concerns to locate in the . . . area to obtain the advantage of its superior terminal facilities [including belt lines] and favorable railroad rates."[125]

In addition to railroad developments, the electrification of urban transportation also carried far-reaching implications for the metropolitan concentration of population and manufacturing. However, unlike the changes associated with the railroad that *directly stimulated* agglomeration and the growth of some cities at the expense of others, the transformations wrought by electrically powered trolleys, subways, elevated lines, and interurban commuter railways, were significant only because they permitted the selective urban accretion of people and factories *to continue* in a modified form.

During the 1880's and early 1890's a number of expansion-threatening diseconomies began to loom large on the horizon in those favored cities where the circular and cumulative growth process was advancing most rapidly. Spiraling land values in existing industrial districts represented the greatest cost obstacle to entrepreneurs wishing to opt for a plant site in a major city. Typically, front foot values in Chicago's wholesaling-industrial areas increased from $600 in the depression of 1879, to upwards of $5,000 in 1891, and in roughly the same period the aggregate value of the 211 square miles of land in the city's 1933 corporate limits went from $250,000,000 to $1,500,000,000.[126] At the same time that residential, commercial, and industrial congestion were making land scarce and expensive in the urban core, local taxes and nuisance legislation were also proving less conducive to the downtown location of truly massive production facilities. Furthermore, so long as horse-drawn vehicles served as the principal nonpedestrian form of circulation, new industrial establishments had relatively little freedom

---

[124] Homer Hoyt, *One Hundred Years of Land Values in Chicago: The Relationship of the Growth of Chicago to the Rise of its Land Values, 1830–1933* (Chicago: University of Chicago Press, 1933), p. 143. For a discussion of the impact of the railroads during the initial decades of Chicago's expansion see Wyatt Winton Belcher, *The Economic Rivalry between St. Louis and Chicago, 1850–1880* (New York: Columbia University Studies in History, Economics and Public Law, No. 529, 1947).

[125] Hoyt, *op. cit.*, pp. 143–144.

[126] *Ibid.*, pp. 175, 470. The aggregate land value of Chicago was $60,000,000 in 1861, and while oscillating after the early nineties, the figure rose to $2,000,000,000 in 1915.

of site selection within large urban centers unless the firm chose to construct residences adjacent to relatively isolated suburban operations; for, although speeds of six miles an hour could occasionally be attained by horsecars, they were usually so slow that two and a half miles was both the approximate limit of effective commuting services and the maximum radius from within which any plant could hope to attract laborers.[127]

Evasion of land-cost diseconomies and solution of the journey-to-work dilemma were made possible by the well-timed appearance of the electric streetcar and other forms of electric traction. In 1887, the year prior to Frank J. Sprague's perfecting experiments, only 35 miles of track and 60 cars were operated by electric street railways.[128] Three years later, 2,350 cars were in daily use on 1,262 miles of track, and the rapid replacement of the horsecar was well under way (Table 2.6).

TABLE 2.6 *Miles of Track Operated by Animal-Powered and Electric-Powered Commuter Services, 1890–1907*

	Miles operated by animal power	Miles operated by electric power
1890	5,661	1,262[a]
1902	259	21,908[b]
1907	136	34,060[b]

SOURCE: Bureau of the Census, Special Reports, *Street and Electric Railways, 1907* (Washington, D. C.: 1910), p. 23.

[a] Includes lines "confined mainly to urban districts and operated on public streets."

[b] Includes interurban passenger lines passing through rural areas.

Shortly after the turn of the century, every rapidly growing city was the hub of an intricate network of electrified commuter transportation (Table 2.7). Permissive of longer journeys to work and of factory construction at the urban periphery, where lower land costs prevailed and larger sites were available, the coming of electric traction heralded the decentralization of metropolitan manufacturing. The story was nearly

---

[127] For related remarks see James E. Vance, Jr., "Labor-Shed, Employment Field, and Dynamic Analysis in Urban Geography," *Economic Geography*, Vol. 36 (1960), pp. 189–220; Sam B. Warner, Jr., *Streetcar Suburbs: The Process of Growth in Boston, 1870–1900* (Cambridge: Harvard University Press and the M.I.T. Press, 1962); and David Ward, "A Comparative Historical Geography of Streetcar Suburbs in Boston, Massachusetts and Leeds, England: 1850–1920," *Annals of the Association of American Geographers*, Vol. 54 (1964), pp. 477–489.

[128] Passer, *op. cit.*, pp. 248–254.

TABLE 2.7 *Miles of Electric Traction Operating Entirely within, or Terminating in, Selected U.S. Cities, 1907*

	Miles of track
New York	1,595[a]
Chicago	1,354
Philadelphia	756[b]
Boston	1,362
Pittsburgh	649
St. Louis	502[c]
San Francisco–Oakland	478[d]
Baltimore	413
Cleveland	586
Detroit	704
Los Angeles	926

SOURCE: Compiled from *Street and Electric Railways, 1907,* op. cit., pp. 330–376.
[a] Not including lines or tubes extending into Connecticut and New Jersey.
[b] Not including lines terminating in Camden, New Jersey.
[c] Not including lines terminating in East St. Louis, Illinois.
[d] Not including lines terminating in Richmond and other Bay Area centers.

everywhere the same: in Chicago, the iron and steel, cement, chemical, railroad equipment, and food products industries began to flourish in the Calumet region, South Chicago, and the Indiana suburbs; in the San Francisco Bay Area, removal of the necessity to integrate spatially housing and production brought about the development of industrial districts in Emeryville, Berkeley, Richmond, East Oakland, and San Leandro;[129] and in Detroit, large plants arose near commuter lines around the city's perimeter.[130] In summary, where other conditions were conducive to the size growth of large urban-industrial agglomerations, electric traction facilitated the perpetuation of concentration by allowing the unit of concentration (the metropolis) to lessen its density and to assume a more spatially dispersed or "subcentralized" form.[131]

[129] See James E. Vance, Jr., *Geography and Urban Evolution in the San Francisco Bay Area* (Berkeley: University of California, Institute of Governmental Studies, 1964), pp. 58–59.

[130] See maps in L. S. Wilson, "Functional Areas in Detroit, 1890–1933," *Papers of the Michigan Academy of Science, Arts and Letters,* Vol. 22 (1947), pp. 399–404; or Amos H. Hawley, *Human Ecology* (New York: The Ronald Press, 1950), pp. 386–388. For greater details on the emergence of industrial suburbs that incidentally underwent unprecedented growth in the first decade of the twentieth century, see Graham Romeyn Taylor, *Satellite Cities: A Study of Industrial Suburbs* (New York: D. Appleton and Company, 1915).

[131] In somewhat different terms it has been argued that

... the peripheric expansion of urban population and the centrifugal scattering of manufacturing plants do not [as some nongeographers would have it] indicate

In a different vein, none of the forementioned repercussions of improved railroad transportation can be wholly divorced from the historical distinction between cities with superior, and those with inferior, trade routes. Traditionally, the selective growth of cities was interpreted almost entirely in terms of site and situation,[132] and this is understandable; for nine of today's eleven most important industrial metropolises occupy superior Atlantic, Great Lakes, or Pacific coastal sites, and the remaining two, St. Louis and Pittsburgh, thrive at or near a strategic river confluence. In other words, all eleven centers are located in the proximity of major break-in-bulk points where the manufacture of some products is made all the more economical by the need to transfer potential inputs from one carrier to another locally (production elsewhere would require the movement of an unreduced weight and an additional and unnecessary incurrence of transshipment costs) and where, because of the convergence of transport nets, the expectation of interregional and/or international trade has been high since a very early phase of local development.[133] However, site and situation arguments fail to shed light on the *processes* underlying the selective growth of cities. As Dean and others have pointed out,[134] transport advances do not bring equal benefit to all existing routes but instead increase the relative importance of a few "primary nodes" by precipitating either a "radical change in the strategy of the flow of traffic" or "an intensification in the utilization of certain routes and sites." Radical changes in traffic media and prevailing routes certainly contributed to the stunting of the relative growth of New Orleans, Cincinnati, and Louisville (the fifth, sixth, and tenth cities of the country in 1860);[135] on the other

---

a declining tendency towards concentration, but only a modified concentration, a new form of urban growth.

For a more detailed exposition see Edgar Kant, "Suburbanization, Urban Sprawl and Commutation," *Lund Studies in Geography,* Series B, Human Geography, No. 13 (1957), pp. 244–309, especially pp. 244–253.

[132] See, for example, Lawrence V. Roth, "The Growth of American Cities," *Geographical Review,* Vol. 5 (1918), pp. 384–398.

[133] Compare with comments by Smolensky and Ratajczak, *op. cit.,* pp. 101–102.

[134] Dean, *op. cit.,* p. 41; see also pp. 35–38, and Isard, "Transportation Development and Building Cycles," *op. cit.,* p. 93. Remarks on the evolution of "high-priority" transport linkages and on the circular growth of transport demands and transport construction, and other relevant ideas, are contained in Edward J. Taafe, Richard L. Morrill, and Peter R. Gould, "Transport Expansion in Underdeveloped Countries," *Geographical Review,* Vol. 53 (1963), pp. 503–529.

[135] Brooklyn, which was the third largest city in the United States in 1860, is here, as elsewhere in these essays, included with New York City.

hand, intensified use of the route through the Hudson and Mohawk Valleys strengthened New York City's dominance in the late nineteenth century.[136] In short, by definition, highly nodal points on superior routes offer better accessibility to materials and markets, and these favorable conditions are usually translated into scale and agglomeration economies that in turn perpetuate growth and initial advantages. Finally, the theoretically critical importance of some nodal points is consistent with the fact that manufacturing growth in the United States from 1860 to 1910 was most marked in some of the already developed commercial, mercantile cities.

Agglomeration Economies and Reduction of Production Costs

Production innovations, like transport improvements, tended to confer advantages on a few cities rather than on all. Advances in American industrial technology during the period under discussion almost inevitably provoked diminished production (input) outlays per unit of output. New machinery and new techniques also required large capital investment and an increase in the optimal size of operation. Thus the avalanche of post-Civil War innovations brought a tremendous impetus toward shifts in manufacturing scale (production function shifts) and an attendant urban concentration of production that involved both the expansion of existing plants and the establishment of new facilities. The pronounced scale shifts in American manufacturing between 1860 and the outbreak of World War I were partly reflected by changes in establishment size. For example, the average establishment in 1860 had about 9 employees and a product value of $13,420, as compared with more than 25 employees and nearly $88,000 product value in 1914.[137] As these figures imply, scale shifts went hand in hand with almost uninterrupted increases in worker productivity; in the 1899–1914 interval alone, the physical output of U.S. manufacturing doubled, the number of wage earners was amplified 50 per cent, and aggregate wage-earner hours per unit of product dropped more than 25 per cent.[138]

---

[136] The late nineteenth-century shift in importance between canals and railroads in the Hudson and Mohawk Valleys appears to have been at least partly responsible for Albany's modest population growth and steep decline in rank from 1860 to 1910 (see Tables 2.4 and 2.5).

[137] Isaac Lippincott, *Economic Development of the United States* (New York: D. Appleton, 1921), p. 476.

[138] Solomon Fabricant, *Employment in Manufacturing, 1899–1939* (New York: National Bureau of Economic Research, 1942), pp. 9, 19. Value added

Perhaps most revealing and imposing is the fact that, in 1914, 3,819 of 275,791 establishments accounted for 35.2 per cent of the nation's industrial wage earners and 41.4 per cent of the value added by manufacturing.[139]

In neo-Weberian terminology, industrial innovations, by reducing or "compressing" per unit production costs, permitted a substitution of additional output and lengthier shipments (greater transport outlays) for labor and other per unit production savings, and therefore prompted a greater extension of market areas than would have occurred if only transportation improvements had been present. Augmentation of market areas again promised the division of fixed costs over an increasing volume of production, which induced still larger optimal scales of production and higher thresholds.

Consequently, *technical innovations that yielded lower per unit production costs tended to favor growth and industrial agglomeration in those few cities that had originally initiated efficient production* (places with successful adaptors and adopters), *and at the same time arrested the development of nonproducing and inefficient centers* (places with unsuccessful adaptors and adopters, and places with no risk-taking entrepreneurs). As thresholds reached higher and higher levels, and as the optimal scale of operation for raw-material-oriented and footloose (nonthreshold) factories grew, the possibilities of entry into the market or expansion of existing facilities became confined to a smaller and smaller number of cities, and many manufacturing functions shifted from lower-order to higher-order urban places[140] and/or became more

---

per wage earner in manufacturing and mining increased, according to 1879 prices, 18 per cent between 1869 and 1879, 46 per cent in the following decade, and over 9 per cent between 1889 and 1899 (Gallman, *op. cit.*, p. 31). Also note bottom of Table 2.2.

[139] U.S. Bureau of the Census, *Abstract of the Census of Manufactures, 1914* (Washington, D. C.: 1917), p. 390. Another 10.9 per cent of the country's manufacturing establishments accounted for an additional 39.4 per cent of the value added.

[140] Again, this implies that the emergence of a more clearly delineated urban hierarchy is in itself a consequence of the rapid industrialization of any given space-economy (economically integrated geographic area). That is, as technical progress dictates larger production establishments and clusters, once ubiquitously distributed industries and completely new manufactures more or less sort themselves out according to urban size, and the hierarchy develops more levels, or becomes more evident. These suggestions are merely a variation of the economist's notion that "Innovations are not simply inventions or new products, . . . innovation is a structural change that destroys old profitabilities (for firms,

geographically concentrated. Occasionally, urban centers of lesser size and rank, uncharacterized by previous long-term growth momentum, blossomed into "industrial cities" of submetropolitan dimensions via the agglomeration of similar nonthreshold production units (e.g., Youngstown, Grand Rapids, and other currently medium-sized cities in the Great Lakes states).

Industrial innovations bore ramifications for selective urban growth other than those that allowed substitution of transport outlays for labor and other production outlays. Because a single cost-reducing invention was often applicable to a number of industries, innovation bred innovation, frequently creating new input-output linkages or the vertical disintegration of production, thereby often compelling proximity of successive stages of production, that in turn, as earlier mentioned, resulted in a locally concentrated rather than a geographically dispersed multiplier. And because, in addition, a sequence of lower prices and greater demand frequently accompanied production-cost decreases, and the converging technology of locally unlinked industries fostered complementary labor supplies, it is easy to understand why metropolises with innovation-implementing entrepreneurs grew at the expense of lesser cities and settlements. In fact, it once again becomes clear that the scale and external economies associated with urban-industrial activities are (were) not "simply additive" but "multiplicative in a complex fashion."[141]

A study contemporary to the above-described consequences of production innovations depicted the 1880-to-1890 decline of small-town industry in an area stretching from Detroit to Des Moines;[142] and the disappearance of local machine shops, sawmills, flour mills, furniture workshops, brick- and tile-producing establishments, and agricultural-implement manufacture was attributed partly to "the substitution of production on a large scale,"[143] although, admittedly, in assessing specific locational developments of the post-Civil War decades it is ex-

---

industries, and perhaps even regions). . . ." Alfred H. Conrad and John R. Meyer, "Income Growth and Structural Change: The United States in the Nineteenth Century," in *The Economics of Slavery and Other Studies in Econometric History* (Chicago: Aldine Publishing Company, 1964), p. 117.

[141] Isard, *Location and Space-Economy, op. cit.,* p. 188.

[142] Henry J. Fletcher, "The Doom of the Small Town," *Forum,* Vol. 19 (1895), pp. 214–223. A concomitant decline of small towns in Massachusetts and New Hampshire was bemoaned by the *Commercial and Financial Chronicle,* Vol. 52 (February 7, 1891), pp. 221–222; cited in Kirkland, *op. cit.,* pp. 237–238.

[143] Adna Ferrin Weber, *op. cit.,* p. 188.

tremely difficult and perhaps nearly meaningless to segregate the impact of production innovations from that of reduced transport costs.

In view of almost universal population increases, it is even more noteworthy that many Midwestern counties experienced absolute declines in manufacturing employment for periods as long as thirty years (1870–1900); that the industrial work force of a not inconsiderable number of other Midwestern counties decreased absolutely for at least twenty years (1870–1890, or 1880–1900); and that still other Midwestern counties lost manufacturing wage earners for two or more inconsecutive decades during the late nineteenth century (Map 2.1).[144]

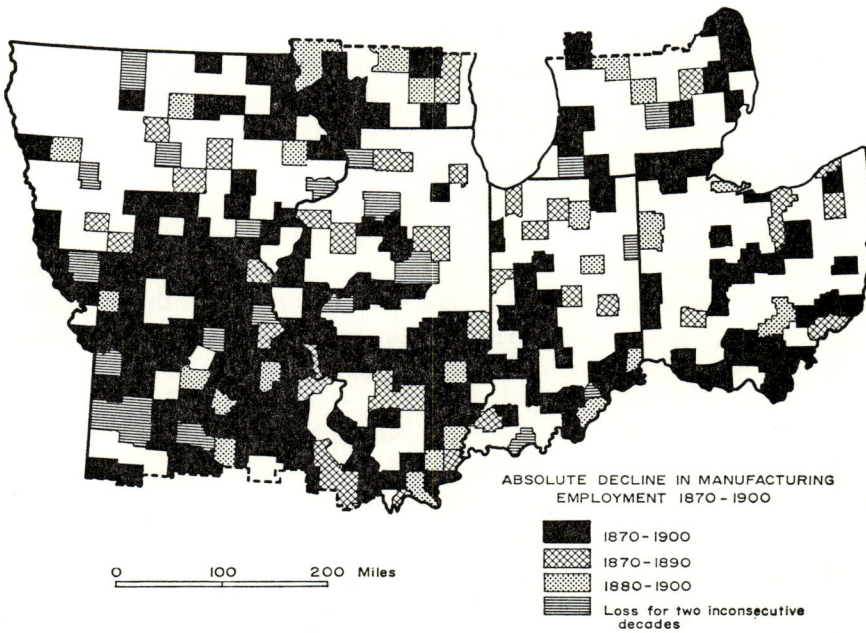

MAP 2.1 Counties in a selected portion of the Midwest with absolute manufacturing losses for at least two decades between 1870 and 1900. Compiled from the 9th through 12th Censuses of the U.S.

It is conjecturable that absolute employment declines in the Midwest and elsewhere could be demonstrated to have been of longer duration if the data for 1860 and 1910 were comparable with those from 1870 to 1900 (the census of 1860 omitted many artisans and workshop

---

[144] Because of changes in worker productivity, there were occasional instances where small increments in value added by manufacture occurred despite absolute decreases in county industrial employment.

activities that were recorded in the increasingly efficient returns of 1870–1900,[145] and the 1910 census no longer tallied "neighborhood and hand" industries). In addition, most of those Midwestern counties that were neither diminishing in absolute manufactural importance, nor included the most rapidly growing cities or their fledgling suburbs, underwent one of two kinds of relative industrial decline between 1870 and 1900.[146] The counties in question either had percentage gains in population that outstripped their percentage gains in manufacturing employment or failed to register percentage increments in their industrial work forces comparable to those of Chicago, St. Louis, Cleveland, or Detroit (Maps 2.2 and 2.3). Both of these conditions, and particularly the former, imply that existing and potential producers in the towns and cities of the relatively declining counties had a portion of their expanded local market usurped by firms in nearby metropolises or in rate-favored Atlantic Coast centers.[147]

The syndrome of reduced production costs, larger optimal scales of factory operation, and geographic concentration conducive to selective urban growth was especially manifest in the agricultural implement and machinery, "malt liquor" (beer and ale), and iron and steel industries, all three belonging to that select group of manufacturing categories whose 1860 and 1910 census returns are relatively comparable.

[145] The custom of the Census Office had been "to exclude from the list of manufacturing establishments all enterprises having a product of less than $500 during the census year. The census of 1860, however, had failed to record many artisans whose activity entitled them to record .... In the census of 1870, however, the omissions appear to have been proportionately less numerous, first, because of a general advance in prices between 1860 and 1870, bringing many enterprises which had not been recorded in 1860 incontestably above the $500 minimum, and, second, because of stringent instructions to the assistant marshals concerning establishments of this smaller type." Thorp, *op. cit.*, pp. 29–30.

[146] The few nonmetropolitan counties of the Midwest that had neither absolute nor relative industrial setbacks in their urban settlements during the 1870–1900 period were predominantly composed of cases where the virtual absence of manufacturing in 1870 distorted meager absolute gains into impressive percentage increases. For example, 17 of Iowa's 18 "nonconforming" counties had under 2.5 per cent of their respective 1900 populations employed in manufacturing (Map 2.2), and in most of these instances the figure was actually well below 1.0 per cent.

[147] The presence of absolute gains in the relatively declining counties does not preclude the elimination or disappearance of some production categories. Some small cities recorded net employment gains while expanding output in some ubiquitous (baking, printing and publishing, etc.) and specialized foot-loose categories, and shrinking or ceasing production in industries with mounting thresholds.

64   AMERICAN METROPOLITAN GROWTH

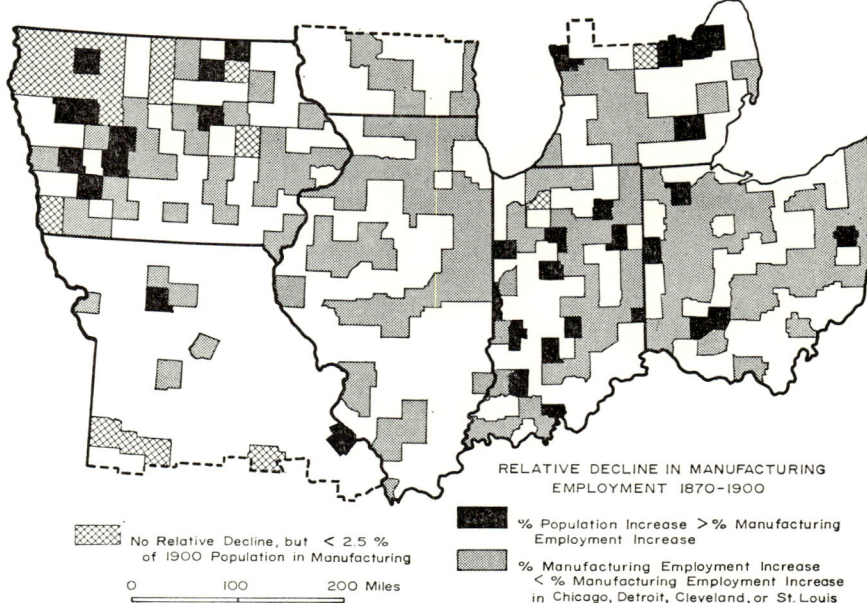

MAP 2.2   Counties in a selected portion of the Midwest with either relative manufacturing employment decreases between 1870 and 1900, or less than 2.5 per cent of their 1900 population employed in manufacturing.

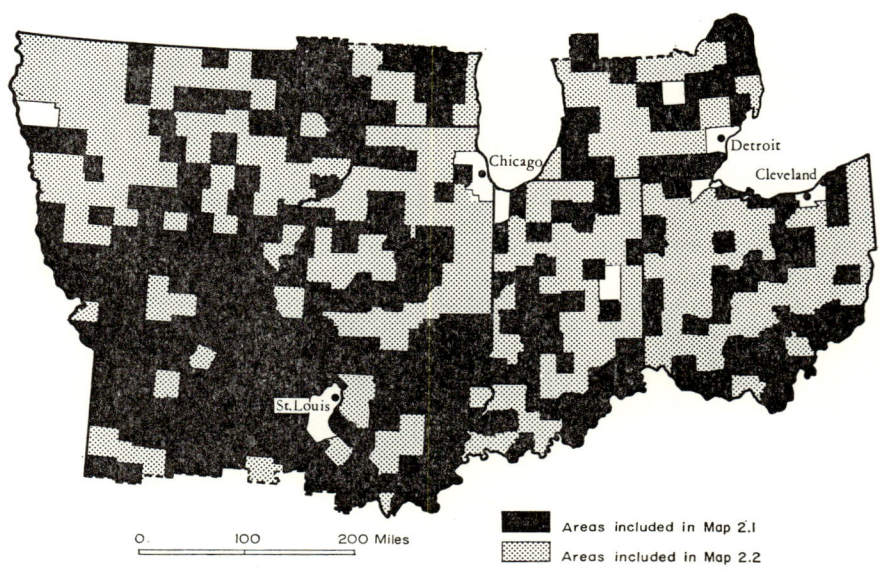

MAP 2.3   Maps 2.1 and 2.2 combined and generalized.

In the agricultural implement and machinery industry, where output became increasingly characterized by reapers, threshers, mowers, and other large pieces of equipment, rather than by hand tools, there was a steady decrease in the number of producing units following 1870, despite an enormous expansion of total production. Moreover, the elimination of most workshop production and technically stimulated scale increases combined to bring about a better than twenty-fold magnification of value added per establishment in the interval from 1860 to 1910 (Table 2.8). For decades the industry had been market oriented (transport sensitive) and had slowly shifted westward in the footsteps of agricultural expansion; thus, the emergence of a major concentration in Chicago (which may be viewed as having grown at the expense of less efficient agricultural implement and machinery centers) was only logical, given the city's hub position in the emerging Midwestern rail network, its cheap freight rates, its local iron production, and *its extremely early start in factory-scale operations*.[148] While Chicago only accounted for 3.5 per cent of the national industry's value added in 1860, it answered for almost 25 per cent of the same total in 1900, and, during the course of 40 years, value added by agricultural machinery production multiplied at a rate better than 2.5 times that of population growth in the Windy City (Table 2.9).

Until the late 1870's, the scale of brewing establishments was limited by their dependence upon natural ice for the mandatory performance of cooling operations. Ice could move only short distances and be assembled in relatively small quantities because of its highly perishable quality and extremely low value per unit weight, and therefore breweries were almost ubiquitously distributed throughout the country's northern and western states. With the introduction of ammonia compressors and other forms of mechanical refrigeration, and with the adoption of the refrigerated railroad car, mass production breweries began to increase in number and size while the competitive position of the small-scale, small-city beer producer was imperiled. Despite a growing population and increasing per capita consumption, from 1880 to 1910 there was a net decrease of at least 775 in the number of breweries operating in the United States (Table 2.8).[149] During this period

---

[148] The McCormick Manufacturing Company founded its Chicago reaper-producing facilities in 1847; and John S. Wright and Company, makers of reapers and mowers, appeared in the same city in 1853.

[149] There are indications that the disappearance of small-scale and inefficient establishments may have assumed much greater proportions. One survey, which

the production of "malt liquors" gravitated to larger cities (i.e., the threshold level was raised), and these more populous centers, benefiting from the industry's linkages with machine shops and cooperies or bottle manufactories, as well as from other multiplier effects, grew in some measure at the expense of former producing communities. The embellished concentration of brewing in New York City and its environs is representative of what occurred to one degree or another near the turn of the century in every city at the top of the U.S. urban hierarchy (Table 2.9).

The post-Civil War parade of technical innovations that yielded lower per unit production costs in the U.S. iron and steel industry was long and swift. Propelled by the rapid evolution of larger and hotter blast furnaces, and by the introduction of the Bessemer process in 1867 and the spread of the open-hearth process in the 1890's — more than 20 years after its first appearance — productivity rates[150] and average size of establishment figures soared (Table 2.8). After 1880 the expansion of new blast furnace capacities accelerated to such a degree, roughly doubling from 1885 to 1890,[151] and the capital requirements of up-to-date iron and steel production facilities became so great, that the competitive position of small-scale plants deteriorated to a point where many of them could no longer maintain operation. As a consequence, geographic concentration in already large and efficiently producing cities, to the presumed detriment of size growth in lesser abandoned centers, was the hallmark of the 1880–1910 era. Although the circular and cumulative growth process was enhanced in Chicago, Cleveland, and Detroit by the growing agglomeration of iron and steel output, it was in Pittsburgh and its suburbs, where development was aided by the advantages of an early start in large-scale production, raw material

---

apparently included basement and back-of-the-bar producers who may not have been tallied by the census marshals, reported that the number of breweries operating in the United States oscillated downward from a peak of 3,293 in 1876, to 2,741 in 1880, to 1,816 in 1900, to 1,568 in 1910 (the decline continued after this date, and was spurred on by the spread of "dry" legislation in rural areas). See John P. Arnold and Frank Penman, *History of the Brewing Industry and Brewing Science in America* (Chicago: 1933), pp. 74–75.

[150] For steel-mill products alone, the number of wage earners per unit of product decreased about 75 per cent between 1869 and 1909; while for blast-furnace products alone, the number of wage earners per unit of output fell better than 60 per cent in the relatively brief period from 1899 to 1914. Fabricant, *op. cit.*, pp. 61–62.

[151] Clark, *op. cit.*, Vol. 3, pp. 74–75.

availability, and the notorious "Pittsburgh plus" pricing system,[152] that the ramifications were most spectacular. By 1910, when the Smoky City's blast furnaces had been the largest in the world for several years,[153] there were over 61,000 laborers, clerks, and salaried officials directly employed by the iron and steel industry in the Pittsburgh "Metropolitan District," and local value added in that industry, which had accounted for 7.7 per cent of the national aggregate in 1860, stood at 23.2 per cent of the U.S. total (Table 2.9).

Except for anomalies due to competitive strategy, the area in which the large-scale and/or localized (concentrated) urban producers of any industrial category could theoretically eliminate less efficient establishments was limited only by the locus of points where their marginal production costs plus costs of transport inputs equaled market price. However, this is not to say that the market usurpation associated with the growth of large urban-industrial complexes in any sense involved the total elimination of inefficient firms. Elimination was typically kaleidoscopic inasmuch as there presumably was a constant procession of unsuccessful adaptors and adopters making their temporary entrances on the locational stage. Furthermore, although inefficient production units were most likely to fall by the wayside when they were jeopardized by the overlapping critical isodapanes (potential market boundaries) of factories in two or more favored metropolises, there were at least two sets of circumstances whereunder vulnerable, outmoded plants could survive in the face of market expansion by larger and more efficient enterprises. In one instance, factories in rapidly growing centers would assimilate all or part of the inefficacious plant's local-growth market; that is, the jeopardized unit would retain its previous level of output but fail to capture its share of increases in the local market that arose from population growth, purchasing power increments, or wider consumer acceptance of the products involved. Alternatively, the higher-cost small-scale manufacturing unit that had a discontinuous market

---

[152] Under the "Pittsburgh plus," or single-basing-point system that was operative in the early years of the twentieth century, "steel was sold at the Pittsburgh base price plus the rail freight from Pittsburgh to the consuming center, *regardless of the location of the producing plant* [underlining added]. As a result Pittsburgh producers were able to quote the same prices as competitors whose products were closer to the new market centers." See Allan Rodgers, "Industrial Inertia: A Major Factor in the Location of the Steel Industry in the United States," *Geographical Review*, Vol. 42 (1952), pp. 56–66, especially pp. 60–61.

[153] Clark, *op. cit.*, p. 73.

TABLE 2.8 *Scale Shifts and Concentration in the Agricultural Implement and Machinery, Malt Liquor, and Iron and Steel Industries, 1860–1910*

	1860	1870	1880	1890	1900	1910
	Agricultural implements and machinery					
Establishments	1,982	2,076[a]	1,943	910	715	640
Wage Earners	14,814	25,249	39,580	42,544	46,582	50,551
Wage Earners per Establishment	7.5	12.2	20.4	46.8	65.1	79.0
Value Added (1,000's of current $)	11,862.8	30,593.0[b]	37,109.3	49,668.4	57,262.8	86,022.0
Value Added per Establishment (1,000's of current $)	6.0	14.7[b]	19.1	54.6	80.1	134.4
	Malt liquors					
Establishments	1,269	1,972[a]	2,191	1,248	1,509	1,414
Wage Earners	6,433	12,443	26,220	34,800	39,532	54,579
Wage Earners per Establishment	5.1	6.3	12.0	27.9	26.2	38.6
Value Added (1,000's of current $)	11,313.6	27,529.0[b]	44,221.9	118,728.3	185,594.8	278,134.0
Value Added per Establishment (1,000's of current $)	8.9	14.0[b]	20.2	95.1	122.9	196.7
Output (1,000's of barrels)	[c]	6,600	13,300	27,600	39,500	59,500
Output per Establishment (1,000's of barrels)		3.3	6.1	22.1	26.2	42.1

TABLE 2.8 (continued)

	Iron and steel					
	1860	1870	1880	1890	1900	1910
Establishments	559	426	1,005	645	668	654
Wage Earners	36,058	50,328	140,978	152,535	222,490	278,505
Wage Earners per Establishment	53.8	118.1	140.3	236.5	333.1	425.8
Value Added (1,000's of current $)	22,244.7	48,672.3[b]	105,286.5	135,176.5	281,569.3	399,013.1
Value Added per Establishment (1,000's of current $)	39.8	114.3[b]	104.8	209.6	421.5	610.1

SOURCES: Ninth through 13th censuses of the United States; and *Historical Statistics of the United States, Colonial Times to 1957*, op. cit., p. 415.

[a] Increase over 1860 figures probably exaggerated by more complete returns (see text).
[b] Considerably exaggerated by inflationary prices.
[c] No data available.

TABLE 2.9 *Concentration of the Agricultural Implement and Machinery, Malt Liquor, and Iron and Steel Industries in Selected U.S. Cities, 1860–1910*

Agricultural implements and machinery in Chicago		
	1860	1900[a]
Establishments	4	6
Wage Earners	294	10,245[b]
Wage Earners per Establishment	73.5	1,707.5
Value Added (1,000's of current $)	410.9	14,006.4
Value Added per Establishment (1,000's of current $)	102.7	2,334.4
% of U.S. Wage Earners	2.0	22.0
% of U.S. Value Added	3.5	24.5
1900 population/1860 population		15.1
1900 wage earners/1860 wage earners		34.8
1900 value added/1860 value added		40.3

Malt liquors in New York City			
	1860[c]	1900	1910[d]
Establishments	70	89	100
Wage Earners	689	4,824	7,836[e]
Wage Earners per Establishment	9.8	54.2	78.4
Value Added (1,000's of current $)	1,240.2	31,417.3	55,334.8
Value Added per Establishment (1,000's of current $)	17.7	353.0	553.3
% of U.S. Wage Earners	10.7	12.2	14.4
% of U.S. Value Added	11.0	16.9	19.9
1900 population/1860 population		2.9	
1900 wage earners/1860 wage earners		7.0	
1900 value added/1860 value added		29.9	

Iron and steel in Pittsburgh			
	1860[f]	1900	1910[g]
Establishments	16	36	64
Wage Earners	2,473	24,418	56,721[h]
Wage Earners per Establishment	154.6	678.3	886.3
Value Added (1,000's of current $)	1,715.6	36,002.8	92,609.1
Value Added per Establishment (1,000's of current $)	107.2	1,000.1	1,447.0
% of U.S. Wage Earners	6.9	11.0	20.4
% of U.S. Value Added	7.7	12.8	23.2
1900 population/1860 population		6.5	
1900 wage earners/1860 wage earners		9.9	
1900 value added/1860 value added		24.7	

SOURCES: 8th Census of the U.S., 1860, *Manufactures, op. cit.,* pp. 86, 373, 382, 494; 12th Census of the U.S., 1900, *Manufactures* (Washington, D. C.: 1902), Part II, pp. 180–181, 624–625, 792–793; and 13th Census of the U.S., 1910, *Manufactures: Reports for Principal Industries, op. cit.,* pp. 921, 981.

TABLE 2.9 (continued)

a Because of disclosure regulations, 1910 statistics were not revealed either for the municipality of Chicago or the Chicago "Metropolitan District."
b Does not include 3,509 salaried officials and clerks.
c New York and its boroughs as constituted after the consolidation of 1898.
d New York "Metropolitan District."
e Does not include 1,547 salaried officials and clerks.
f Allegheny County.
g Pittsburgh "Metropolitan District."
h Does not include 5,074 salaried officials and clerks.

area with nonlocal as well as local fragments could persist at a given level of output by relinquishing its distant customers to metropolitan competitors and substituting a portion of the local-growth market through exploiting established local consumer preferences and habits (allegiances). For specific industries, detailed capabilities for market expansion of agglomerated metropolitan producers can be put in the cost structure and relative location terms used elsewhere to develop a typology of modern manufacturing flows.[154]

Before leaving the question of reduced production costs and the selective growth of urban-industrial concentrations, it must be reiterated that urban diseconomies also accumulated and eventually became oppressive to *some* types of industries, even after the advent of electric traction. Nothing that has been said should be interpreted as meaning that advantages accrued indefinitely to the emerging major metropolises. In the half-century following 1860, urban diseconomies mounted, "diseconomies engendered by rises in the cost of living and money wages, in the costs of local materials produced under conditions of diminishing returns, in time-cost and other costs of transportation, and in land values and rents."[155] If it had not been for the continued amassing of these diseconomies, and for the maturing of automotive transportation, a cessation in the falling trend of long-haul railroad rates, new raw-material requirements, and regional population growth leading to the more widespread attainment of specific thresholds, it is highly probable that the eleven largest industrial metropolises would account for even more than their present 38.3 per cent of national value added by manufacturing.

[154] Note subsequent comments on relative accessibility, and Allan Pred, "Toward a Typology of Manufacturing Flows," *Geographical Review,* Vol. 54 (1964), pp. 65-84.

[155] Isard, *op. cit.,* p. 183. Isard's statement does not specifically refer to the period 1860-1910, but it nonetheless applies in varying degrees to conditions in each of that period's most rapidly growing cities.

Relative Accessibility

Relative accessibility, here defined as the accessibility of a city to the population or market of the country as a whole,[156] also influences the selective growth of cities. In general, *transportation improvements and lower unit production costs work to the advantage of points with high accessibility as opposed to points with low accessibility.*[157] This is partly because, by definition, low-accessibility areas have relatively small aggregate populations and incomes and consequently encounter difficulties in meeting scale thresholds for other than essential consumer goods. In addition, in serving a regional market of given sales volume, manufacturers in low-accessibility cities would have longer average shipments, and greater allocations for transport, than their counterparts in high-accessibility cities. The late nineteenth-century, low-accessibility firm, being in a comparatively undeveloped area, was probably further throttled in its development by the distribution and raw-material assembly disadvantages of a small-mileage railroad network that had few intersections and a low degree of connectivity.[158]

Despite these handicaps, some large metropolises should eventually arise in low-accessibility areas, even in the absence of the mass population shifts that have been characteristic of the United States in the twentieth century. Large metropolises are not totally alien to low-accessibility areas, but their potential numbers are limited. Growth of urban centers is possible partly because transportation economies may occasionally be substituted for production diseconomies; that is, for *some* goods, lower (suboptimal) scales of production, and consequently higher unit costs, are compensated by avoidance of the transcontinental

---

[156] Relative accessibility is measured in terms of population or market potential. For original definitions see John Q. Stewart, "Empirical Mathematical Rules Concerning the Distribution and Equilibrium of Population," *Geographical Review*, Vol. 37 (1947), pp. 461–485; and Chauncy D. Harris, "The Market as a Factor in the Localization of Industry in the United States," *Annals of the Association of American Geographers*, Vol. 44 (1954), pp. 315–348.

[157] It has been demonstrated that similarly sized cities "with high accessibility tend to have higher levels of manufacturing activity than those with low accessibility." Duncan and others, *op. cit.*, p. 128. Alfred Weber was also cognizant of the relationship between population concentration and degree of industrial agglomeration (*op. cit.*, p. 168).

[158] Cf. K. J. Kansky, *Structure of Transportation Networks* (Chicago: University of Chicago, Department of Geography, Research Paper No. 84, 1963), pp. 93–104.

freight costs that would be incurred if the product were imported from high-accessibility cities.[159] Expressed somewhat differently, a small number of low-accessibility cities can achieve metropolitan proportions because they are beyond the critical isodapanes of many market-oriented industries in high-accessibility centers, or, alternatively, because they are at great distances from cities of the same class in the urban hierarchy. Under such low-accessibility conditions, it is probably regional incapacity for duplicating many production and specialized service thresholds that, more than anything else, confines massive urban-size expansion to one or two large cities and inhibits the emergence of medium-sized centers.[160]

Regardless of these circumstances, the low-accessibility centers that do grow quickly during periods of rapid industrialization, like the corresponding cities in older high-accessibility areas, almost invariably possess some pertinent initial advantages. This is well illustrated by the 1860–1880 growth of San Francisco that occurred prior to the southern California land boom and the fleshing out of the entire state's extremely low market potential (accessibility). Although the city that controlled the gateway to the Sacramento and San Joaquin Valleys had only 2.6 per cent of its population employed in workshops and small factories as of 1860 (Table 2.2), it nonetheless accounted for 25 per cent of the state's industrial employment and 40 per cent of its value added by manufactures. Twenty years later, San Francisco had exploited transport improvements and agglomeration economies and thereby parlayed its initial advantages to a point where the city contained 65 per cent of the state's industrial employment and 69 per cent of its value added by manufacturing.[161] During this same score of years, San Francisco increased its population more than fourfold, to

[159] This would be especially true when the spreading of the low-accessibility city's skeletal transportation network promised to bring its market area closer to some unfulfilled threshold levels.

[160] See recent remarks on the abnormally low number of medium-sized central places in Sweden's low-accessibility areas in Gunnar Olsson and Åke Persson, "The Spacing of Central Places in Sweden," Papers and Proceedings of the Regional Science Association, Vol. 12 (Europe Congress, 1963), Philadelphia, 1964, pp. 87–93. Also note Olsson, *op. cit.*, pp. 11–12.

[161] 8th Census of the U.S., 1860, *Manufactures, op. cit.*, pp. 28–29, 35; and 10th Census of the U.S., *Statistics of Manufactures* (Washington, D. C.: 1883), pp. 92, 435–437. Fisheries and mining activities were deducted from the 1860 state totals.

nearly 234,000, while its largest "rival," Sacramento, had failed to double in size and had only 21,420 inhabitants.[162]

The more general influence of relative accessibility on American urban development in the late nineteenth century is roughly indicated by Maps 2.4 and 2.5. In 1860 the four largest cities in the country, New York (including Brooklyn), Philadelphia, Baltimore, and Boston, were in the highest-accessibility area. By 1900 such centers as Chicago, St. Louis, Cleveland, and Detroit had achieved large populations, though they were not in the area of highest accessibility. Agricultural development of the Midwest and the Great Plains, as well as urban-industrial growth itself, had created levels of accessibility between the Mississippi and the northern Appalachians that far exceeded those of any of the Atlantic Coast cities in 1860. The persistent growth of the older eastern metropolises (Table 2.3) is understandable in the light of the more than doubling of their accessibility during the forty years.[163] By the same token, no city on the low-accessibility Pacific Coast, including San Francisco and Los Angeles, had grown to the size of the largest Midwestern and Eastern cities, though the rise of the two California centers had been impressive. In addition, the high levels of accessibility existing by 1900 in both the Midwest and East facilitated the development of some specialized regional-threshold and nonthreshold manufacturing outside the major metropolises, and by extension, the emergence and size growth of submetropolitan "industrial cities" that filled in the middle ranks of the solidifying American urban hierarchy. On the other hand, already existing, lesser, high-accessibility urban units, such as Portland, Maine, and Albany, that failed to develop viable specialities on a large scale were doomed to tremendous declines in relative importance (Table 2.4).

[162] *Census of Population: 1960*, op. cit., pp. 6-18–6-22. Actually Oakland had a somewhat larger population than Sacramento by 1880, but there are strong grounds for not divorcing the former city's growth from that of San Francisco.

[163] In constructing isarithmic maps of transport costs to the national market for specific Swedish industries, Törnqvist assigned all exports to the market total of the ports of shipment. Gunnar Törnqvist, *Studier i Industrilokalisering* (Stockholm: Meddelanden från Geografiska Institutionen vid Stockholms Universitet, No. 153, 1963), pp. 215–274; and "Transport Costs as a Location Factor for Manufacturing Industry," *Svensk Geografisk Årsbok*, Vol. 38 (1962), pp. 37–60. If industrial exports were similarly assigned to New York, Philadelphia, Baltimore, and Boston, and if Maps 2.4 and 2.5 were maps of market potential rather than population potential, then the amplification of these cities' relative accessibility between 1860 and 1900 would be even more striking.

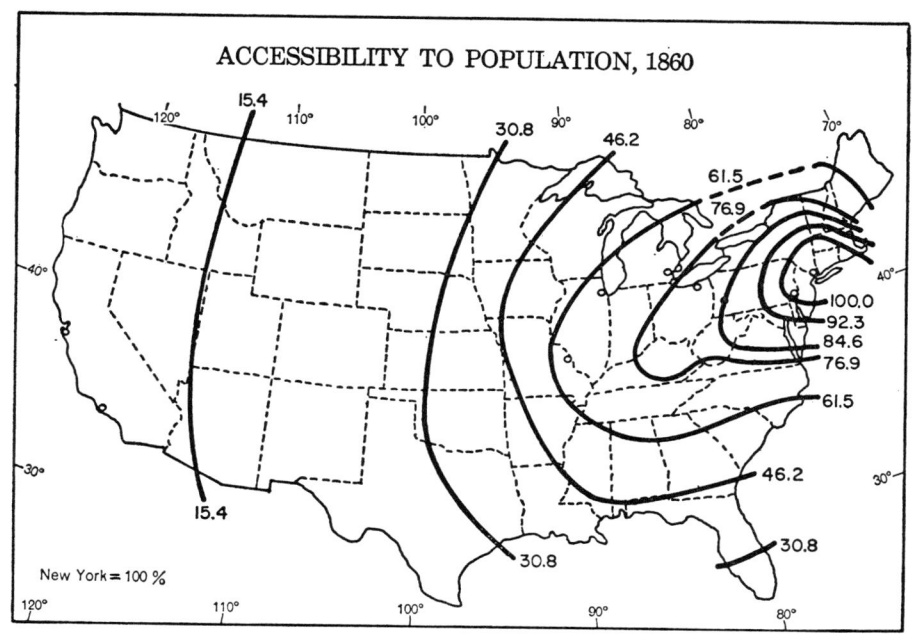

MAP 2.4 Accessibility to population, 1860. Adapted from John Q. Stewart and William Warntz, "Macrogeography and Social Science," *Geographical Review,* Vol. 48 (1958), Figure 7, p. 181.

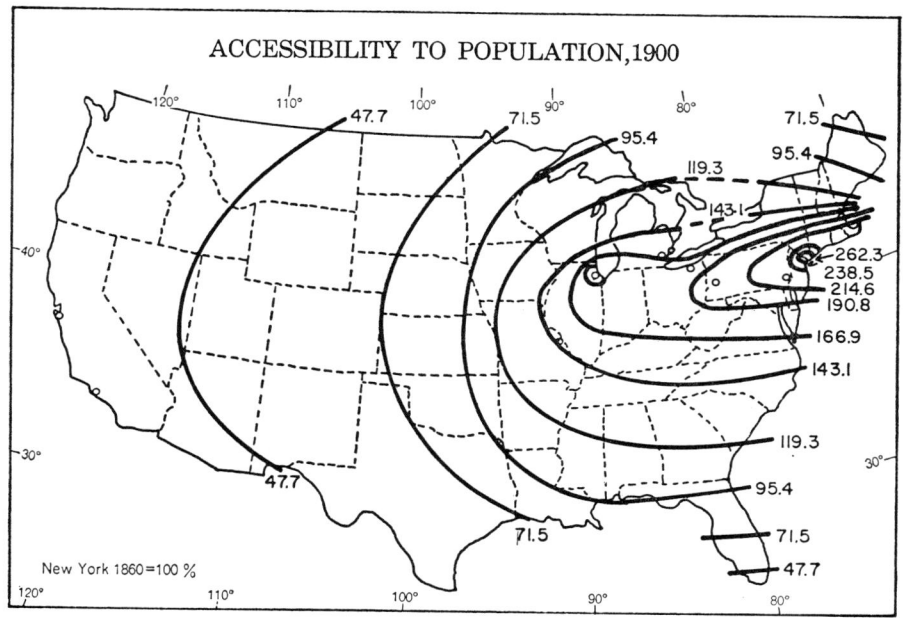

MAP 2.5 Accessibility to population, 1900. Adapted from John Q. Stewart, "Empirical Mathematical Rules Concerning the Distribution and Equilibrium of Population," Figure 11, p. 479 (see footnote 156).

Combination and Competition

The growth of trusts and mammoth corporations, the vertical and horizontal integration of previously independent firms, and the consolidation of small railroads into vast systems also had ramifications that confirmed the ascendancy of a few cities at the expense of others. The previously cited size-of-establishment statistics and specific discussion of the agricultural implement and machinery, malt liquor, and iron and steel industries provides only an inkling of the combination activity that gathered momentum after business recovered from the "panic" and depression of the seventies, and climaxed its first major crescendo in the late nineties (1898–1902) when traditional nonindustrial capital outlets were somewhat curtailed. The proliferation of limited-dividend manufacturing corporations, almost nonexistent outside of the textile industries in 1860 and numbering more than forty thousand in 1900, was another manifestation of the increasing concentration of industrial capital. By the turn of the century limited-dividend corporations "comprised barely a tenth of all establishments, [but] they produced 60 per cent of the value, and almost completely dominated the metal and technical branches."[164]

Although risk, irrational entrepreneurial behavior, and other factors sometimes prevented response to small local demands and prompted dependence on larger producers in big cities, the consequences of corporate manufacturing were particularly far-reaching in the industries that distributed to a large regional or national market. In such industries, excess-profit taking and the strategies of oligopolistic competition often prevented the appearance of new plants when minimum thresholds were fulfilled, or resulted in the corporative purchasing and closing of independent establishments with marginally profitable or inferior small-city locations. For these reasons, reality ran counter to Lösch's idealistic conditions of locational equilibrium (the third and fourth of Lösch's five conditions stipulate that "abnormal profits must disappear," and that "areas of supply, production, and sales [market areas] must be as small as possible").[165] In other words, the piratical competitive strategies of a few industrial giants fighting it out on a national or extensive re-

[164] McKelvey, *op. cit.*, p. 41.
[165] Lösch, *op. cit.*, pp. 95–96. Admittedly, after later reiterating that, in general, "a single good is *produced in as many localities as possible,*" Lösch added the following footnote: "This is true only for given techniques. Technical progress may bring about the opposite tendency — to decrease the number of producers." P. 259.

gional scale frequently hindered entry into the market, and/or jeopardized small-scale survival in the market, and generally favored the growth of producing cities to the detriment of inefficient and nonproducing centers. As a case in point, Westinghouse and General Electric, which had grown through mergers in the late eighties and early nineties, were able to restrict the entry of new locations (firms) into the production of generators, motors, and other heavy electric equipment by setting low prices, maintaining small profit margins, and colluding in a patent agreement (1896).[166] Moreover, it was often possible under oligopolistic competition that no single corporation could monopolize threshold markets in the South and West, and therefore exploitation of the threshold of scale economies was occasionally confined to producers in the somewhat older, higher-accessibility cities in the Manufacturing Belt (the industrialized Midwest and Northeast).[167] As consolidation sometimes limited production in such industries to a handful of plants, and as opportunity costs, or even chance or entrepreneurial whim, sometimes determined locational decisions within the older industrialized area of the country, it is still more comprehensible that similar-sized metropolises have (had) asymmetrical manufacturing structures.

As indicated earlier, preferential and discriminatory freight rates were an important by-product of railroad combination and competition, and they too had repercussions on the selective growth of cities. In spite of the formation of the Interstate Commerce Commission in 1887, it was some decades before discriminatory rates began to be effectively abolished on a wide scale. Throughout the period under discussion, below-average unit cost and below-operating-cost freight rates were not uncommon. Deficits were recouped on noncompetitive commodities and in areas where rivalry was lacking.[168]

---

[166] Passer, *op. cit.*, especially pp. 349 ff. Production competition, or competition through changes in the product, was also an important factor in the late nineteenth-century concentration of the electrical industries (pp. 316–318).

[167] See Ullman, *op. cit.*, pp. 186–187.

[168] For some period differential freight assessments by individual carriers took the form of imposing a higher rate on short-distance movements emanating from cities where other lines were not competing than on long-distance hauls from larger cities where shipping alternatives were many and competition was intense. The prevalence of various forms of preferential tariffs as late as 1908 is in part manifested by testimony that "the rate on merchandise of the first class per 100 pounds for fifty miles ranges from 12 cents to 32 cents in various districts between the Atlantic Ocean and the Missouri Valley." Logan G. McPherson, *Railroad Freight Rates in Relation to the Industry and Commerce of the United States* (New York: Henry Holt & Co., 1909), p. 172.

In general, rates were most propitious for diversely served terminal cities within "Official Territory" (a rate zone that included all the cities in Table 2.3 but San Francisco and Los Angeles). Rates were low for raw materials coming into the territory and high for goods manufactured outside it, and this arrangement "undoubtedly discouraged and retarded the diffusion of manufactures into outlying regions."[169] Besides, the oversupply of facilities in major terminal cities constantly forced the railroads to succumb to the badgering and clamoring of producers who wished to receive special concessions that would enable them to expand their market areas.

Typically, for a time, the "railroads west of Chicago followed the general policy of maintaining, as their share of all through tariffs, the rate charged for the transportation of products from interior points to Chicago or from Chicago to interior points."[170] This policy inevitably reduced through traffic between points east and west of Chicago and promoted manufacturing and other economic activities in the Illinois metropolis. Not surprisingly, at a later date Iowans complained that the growth of their urban centers was dampened by the railroad rates proffered to both Chicago and St. Louis.[171] In fact, for all benefiting cities, discriminatory rates had the tumbling-domino effect of lessening the significance of distance, of permitting greater agglomeration economies and multiplier effects through a widening of the market, of generating higher thresholds of entry for nonproducing centers, of eliminating small-scale inefficient competition, and of perpetuating the circular and cumulative size-growth process.

Availability of Labor and Capital

The external economies of labor and capital availability also operated as initial advantages favoring the growth of existing commercial foci over smaller places.

Many new or expanding industries may be viewed as having minimum labor as well as market thresholds, and within this context it fol-

---

[169] Perloff and others, *op. cit.*, p. 219. See also Fletcher, *op. cit.*, p. 219.
[170] Belcher, *op. cit.*, p. 198.
[171] Adna Ferrin Weber, *op. cit.*, p. 33. The more general impact of inequitable freight rates on small-city growth is indicated by some of the complaints brought before the 1887 Senate Select Committee on Interstate Commerce. There it was frequently charged in regard to rate discrimination "That such favoritism and secrecy introduce an element of uncertainty into legitimate business that greatly retards the development of our industries and commerce." Cullom, *op. cit.*, p. 181.

lows that "the [labor-sensitive] manufactures with the greatest number of wage earners can only be located in the larger cities, whereas the smaller ones may also be in the larger cities."[172] Therefore, older commercial and manufacturing centers were often the most probable places in which the undecided entrepreneur, making a marginal locational decision, would seek skills and manpower. Although semiskilled and unskilled labor might have been duplicated fairly easily from place to place, the significance of the size of the local labor pool became magnified as the average size of establishment increased and as technological advances demanded less and less in the way of previous experience or training from the potential factory hand. Work-force requirements were usually satisfied with particular ease in established large urban-industrial complexes because the migration mechanism channeled much of the cheap labor of European immigrants and rural-to-urban migrants into these relatively few places where relatives and friends had preceded them,[173] where foremen spoke the arrival's native tongue, and where public, private, and philanthropic job-placement institutions had arisen in great numbers.

The singular advantages of established industrial cities were even more pronounced with respect to skilled labor; for location or expansion elsewhere put the firm in the dilemma of finding "a labor market big enough to provide an adequate number of workers with the necessary aptitudes" or resigning itself "to a prolonged training period for a major segment of its labor force."[174] Furthermore, the skilled labor market in major ports of entry was such that, when existing local supplies temporarily dwindled, individual manufacturers could usually expand their skilled employment without resorting to costly recruitment from Europe or other American cities. "They were willing to take their chances of filling their requirements from a high immigrant stream. Confident that, when necessary, they could get European workers for particular tasks, and to oversee learners, ..."[175]

[172] George Kingsley Zipf, *Human Behavior and the Principle of Least Effort* (Cambridge: Addison-Wesley Press, 1949), p. 384.

[173] The cumulative character of the migration process, whereby over 37,000 Swedes and Norwegians could arrive in Chicago in a single year, not infrequently caused temporary gluts in the labor markets of major cities (Erickson, *op. cit.*, pp. 88–89) and thereby increased their locational attractiveness to new or expanding producers.

[174] Martin Segal, *Wages in the Metropolis* (Cambridge: Harvard University Press, 1960), p. 20. Also see Ohlin, *op. cit.*, p. 219.

[175] Erickson, *op. cit.*, pp. 33–34.

Capital availability (a province of the economist and only cursorily treated here) and knowledge of capital sources were crucial to industrial entrepreneurs. Although post-Civil War institutional innovations began to lower the barriers to interregional capital movements,[176] investment funds remained more readily available to manufacturing interests in traditional banking capitals such as New York, Philadelphia, Boston, and Baltimore, and in Chicago and St. Louis, the new central reserve cities created by law in 1887. The diffusion of knowledge regarding investment opportunities was most efficient in these and other centers, such as Cleveland, Detroit, and San Francisco, where the lines of commercial communication were of comparatively long standing. It again follows that these few cities exerted a strong attraction on the undecided marginal locator, and that elsewhere the chances for a new round of growth were correspondingly diminished. Along these same lines, it is significant that banks in the most rapidly growing urban-industrial centers offered lower interest rates than most or all of their counterparts in smaller competing cities of the same region. For example, the average weekly rate of discount from 1893 to 1897 was 3.932 per cent in Boston, but 4.982 per cent in Providence, and 6.000 per cent in Portland, Maine; and the corresponding rates in San Francisco and Los Angeles, while much higher (6.216 per cent and 7.057 per cent, respectively), were the lowest prevailing in any city in the Rocky Mountain and Pacific Coast States.[177] Virtually all of the slowly expanding Southern cities were not only encumbered with high local interest rates after the 1870's, but also with a small number of banks offering these rates — banks that were both unaggressive and antagonistic toward manufacturing.[178]

[176] This was especially true of short-term, as opposed to long-term, movements. "In the period from 1870 to 1914, barriers to short-term mobility were overcome (or at least reduced) by direct solicitation of interregional funds, by commercial bank rediscounting, and most important, by the evolution of a national market for commercial paper." For greater details see Lance E. Davis, "The Investment Market, 1870–1914: The Evolution of a National Market," *Journal of Economic History*, Vol. 25 (1965), pp. 355–399.

[177] *Ibid.*, p. 359; and R. M. Breckenridge, "Discount Rates in the United States," *Political Science Quarterly*, Vol. 13 (1898), p. 126. It is true that there was some tendency for banks in large low-interest cities to seek more lucrative investment opportunities elsewhere. However, even under these circumstances large cities in other regions were probably favored by being a common destination of flows (rates in large Midwestern cities were higher than those of large Eastern cities, those in Western centers higher than those in Midwestern centers).

[178] Davis, *op. cit.*, p. 389. As late as 1914 discount rates in Southern cities remained much above those of Eastern and Midwestern cities.

Along related lines, as the size of the capital-goods sector became more important vis-à-vis the consumer-goods sector,[179] capital availability also became more important, since, on the whole, "the food and clothing industries need less capital to build and equip [and operate] their factories . . . than such industries as iron, steel and engineering."[180] According to the logic of the circular and cumulative growth model, investment in new or expanded capital-goods factories created additional capital outlets because the multiplier effects of these new facilities called forth a greater demand for ubiquitous industries, tertiary activities, construction, and local government services.[181]

Other Considerations

The compilation of an encyclopedic roster of other factors and initial advantages affecting selective urban growth is hardly feasible, for the fabric of reality is woven of an infinitely complex warp and woof. Moreover, to go beyond the vital and most conspicuous, to interpret imprecisely the plethora of apparent minutiae, would be to indulge in unnecessary turgidity, and to becloud the vivid pattern of that fabric. The enumeration of additional influences is therefore restricted to a minimum.

The achievement of a given threshold, and the consequent establishment or expansion of nearly equal scales of production in different geographical locales, is not normally followed by exactly equivalent patterns of growth at each manufacturing site. All cities and firms are unique, and the manner in which their singularities interact in the circular and cumulative growth process cannot be duplicated like prints from a lithographic plate. Some plants expand more rapidly than others in the same industry, either because of entrepreneurial aggressiveness, willingness to innovate, and ingenuity, or because of some permutation

---

[179] In 1860 the clothing, shoemaking, and food-processing industries were typically of primary importance in the manufacturing structure of most large cities, but by 1910 the metal-fabricating and machinery industries usually predominated.

[180] W. G. Hoffmann, *The Growth of Industrial Economies* (translated from the German by W. O. Henderson and W. H. Chaloner; Manchester, England: Manchester University Press, 1958), p. 38.

[181] Obviously, investment in ubiquitous industries and other local activities "has to be located where the demand is." James S. Duesenberry, "Some Aspects of the Theory of Economic Development," *Explorations in Entrepreneurial History*, First Series, Vol. 3 (1950–1951), p. 97. Also see Conrad and Meyer, *op. cit.*, p. 152.

of the factors discussed under the immediately preceding subheadings. Similarly, within a given industry some plants have a greater propensity than others to survive downswings in the business cycle.[182] Because variable rates of establishment growth imply variable multiplier effects, the selective growth of plants is logically both an instigator and a corollary of the selective growth of cities. Not uncommonly, faster-growing plants obtain economies of scale that enable them partially or totally to usurp the market area of slowly expanding factories. Such a sequence of events likewise tends to favor some cities at the expense of others. Moreover, different rates of plant growth also contribute to the dissimilar industrial structures of multimillion metropolises.

In Southern cities, where the normal growth pattern of many infant industries was adversely affected by the Civil War for periods of a decade or longer, the pace of population expansion was slower than that prevailing in comparably sized units elsewhere presumably because, among other reasons, manufacturing salaries were substantially lower than in cities of other regions. In 1870 the average annual earnings of Southern laborers in 17 major manufacturing categories were 73 per cent of those of similar workers in the Middle Atlantic States. By 1880 the ratio had fallen to 70 per cent, and gains registered in the next decade could only bring the 1890 figure up to 75 per cent.[183] The relatively low wage levels prevalent in Southern urban manufactures must have abbreviated their multiplier effects and thereby slowed local size growth. To the extent that abnormal manufacturing pay levels

[182] In many instances, the adoption of cost-cutting innovations or other strategies implemented during periods of depression served to solidify the position of selected firms and establishments by conferring advantages upon them that were *above and beyond* those associated with the collapse of unsoundly operated and financed competitors. Passer's ensuing remarks regarding the electrical industry are exemplificative: "It is important to note that the 1893 depression, severe as it was, did not dampen the enthusiasm of many entrepreneurs in the electrical industry; they continued to believe that rapid growth of the industry would soon begin again. With such a viewpoint, an entrepreneur can take advantage of a general business depression to prepare for further expansion. Westinghouse did just that in consolidating his manufacturing activities in a very large and modern factory at East Pittsburgh. Low construction costs in 1893 and 1894 made this an extremely attractive investment." Passer, *op. cit.*, p. 8.

[183] Long, *op. cit.*, p. 84. The following industrial categories were included in Long's sample: agricultural implements, brick and tile, carriages and wagons, chewing and smoking tobacco, cigars and cigarettes, cotton goods, distilled liquors, flour and grist mills, foundries and machine shops, glass, iron and steel (blast furnaces), iron and steel (rolling mills), leather, malt liquors, paper, sawed lumber, and woolen goods.

"roll out into the local service sector and produce atypical service industry wage rates,"[184] such pay levels must have further reinforced a braking of the growth process. In a sense, the subnormal wages of Southern cities can be construed as initial *dis*advantages whose cumulative negative effect contributed to their almost universal decrease in relative importance within the national system of cities (Table 2.4).

The Southern urban experience of the post-1865 era is illustrative of a more general principle. To wit, the circular and cumulative growth of smaller cities with unimposing initial advantages (low relative accessibility, limited availability of capital, etc.) is often, but not always, impeded or short-circuited because the new or enlarged manufacturing that they generate does not have a multiplier effect capable of drawing a train of higher thresholds and new innovations. When such stagnancy occurs, many local demands must be satisfied with goods produced in regional and national metropolises whose growth is unobstructed.

Finally, no inquiry into the growth of some cities at the expense of others would be complete without passing mention of the part played by factor immobility. Because management is more prone to augment existing facilities than to relocate where large initial capital expenditures would be necessary, "the ability of a locality to hold an industry greatly exceeds its original ability to attract."[185] On a considerably grander scale, large cities themselves obviously "are much less subject to relocation than are individual units of production." This is so because "the accumulated fixed investments of an urban mass in conjunction with its vested social institutions entail major geographic immobilities and rigidities."[186] These immobilities, as much as any other factor, lie at the crux of initial advantage.

Concluding Remarks

The evolution of a system of cities in the United States and of a disproportionate concentration of manufacturing in the highest-order centers of that system, has been, and continues to be, a process of fog-enshrouded and gigantic complexity. For some time, tertiary activities have been the most important component perpetuating the growth of the nation's largest metropolises. Therefore, an attempt has been made to get at the functioning of this involuted process of urban-industrial

---

[184] Thompson, *op. cit.*, p. 73.
[185] Ohlin, *op. cit.*, p. 236.
[186] Isard, *op. cit.*, p. 183.

concentration by focusing on that period of time when manufacturing was the most instrumental, but by no means the sole, determinant of American growth, and by posing two questions: How and why does the magnitude of cities expand precipitately during periods of rapid industrialization? Why do some cities grow more rapidly than, and at the expense of, other cities?

In response to the first question, a descriptive model was constructed depicting urban-size growth as a circular and cumulative process in which multiplier effects promoted the fulfillment of successive industrial thresholds, and the possibilities of invention and innovation within both threshold and nonthreshold industries were continuously enhanced by an intensifying network of interpersonal communications and confrontations. It was further proposed that the circular and cumulative growth process was reinforced by migration, natural population growth, real wage increases, accumulating external economies, the declining locational influence of primary raw materials, and the concurrent operation of adaptive and adoptive locational processes. Answers to the second question were founded on the premises that transport improvements and reduced per unit production costs worked to the benefit of a limited number of efficiently producing centers; that other initial advantages in the guise of site and situation, relative accessibility, labor and capital availability, and factor immobility, favor the growth of already identified commercial centers at the expense of other cities; and that the combination movement and oligopolistic competition supported the tendency of manufacturing to concentrate in a relatively restricted number of cities.

No pretense at originality is made for any of the ideas presented here, though it is hoped that they gain new ramifications through unification and juxtaposition in a model that seeks to provide insightful generalizations, rather than to identify incontrovertible cause and effect relationships. Nor is it argued that the logical cement holding the model's eclectic conceptual bricks together is flawless, lacking in conjecture, uncontroversial, or unrepetitious. It is also conceded that there are numerous other shortcomings. Historical intricacies have been pared down and impressionistically sketched in an oversimplified manner; business cycles and other important contingencies are almost unmentioned; the empirical evidence presented is not overwhelming and its grain is coarse; the roles of capital, the entrepreneur, migration, and tertiary activities have been somewhat underplayed; the intraurban locational shifts of manufacturing that accompanied the growth of cities are only grossly outlined; allusions to the post-1890 expansion of the "late-coming," or presently medium-sized, urban-industrial concentrations is minimal; and no parallel is drawn with the experience of West European countries that also underwent rapid urbanization and industrialization within a framework of capitalistic institutions.

Although these and other criticisms are justifiable, it should be acknowledged that broad generalizations always have their imperfections, exceptions, and drawbacks, and that the countless interlocking pieces of the locational mosaic do not lend themselves to more than partial reassembly in verbal abstractions. At best one achieves some comprehension of the economy's spatial organization and the distribution of population, but never a faithful reproduction of their infinite nuances.

3

Industrial Inventions, Industrial Innovations: Some Locational Relationships with Urban Growth

"*Plus ça change, plus c'est la même chose.*" This time-worn Gallic adage applies in no small measure to scholarly attitudes regarding the significance of the role of technological progress in the process of economic development. The relationships between the state of knowledge of a nation's industrial population, its aggregate output, and new production techniques were in one way or another first greatly appreciated by such titans as Adam Smith, John Stuart Mill, and Karl Marx, and somewhat later by the likes of Frank W. Taussig and Alfred Marshall; but, because of a long-term, involved, and generally faithful romance with the theory of capital formation, it is only relatively recently that post-Schumpeterian economists have become more and more inclined to the viewpoint that technological change rather than capital formation is the most important component of economic growth.[1] The full cycle completed by economists stands in stark contrast to the persever-

---

[1] For examples of the post-Schumpeterian evidence and arguments see Jacob Schmookler, "The Changing Efficiency of the American Economy, 1869–1934," *Review of Economics and Statistics*, Vol. 34 (1952), pp. 214–231; Moses Abramovitz, "Resource and Output Trends in the U.S. since 1870," *American Economic Review*, Vol. 46 (May, 1956), pp. 1–23; Robert Solow, "Technical Change and the Aggregate Production Function," *Review of Economics and Statistics*, Vol. 39 (1957), pp. 312–320; Benton Massell, "Capital Formation and Technological Change in U.S. Manufacturing," *ibid.*, Vol. 42 (1960), pp. 182–188; and Everett E. Hagen, *On the Theory of Social Change: How Economic Growth Begins* (Homewood, Ill.: Dorsey Press, 1962), pp. 49, 217. Also note Jacob Schmookler, "Technological Change and Economic Theory," *American Economic Review*, Vol. 55 (May, 1965), pp. 333–341.

ing lack of concern geographers have evinced toward the spatial attributes of industrial inventions and innovations. It is true that geographers have periodically shown some interest in the impact of technological change upon the location patterns of economic phenomena; however, the chain from invention to manifestation on the landscape has been virtually ignored, and many have been content implicitly or explicitly to take the position that inventions are locational "accidents."

Inasmuch as there has been a resurging emphasis on the interplay between technological progress and economic growth, inasmuch as the model of urban-size growth and industrial concentration presented in the previous essay placed such emphasis on the city's increasing propensity for invention and innovation (a propensity that supposedly devolves from the increasingly more complex network of interpersonal communications and confrontations in an expanding urban population), and inasmuch as a geographic dimension may be grafted upon Schumpeter's observation "that innovations are not at any time distributed over the whole economic system at random, but tend to concentrate in certain sectors and their surroundings,"[2] it appears as if there is a need for some further elaboration upon the spatial attributes of industrial inventions and innovations. More specifically, at least two further lines of inquiry immediately suggest themselves for detailed consideration: To what degree, and why, are manufacturing inventions and innovations a function of the size and rate of growth of cities during that period (the post-Civil War decades in the United States) when the foundations of an economy complete their metamorphosis from the commercial-mercantile to the industrial-capitalistic? How, at any period of time, and especially in the era prior to the institutionalization of industrial-technological development,[3] do (did) the spatial patterns of

---

[2] Joseph A. Schumpeter, *Business Cycles* (abridged, with an introduction, by Rendigs Fels; New York: McGraw-Hill, Inc., 1964), p. 75.

[3] Although it is not possible to pinpoint a date after which one could qualitatively describe inventive activity within the manufacturing sector as being characteristically institutionalized, it seems safe to say that individual rather than deliberately organized corporate effort prevailed overwhelmingly between the termination of the Civil War and the turn of the century. In 1901, the first date for which a breakdown is available, 82.7 per cent of the U.S. patents granted to individuals and domestic corporations went to individuals. By 1916, corporate grants accounted for 37.1 per cent of the same total, and ever since the mid-thirties well over half the grants have annually gone to corporations. See U.S. Bureau of the Census, *Historical Statistics of the United States: Colonial Times to 1957* (Washington, D. C.: 1961), p. 607.

innovation diffusion for different broad categories of urban-industrial activity theoretically behave and vary from one another?

A Distinction Between Invention and Innovation

Semantic jungles abound in the hot and humid climate of academic investigation — jungles where meanings of simple words are frequently entangled and suffocated in the dense undergrowth of contradiction, convolution, and confusion. Therefore, any reasonable approach to the problems just mentioned precludes that a logically consistent but arbitrary distinction be drawn between the oft-used terms "invention" and "innovation."

As employed here, "invention" does not refer to scientific discovery, but to individual (discrete) technical advances that are comprised of "new combinations of existing knowledge for practical use in production."[4] Such a definition is not inconsistent with that view of invention which de-emphasizes the dramatic and stresses the "perpetual accretion of little details."[5] This delimitation is intentionally qualitative rather than quantitative, for while it is obvious that "inventions differ widely with respect to the magnitude of technical problem overcome, technical potential, and economic contribution,"[6] it is equally apparent that evidence is lacking that would indicate that the infrequent revolutionary technical advance is invariably more important to economic progress and urban growth than the multitude of more closely timed, smaller improvements.[7] In substantiation of the last point, studies have shown that minor improvements, rather than changes in basic production methods, were responsible for a 50 per cent increase of potential labor productivity in the cotton textile industry between 1910 and 1936, and that in the manufacture of electric light bulbs detailed, rather than major, advances induced a fivefold increment in output per man-hour from 1925 to 1931.[8]

---

[4] Simon Kuznets, "Inventive Activity: Problems of Definition and Measurement," in *The Rate and Direction of Inventive Activity: Economic and Social Factors* (A Report of the National Bureau of Economic Research; Princeton: Princeton University Press, 1962), p. 21.

[5] S. C. Gilfillan, *The Sociology of Invention* (Chicago: Follet Publishing Company, 1935), p. 5.

[6] Kuznets, *op. cit.*, p. 30.

[7] John Jewkes, David Sawers, and Richard Stillman, *The Sources of Invention* (New York: St. Martin's Press, 1959), p. 6.

[8] Note the studies cited in W. E. G. Salter, *Productivity and Technical Change* (Cambridge, England: The University Press, 1960), p. 5.

"Innovation," because of its connotation of originality, is occasionally used interchangeably with "invention." However, in partial keeping with Schumpeter's view of "innovation" as any change which brings about a new production function and a shift in a firm's total or marginal cost curve,[9] the term is here defined as occurring when "an invention is introduced commercially as a new or improved product or process";[10] and *hence, any originality that might be legitimately associated with "innovation" is derived from implementation rather than conceptualization.* In fact, by going one step further and making our definition of "innovation" loose enough to subsume implementation and adoption by imitation, or what is sometimes termed "secondary innovation" and/or "the diffusion of innovation," we deprive the act of most of its connoted originality, but not necessarily any of its daring.[11] In other words, any act by an individual or firm can be construed as an innovation, even if it has already been performed by others, so long as the imitator has heretofore not carried it out.

By defining "innovation" in a solely technological dimension its implications and innuendos are kept intentionally narrow. Admittedly, innovations may be depicted so as to subsume new financing, advertising, or competitive strategies, or to include new managerial or organizational tasks and alignments. However, because of the orientation of this essay, because of its intimate bonds with the urban-size growth model of the previous essay, "innovation" has been deliberately confined to acts that directly lead to new or expanded manufacturing production, and thereby a multiplier effect and urban population expansion. While nontechnological innovations may also, and often do (did), lead to changes in output, they are not as unambiguously associated with new or enlarged production and therefore are not considered here.

Finally, it should be underscored that "invention" and "innovation" are for the purposes of this essay mutually exclusive terms. In any given place, at any given time, innovation may or may not follow upon the heels of a particular industrial invention; i.e., invention can occur without local innovation (due, for example, to the marginal quality

[9] Schumpeter, *op. cit.*, pp. 62–66.
[10] W. Rupert Maclaurin, "The Sequence from Invention to Innovation and its Relation to Economic Growth," *Quarterly Journal of Economics*, Vol. 67 (1953), p. 105.
[11] Under conditions of market uncertainty the adoption of a well-tried production technique may require as much boldness as an act of initial innovation. Note Alister Sutherland, "The Diffusion of an Innovation in Cotton Spinning," *Journal of Industrial Economics*, Vol. 7 (March, 1959), pp. 118–135.

of the invention or to the absence of risk-taking entrepreneurs), and, conversely, innovation can occur without local invention (due, for example, to the importation of ideas or the imitation of exogenous practices).

The Urban Concentration of Inventive Activity

Current scholarly concern with inventive activity is almost exclusively economic, historical, and sociological, although one recent study with a locational orientation indicated that in the early 1950's there was a linear coefficient of correlation of 0.964 between the number of U.S. patents granted to the individual states and the number of persons residing in the metropolises of those states.[12] The urban concentration of inventiveness, while not measured in such explicit terms elsewhere, is implicit in most relevant economic and historical studies. Hence, if we are to examine evidence and ultimately to offer empirically based generalizations regarding the occurrence of inventions and the size and rate of growth of cities during periods of rapid industrialization, we ought first explore the more general proclivity of inventive efforts to be associated with any urban environment of appreciable magnitude.

Inventive output is, to a considerable degree, a function of unique supply-and-demand conditions that prevail in the cities of an industrializing economy such as that of the United States between 1860 and the early twentieth century. More precisely, many technological advances in the late nineteenth century were reliant upon a demand for inventions. This demand was most likely to occur in the burgeoning cities where manufacturing was agglomerating, where there already was an adequate supply of both potential inventors (including skilled laborers) and investment capital.

Expressed alternatively, techniques may be feasible, but they are not likely to materialize into inventions unless specific economic pressures are present. If the demand for manufactured goods is increasing quickly, as it was in many U.S. cities for much of the late nineteenth century, then entrepreneurs are likely to be on the alert, *or searching,* for new

---

[12] Wilbur R. Thompson, "Locational Differences in Inventive Effort and Their Determinants," in *The Rate and Direction of Inventive Activity: Economic and Social Factors, op. cit.,* pp. 253–271. Earlier attempts to treat the locational aspects of inventiveness are apparently confined to Mark Jefferson, "The Geographic Distribution of Inventiveness," *Geographical Review,* Vol. 19 (1929), pp. 649–661; and S. C. Gilfillan, "Inventiveness by Nation: A Note on Statistical Treatment," *ibid.,* Vol. 20 (1930), pp. 301–304.

cost-reducing production techniques with which to embellish their profit-making opportunities,[13] — "the incentive to make an invention, like the incentive to produce any good, is affected by the excess of the expected returns over expected costs."[14] If a specific firm or industry is going through an expansion of sales, as certain late nineteenth-century urban units were, at the expense of other smaller-scale urban, small-town, and rural units, then the amount (supply) of capital it may allocate to inventive effort expands parallelly.[15] This supply-and-demand argument is well substantiated by the experience of the machine tool industry in the post-Civil War decades, when "new skills and techniques were developed or perfected . . . in response to the demand of specific customers";[16] and by the history of the electrical industries during that period, when much of the progress in the development of arc lighting, telegraphic devices, electric lighting, and the subsequent range of more complicated electrical devices took place in the Cleveland, Philadelphia, and New York metropolitan areas, where capital was available at critical moments.[17]

The interaction between demand for technological improvements, the supply of inventors provided by manufacturing itself, and the urban preponderance of inventions is made clearer by introducing the corollary that advances in production technology usually occur as a response to particular problems *that in themselves are most apt to arise in existing centers of industrial concentration.* In proposing a formal theory of the inventive process, Usher persuasively reasoned that individual inventions rarely evolve in a vacuum but instead are interrelated events deriving from a cumulative technological synthesis, events that are periodically set in motion by "the perception of an unsatisfactory pattern."[18] Employing the logic of Gestalt psychology, Usher argued that

---

[13] Note Alfred D. Chandler, "Entrepreneurial Opportunity in Nineteenth Century America," *Explorations in Entrepreneurial History, Second Series,* Vol. 1 (Fall, 1963), pp. 106–124.

[14] Jacob Schmookler, "Economic Sources of Inventive Activity," *Journal of Economic History,* Vol. 22 (1962), p. 19.

[15] Compare *ibid.,* p. 17.

[16] Nathan Rosenberg, "Technological Change in the Machine Tool Industry, 1840–1910," *Journal of Economic History,* Vol. 23 (1963), p. 426.

[17] Harold C. Passer, *The Electrical Manufacturers 1875–1900* (Cambridge: Harvard University Press, 1953), pp. 14–15, 22, 78, 85.

[18] Abbott Payson Usher, "Technical Change and Capital Formation," in *Capital Formation and Economic Growth* (A Report of the National Bureau of Economic Research; Princeton: Princeton University Press, 1955), pp. 527–528; and *idem, A History of Mechanical Inventions* (revised edition; Cambridge: Harvard University Press, 1954), pp. 60 ff. For related remarks see Gilfillan, *The Sociology of Invention, op. cit.,* pp. 44–45, 60, 91.

once particular data (partly composed of the initial problem perception) create tension, "some favorable configuration of thought or things will [sooner or later] *reveal* the solution by the 'intrinsic properties of the data.' "[19] More precisely, problem perception is seen as being followed by "the setting of the stage" or the fortuitous assembly of all other data (thoughts or events) pertinent to problem solution; the act of insight (problem solution or invention); critical study and comprehension of the solution (perfection of the invention). These four stages were given diagrammatic representation (Figure 3.1), and, most im-

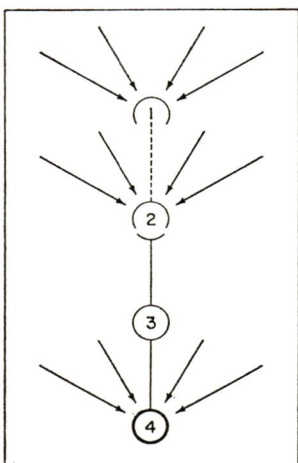

FIGURE 3.1 "The emergence of novelty [invention] in the act of insight: 1) perception of an incomplete pattern; 2) the setting of the stage; 3) the act of insight; 4) critical revision and mastery of the new pattern.

"Progressive synthesis is suggested by arrows leading in toward the various steps in the process. The discontinuities in the process are indicated by the gaps between the arrows and the steps in the process, and by the broken line between the perception of the incomplete pattern and setting of the stage."

Source: Usher, *A History of Mechanical Inventions*, pp. 65–66 (see footnote 18).

portant, arrows were introduced at three of the stages to symbolize progressive synthesis. Within a late nineteenth-century, pre-mass-communications context, *each of the arrows may be interpreted as taking the form either of intentional or unintentional exposure to other manufacturing production techniques relevant to problem solution and perfection, or intentional or unintentional personal confrontation with other information-bearing individuals — both forms having their highest probability of transpiring in urban-industrial centers.*

In a not unrelated fashion Schmookler has maintained that industrial inventions devolve from the interplay between the state of knowledge and the state of industry[20] (which implicitly influences problem awareness and expected benefits from problem solution).

[19] Usher, *op. cit.*, p. 64.
[20] Jacob Schmookler, "Changes in Industry and in the State of Knowledge as Determinants of Industrial Invention," in *The Rate and Direction of Inventive*

These lines of thought do not comprise the full arsenal of support that may be mustered for the contention that late nineteenth-century inventive activity tended to transpire at manufacturing clusters (urban environments) where particular problems arose, for the problem-awareness phenomenon of "technological disequilibrium" also presumably fostered a locational coincidence of productive and inventive efforts.

"Technological disequilibrium" occurs when there is a discrepancy between the ability of different steps in a given manufacturing process to equal or exceed expected levels of performance. Such disequilibrium normally evokes an Usherian sequence of problem perceptions and inventive responses. In other words, "Any important improvement in the operation of a component [or in the technical efficiency of a stage of production], whether it be the currently limiting one or not, is likely to create new obstacles, in the form of limitations imposed by another component [stage], to the achievement of a higher level of performance. Thus single improvements tend to create their own future problems, which compel further modification and revision."[21] Invention-inducing discrepancies in level of output need not be confined to production stages within an individual factory or firm; they may also be associated with backwardly or forwardly linked manufacturing establishments. In this light, the late nineteenth-century multiplication of urban-industrial linkages can be interpreted as going hand in hand with a concurrent urban concentration of inventive activity. "Technological disequilibrium" within individual firms is presumably reflected in part by the fact that in the production of railroad equipment, and in several other industries, there has been since the mid-nineteenth century "a marked tendency for output and invention to move together in the long run, in the short run and in intermediate periods";[22] that is, invention rates are high when sales are high not only because of the influence of expected profits, but also because under such circumstances discordancies

---

Activity: Economic and Social Factors, op. cit., pp. 195–232; especially p. 196. Again, Schmookler's evidence indicates that demand influences invention to the extent that regardless of when an idea is conceived "an inventor . . . will tend to press for a solution [be mentally preoccupied with the relevant data] when sales are high and slacken his efforts when sales are low" [p. 215].

[21] Rosenberg, *op. cit.,* p. 440. Also note Erik Dahmen, "Technology, Innovation and International Industrial Transformation," in Leon H. Dupriez, ed., *Economic Progress* (Louvain: Institut de Recherches Economiques et Sociales, 1955), pp. 293–306; especially p. 297.

[22] Schmookler, "Economic Sources of Inventive Activity," *op. cit.,* p. 11.

between production stages are likely to become magnified and less tolerable. Perhaps most strikingly, "technological disequilibrium" was largely responsible for the quick parade of inventions in the pre-World War I American iron and steel industry, for increases in the scale of plant output were not feasible unless hot-blast ovens, blowing machines, cooling jackets, steam blasts, mechanical loaders, automatic pig-casting machines, furnace linings, and other devices functioned at a nearly equivalent rate of efficiency and productivity.[23] Significantly, the majority of domestic inventions in this realm were associated with Pittsburgh and its later incorporated environs.

No outline of the interrelationships between the urban concentration of invention and the dovetailing and multiplicative character of inventive output would be complete without referring to the existence of "technological convergence." The tendency for individual industrial inventions to fall frequently into orderly sequences stems from the fact that solution-awareness as well as problem-awareness can set the inventive process in motion. And this was sometimes the case in the late nineteenth-century United States, where "industrialization was characterized by the introduction of a relatively small number of broadly similar productive processes to a large number of industries."[24] Thus, as new techniques developed in the manufacture of one product that were applicable in a variety of related industrial activities, the possible permutations of combined knowledge expanded (solution-awareness grew through exposure) and inventions multiplied in number. Expressed differently, each new invention had the possibility both of calling forth additional inventions in the same production process because of "technological disequilibrium" and of precipitating new mechanical creations to serve other production processes. Or, as Schumpeter put it, "Whenever a new production function has been set up successfully and the trade beholds the new thing done and its major problems solved, it becomes much easier for other people to do the same thing *and even to improve on it. . . . [and] it becomes easier not only to do the same thing, but also to do similar things in similar lines.*"[25] The easing of in-

---

[23] For greater detail see W. Paul Strassmann, *Risk and Technological Invention: American Manufacturing Methods during the Nineteenth Century* (Ithaca: Cornell University Press, 1959), pp. 32–75.

[24] Rosenberg, *op. cit.*, p. 422.

[25] Schumpeter, *op. cit.*, p. 75 (italics added). Schumpeter described "those additional improvements which present themselves in the process of copying the first innovators" as "Induced Innovations [inventions]."

vention by "the employment of similar skills, techniques, and facilities at some of the 'higher' stages of production for a wide range of final products," has been termed "technological convergence,"[26] and in the late nineteenth century was most prominent in the machinery and metal-consuming industries.

Examples of "technological convergence" and related forms of cumulative technological synthesis are so numerous and varied that only an arbitrary few need be succinctly cited here: the prodigious inventive career of George Westinghouse and his associates can be traced from his initial perfection of a device for returning derailed railroad cars to the track, to development of the air brake, to the use of compressed air and electricity in railroad switches and signaling devices, and ultimately into the broader field of electrical machinery; bicycle manufacture in the 1890's led to the widespread utilization of ball bearings and the development of the flat-link chain, and these two technical advances, after minor modifications and redesigning, had far-reaching consequences in numerous other industries where the reduction of wear and friction or an increase in the efficiency of power transmission were inventive objectives; and improvement of the sewing machine resulted in significant production changes in the post-Civil War boot and shoe, bookbinding, and rubber plastic goods industries, as well as in the output of awnings, tents, sails, pocketbooks, and other items.[27] This variety of cumulative technological progress was by no means born in the late nineteenth century; it had occurred in earlier decades, e.g., in New York City, where brass foundries turned to the manufacture of a diverse array of engines and machinery (brass was in the early nineteenth century quite important as an industrial metal).[28]

If inventions tend to dovetail and multiply through "technological convergence," then it again logically follows that inventive activity is apt to concentrate in urban environments where manufacturing is sizable and where the repertory of know-how accumulates most rapidly. To be explicit, if "technological convergence" is dependent upon the potential inventor's exposure to solutions to related problems outside

[26] Rosenberg, *op. cit.*, p. 423.
[27] *Ibid.*, pp. 435–436, 430; and Passer, *op. cit.*, pp. 129–130. Also see the discussion of the impact of cross-fertilization on the technology of U.S. glass manufacture in Warren C. Scoville, *Revolution in Glass-making* (Cambridge: Harvard University Press, 1948).
[28] Victor S. Clark, *History of Manufactures in the United States* (New York: McGraw-Hill, Inc., 1929), Vol. 1, p. 502.

his own industry or, more accurately, to *multiple exposure* to such solutions (in order both to create the level of tension and to collect the data requisite to solution of his own problem), then in a pre-mass-communications context, such as the relatively compact cities of the late nineteenth century, where diffusion of technical knowledge is highly reliant upon personal interaction,[29] the possibilities for invention ought to be enhanced by the growing network of interpersonal communications and confrontations.

If to this point it has been implicitly demonstrated that "invention in each line centers in a few regions [or cities] which most abundantly produce that line,"[30] it should also be understood that the frequency of invention at any location is partially governed by social conditions. If one chooses, the entire inventive process can be put in the structural-functional terminology of Talcott Parsons and interpreted as something that is triggered by social (consumer) dissatisfaction with industrial productivity or the quality of manufacturing output.[31] Regardless of whether or not such a formulation is construed as a rococo version of the notion that invention springs from an awareness of specific problems or mutable solutions, it is difficult to deny that an achievement-rewarding social environment is conducive to the progress of industrial technology.

In those cities that are, according to the jargon, characterized by "heterogenetic transformation,"[32] and unencumbered with the rigid

[29] This is not to convey the impression that late nineteenth-century exposure to solutions was confined to first-hand visual and verbal experiences. After the Civil War technical knowledge found its way increasingly into *Iron Age* and other newly founded trade journals. However, it seems that the role of these journals should not be overestimated, as only under unusual circumstances could they of themselves have provided the stimuli (multiple exposure and sufficient data) necessary to inventive solution without being supplemented by face-to-face conversations and observations. This is all the more so since it appears as if person-to-person confrontations are crucial to information dissemination even where society is completely steeped in mass communications media. See Elihu Katz, "Communications Research and the Image of Society: Convergence of Two Traditions," *American Journal of Sociology*, Vol. 65 (1960), pp. 435–440.

[30] Gilfillan, *op. cit.*, p. 8.

[31] See Neil J. Smelser, *Social Change in the Industrial Revolution: An Application of Theory to the British Cotton Industry* (Chicago: University of Chicago Press, 1959), particularly pp. 1–157.

[32] Robert Redfield and Milton Singer, "The Cultural Role of Cities," *Economic Development and Cultural Change*, Vol. 3 (1954–1955), pp. 56–59; and Bert F. Hoselitz, "Generative and Parasitic Cities," *ibid.*, pp. 278–294. Also see Rhoads Murphey, "The City as a Center of Change: Western Europe and China," *Annals of the Association of American Geographers*, Vol. 44 (1954), pp. 349–362.

class structure of a traditional society, endemic change is fostered and the inventor is usually accorded position, prestige, and pecuniary incentives. (This is not to suggest that inventive effort will always thrive in cities where occupational or entrepreneurial success and prestige are synonymous; for while an "ethic which places a high valuation on occupational achievement is a necessary condition for economic development [industrial change] . . . it is not a sufficient one. The criteria for occupational success must be such as to encourage the active searching after new ways of doing things."[33]) In a contrasting negative sense, the social milieu of rural areas, and cities of "orthogenetic transformation" in traditional societies, mitigates against change and possesses a limited capacity to stimulate and promote inventive efforts, although this is by no means tantamount to saying that invention is impossible in such environments. Inventions, or changes in manufacturing practices, will be possible under any social circumstances if there are individuals present with psychological (personality) eccentricities or idiosyncracies who are inclined toward deviant behavior. Societal inhibitions toward the promotion of economic growth and, by extension, investment in change through the allocation of resources to inventive effort, may be more dramatically overcome if the local elite become inculcated with a previously absent "rationality that will search out and wherever possible resolve conflicts between ends [and/] or values, ..."[34]

Last, on a slightly more subtle level, at any given location the way in which potential inventors think, and the supply of potential inventors itself, is presumably influenced by the imprint made upon the individual subconscience by social values and sanctions. Values, sanctions, and other social governors of behavior, through encouraging or discouraging the presence of subconscious censorship mechanisms, affect the response evoked in individuals when exposed to stimuli (events or ideas) that are capable of eliciting the constellation of thought necessary to an

---

[33] J. S. Duesenberry, "Some Aspects of the Theory of Economic Development," *Explorations in Entrepreneurial History*, First Series, Vol. 3 (1950–1951), p. 73. Inventiveness is not likely to be associated with prestigeful entrepreneurship if the entrepreneurial role is inherited rather than secured through competitive self-advancement.

[34] Sylvia L. Thrupp, "Tradition and Development: A Choice of Views," *Comparative Studies in Society and History*, Vol. 16 (1963–1964), p. 87; and Joseph J. Spengler, "Theory, Ideology, Non-Economic Values, and Politico-Economic Development," in Ralph Braibanti and Spengler, eds., *Tradition, Values, and Socio-Economic Development* (Durham: Duke University Press, 1961), pp. 3–56.

awareness of either the existence of specific problems or the convertibility of related solutions.[35]

The Urban Concentration of Industrial Innovations

That industrial innovations have been urban concentrated since 1860 and earlier is intuitively even more obvious than the urban focus of invention, and yet the factors underlying this relationship require some delineation if subsequent generalizations are to be as meaningful as possible.

The interaction of forces that brings about an urban concentration of industrial innovation can perhaps be best comprehended by looking initially upon the implementation of invention as a behavioral (decision-making, problem-solving) act on the part of a firm or an individual that (who) is limited in its (his) ability to acquire and utilize information regarding alternatives.[36]

Virtually all economic decisional acts are undertaken in the presence of uncertainty, which in turn derives from "ignorance owing to the lack of information; risk owing to the spread of possible values for a random variable; and economic indeterminacy" owing to the fact that the outcome of the act is itself dependent upon the action of other individuals or firms (i.e., upon a game situation).[37] The uncertainty associated with acts of industrial innovation may be particularly great because the perceived, but not necessarily real, risks can assume manifold shapes. For example: there may be functional risks caused by the mechanical, hydraulic, thermic, electromagnetic, or chemical principles upon which the device or apparatus operates; there may be risks of labor availability and factor availability in general; there is the risk of premature obsolescence; there are "customer risks," centering on adoption or, in the case of senile industries, continued acceptance, of the product by the market; and there are timing risks stemming from the possibility that the innovation may occur close to a business recession or depression.[38]

[35] Compare James G. March and Herbert A. Simon, *Organizations* (New York: John Wiley & Sons, Inc., 1958), p. 139.

[36] This is consistent with the viewpoint, held by March, Simon, and other contemporary behavioral scientists, that depicts the human individual "as a complex information-processing system," as "a choosing, decision-making, problem-solving organism that can do only one or a few things at a time, and that can attend to only a small part of the information recorded in its memory and presented by the environment." *Ibid.*, pp. 9, 11.

[37] Martin Shubik, "Information, Risk, Ignorance, and Indeterminacy," *Quarterly Journal of Economics*, Vol. 68 (1954), p. 639.

[38] Compare with Strassmann, *op. cit.*, pp. 13–15.

Uncertainties of this sort can be intensified and made more perplexing by the incomparability or the incompatibility of alternatives suggested by unrelated forms of risk; by the degree to which over-all strategy is oriented toward minimization of costs (losses), maximization of profits, or some permutation of the two;[39] by a more basic psychological insecurity associated with departures of any kind from the status quo, by fear of things unknown, unencountered, untried; or by risks pervading the political or social, rather than economic, atmosphere.[40]

Now, insofar as uncertainty and imperfect knowledge obviate the possibility of optimal solutions, it is understandable that most economic "decision-making, whether individual or organization, is concerned with the discovery and selection of satisfactory alternatives";[41] and that these chosen alternatives, in turn, are usually ones where the perceived array of uncertainties appear to be reduced. It follows from these observations, plus the fact that "uncertainty has a spatial dimension,"[42] that industrial innovators should usually have a strong locational preference for places or areas where present and anticipated uncertainties appear to be less than elsewhere.

In the overwhelming majority of instances it is the metropolitan environment that both in appearance and in fact confronts the innovation-contemplating entrepreneur with a lesser degree of uncertainty. Even where mass media prevail, the range of daily experience and the web of communications of the large city and its suburbs provide ideas, conceptual stimuli, observations, and other bits of information that are less available under conditions of relative geographic isolation, and that constantly expand the potential innovator's knowledge and thereby

[39] For an extremely structured treatment of the impact of these strategies upon the behavior (locational and otherwise) of entrepreneurs within very narrowly defined situations, see Walter Isard and Michael F. Dacey, "On the Projection of Individual Behavior in Regional Analysis," *Journal of Regional Science*, Vol. 4 (1962), pp. 1–34, 51–83.

[40] See W. T. Easterbrook, "Uncertainty and Economic Change," *Journal of Economic History*, Vol. 14 (1954), pp. 346–360.

[41] March and Simon, *op. cit.*, pp. 140–141.

[42] Julian Wolpert, "The Decision Process in Spatial Context," *Annals Association of American Geographers*, Vol. 54 (1964), p. 547. While Wolpert has given empirical creditability to the notion that uncertainty varies geographically, Isard and Tung have indirectly provided some formality for the conception in their discussion of accessibility to information, the decision-making unit's degree of spatial centralization, and locational cost differences in decision-making. Walter Isard and Tze Hsiung Tung, "Some Concepts for the Analysis of Spatial Organization," *Papers and Proceedings of the Regional Science Association*, Vol. 11 (1963), pp. 17–40, and Vol. 12 (1964), pp. 1–25.

diminish the portion of his uncertainty that grows from ignorance. Likewise, the large labor force, the substantial local market, and the diversity of external economies in the metropolis help to diminish risk uncertainties; and urban proximity to competitors and to manufacturers in general promises to shrink those uncertainties devolving from "economic indeterminacy."[43] In this context it is perfectly reasonable that, from the late nineteenth century to the present, innovative effort in the United States has been disproportionately concentrated in oligopolistic large-firm industries,[44] and that in these industries, where high levels of indeterminacy are common, the typical location pattern has usually been one of a relatively few factories *unsymmetrically concentrated in the major metropolises.*

It is one thing to point out that, other things being equal, "major scale [and urbanization] economies obtain in [securing], processing and beneficiating information,"[45] it is quite another thing to suggest that all potential innovators are capable either of choosing locations where uncertainty is reducible, or, once having made a successful (correct) selection, of procuring and rationally reacting upon the information available in the metropolis. In short, possible reductions in uncertainty are not to be confused with rational exploitation of actual reductions in uncertainty. Presence in the metropolis is no guarantee of "correct" innovative decisions. Differences in performance among potential metropolitan innovators, arising from discrepancies in the volume and quality of information available to decision-makers and variations in their degree of rationality, can be arbitrarily summarized by reinvoking and rephrasing the adaptive-adoptive behavioral permutations introduced in the previous essay. Theoretically, at any point in time, the potential

---

[43] Compare these remarks with those of Richard L. Meier, "The Organization of Technological Innovation in Urban Environments," in Oscar Handlin and John Burchard, eds., *The Historian and the City* (Cambridge: The M.I.T. Press and Harvard University Press, 1963), pp. 74–83, especially pp. 74–75; and C. F. Carter and B. R. Williams, *Industry and Technical Progress: Factors Governing the Speed of Application of Science* (London: Oxford University Press, 1957), pp. 157–158.

[44] If all manufacturing categories are considered simultaneously, the association between innovativeness and oligopoly is not perfect. However, studies repeatedly indicate that, with the exception of some of the most extreme cases of oligopoly, innovational effort increases from category to category more rapidly than the concentration of ownership. See Jesse W. Markham, "Market Structure, Business Conduct, and Innovation," *American Economic Review,* Vol. 55 (May, 1965), pp. 323–332.

[45] Isard and Tung, *op. cit.,* Vol. 11, p. 36.

industrial innovators in a given metropolis will be comprised of some combination of rational and irrational actors; that is, among the adaptors, or those making innovative choices based on large and accurate quantities of knowledge, there are those who elect to make viable innovations (successful adaptors), and those who, through faulty reasoning and improper and inefficient employment of information, accept unprofitable innovations, fail to accept profit-increasing innovations, or undergo an excessively long gestation period prior to accepting a now outmoded innovation (unsuccessful adaptors); and similarly, among the adopters, or those making innovative choices based on small and highly imperfect quantities of knowledge, there are those who unwittingly accept profit-increasing innovations by "chance" (successful adopters), and those who reject viable innovations or accept innovations that are out-of-date or do not permit long-term profits and survival (unsuccessful adopters).[46]

An alternative and supplementary manner of approaching the urban concentration of industrial innovation lies along the less devious route of viewing most innovation as imitation of observed success. Acceptance of this viewpoint leads to the conclusion that innovation is most likely to occur in an urban environment where manufacturing is already agglomerated, and concurrently substantiates the uncertainty argument because observation of success presumably reduces uncertainty (to which it may be relevantly added, "Once formed, opinions about an innovation are reinforced by interaction with others. In the face of a high degree of uncertainty, most individuals wish to validate their opinions with those of others").[47] Furthermore, urban-industrial innova-

---

[46] This fourfold typology may be contrasted with the following classes of entrepreneurial behavior proposed by Danhof:
  1. *Innovating entrepreneurship,* characterized by aggressive assemblage of information and the analysis of results deriving from novel combinations of factors. . . .
  2. *Imitative entrepreneurship,* characterized by readiness to adopt successful innovations inaugurated by innovating entrepreneurs. . . .
  3. *"Fabian" entrepreneurship,* characterized by very great caution and skepticism (perhaps simply inertia) but which does imitate when it becomes perfectly clear that failure to do so would result in a loss of the relative position of the enterprise.
  4. *Drone entrepreneurship,* characterized by a refusal to adopt opportunities to make changes in production formulae even at the cost of severely reduced returns relative to other like producers.
See Clarence H. Danhof, "Observations on Entrepreneurship in Agriculture," in Harvard Research Center in Entrepreneurial History, ed., *Change and the Entrepreneur* (Cambridge: Harvard University Press, 1949), pp. 23–24.
[47] Everett M. Rogers, *Diffusion of Innovations* (New York: The Free Press of

tion by imitation can frequently bring about further innovations because of "technological disequilibrium" and "technological convergence," or because some imitators succeed "by unwittingly acquiring some unexpected or unsought unique attributes"[48] that are subsequently imitated by competitors and other related urban manufacturing units. Pertinently, both the uncertainty and the imitation lines of reasoning are consistent with Mansfield's tested model that demonstrates that because of competitive pressures, "bandwagon" effects, and other forces, the probability of a firm introducing a new production technique is related to the proportion of firms already employing the specific technique.[49]

A supply and demand framework also lends itself to an amplification of the ideas already presented regarding the urban concentration of industrial innovations. The frequency of innovation in a given location may be looked upon as a function of the supply of inventions and capital (entrepreneurs willing to risk capital), and the demand for innovations and information regarding existing technological improvements. It is quite obvious that among the variables "influencing the rate of innovation, invention is one of the more important";[50] and inasmuch as inventions are urban oriented, one would expect the same of innovations, *even* if no other evidence were available. "Stated otherwise, the rate at which opportunities for more satisfactory performance [applicable inventions] are encountered, whether by accident [randomly acquired information] or design [research], will be one of the determinants of the rate of innovations."[51]

Glencoe, 1962), p. 224. The suggestion that imitative industrial innovation is most apt to occur in geographic proximity to preceding innovators is consistent with Rashevsky's mathematical models of imitative behavior, the underlying idea of which is that the performance of an act by a given individual produces an increased stimulation (or tendency) toward the performance of the identical act by other individuals. See, for example, N. Rashevsky, "Imitative Behavior in Nonuniformly Spatially Distributed Populations," *Bulletin of Mathematical Biophysics*, Vol. 15 (1953), pp. 63–73; idem, "Mathematical Biology of Social Behavior: IV. Imitation Effects as a Function of Distance," *ibid.*, Vol. 12 (1950), pp. 177–185; and *idem*, "A Note on Imitative Behavior and Information," *ibid.*, Vol. 13 (1951), pp. 147–151.

[48] Armen A. Alchian, "Uncertainty, Evolution, and Economic Theory," *Journal of Political Economy*, Vol. 58 (1950), p. 218. Also see Strassman, *op. cit.*, pp. 18–19, 208.

[49] Edward Mansfield, "Technical Change and the Rate of Imitation," *Econometrica*, Vol. 4 (1961), pp. 741–766.

[50] Yale Brozen, "Invention, Innovation, and Imitation," *American Economic Review*, Vol. 41 (May, 1951), p. 251.

[51] March and Simon, *op. cit.*, p. 183.

CONCENTRATION OF INDUSTRIAL INNOVATIONS   103

Because of the growing importance of the capital-goods sector vis-à-vis the consumer-goods sector after the Civil War, and because late nineteenth-century technological change in itself so frequently required shifts in the scale of plants, capital availability became progressively more important to successful innovation[52] — and again it was in the cities, where dollars accumulated from commerce, land speculation, and *already existing industrial activities,* that this factor was most readily available.[53] In fact, the increasing "lumpiness" of capital injections required for many innovations (a "lumpiness" that could be distorted by conservative expectations of returns), often limited specific forms of innovation to expanding large-scale firms that were operated by risk-taking (capital supplying) entrepreneurs[54] and were *usually more concentrated in sizable cities than manufacturing as a whole.* In this way the propagation of one innovation by another can be seen in another perspective, i.e., the cost-savings or profits resulting from one "lumpy" innovation can provide the capital for another profit-enlarging "lumpy" innovation at the same locus.[55]

Similarly, the late nineteenth-century demand for innovations, and for information pertaining to inventions, should have been greatest in cities where the growing specialization of industrial functions was multiplying the number of forward and backward local linkages and thereby creating "technological disequilibrium" between separate plants, rather than within individual producing units.[56] Because of the innovations that

[52] For comments that suggest that the importance of capital availability should not be exaggerated, see H. J. Habakkuk, "The Historical Experience on the Basic Conditions of Economic Progress," in Dupriez, *op. cit.,* pp. 149–169, especially pp. 164–166.

[53] Urban capital supplies of nonindustrial origin can also be construed as a factor in the reduction of uncertainty.

[54] It was Schumpeter's assumption that innovations "are always associated with the rise to leadership" of new entrepreneurs or "New Men" willing to make "lumpy" investments. Schumpeter, *op. cit.,* pp. 70–72.

[55] Of course, unless new manufacturing functions are undertaken, this kind of single-firm cycle is unlikely to perpetuate itself indefinitely, for the possibilities of major technological improvements within a given production process sooner or later exhaust themselves.

[56] The process by which innovation in one industry brings about a need for innovation in linked industries is often stated in some variation of the following formal economic terms:

If the consumers' goods industry X requires inputs A and B, an innovation may economize on the amount of A per unit of output. If it is assumed that demand is elastic, output will be increased and therefore the demand for input B will increase. As a result, scale-increasing innovations may become economical in B, which, in turn, can make a further expansion of consumers'

arose from "technological disequilibrium" between linked establishments, and as a joint consequence of the aforementioned patterns of uncertainty and imitation, it again becomes apparent that the sequence of urban-industrial innovations, as well as that of urban-industrial inventions, was dovetailing and multiplicative.

The supply-and-demand framework ought not be abandoned before making a brief allusion to the somewhat less clear-cut effects of an abundant supply of cheap unskilled labor upon the urban location of industrial innovations. It is sometimes argued that a large supply of unskilled labor, such as that provided by European immigrants in many American cities of the late nineteenth and early twentieth centuries, encourages the adoption of mechanized production techniques (innovations) in order to substitute workers from this pool for more expensive skilled labor. However, "It may be doubted whether there were many new methods [post-Civil War innovations] which depended for their effect solely on replacing skilled by unskilled labour: it was usually the reduction of *all* grades of labour per unit of output that was important rather than the change in grades."[57] On the other hand, methods permitting lower labor inputs per unit of output often heightened the importance (locational attractiveness) of cheap labor supplies by requiring larger scales of output and an increase in total factory hands. In either case, technological advancements most often required *an embellishment, rather than a replacement,* of skilled labor by cheaper forms of labor.

Finally, it should be pointed out that innovations, like inventions, can be envisaged as being propagated by social dissatisfaction with the quality of manufacturing output or the level of industrial productivity, and/or by the milieu of an achievement-rewarding urban society. In more explicit terms, the latter possibility again suggests that the entre-

---

goods industry X possible. Moreover, if input B is also used in consumers' goods industry Z, innovations become possible there which may increase the demand for its inputs C and D. The increase in the production of B can make possible further innovations in the industries that supply industry B, ...

Strassmann, *op. cit.*, p. 206. Also note Marcus Fleming, "External Economies and the Doctrine of Balanced Growth," *Economic Journal,* Vol. 65 (1955), pp. 241–256; and Albert O. Hirschman, *The Strategy of Economic Development* (Yale Studies in Economics, No. 10; New Haven: Yale University Press, 1958), pp. 98–119.

[57] H. J. Habakkuk, *American and British Technology in the Nineteenth Century* (Cambridge, Eng.: The University Press, 1962), p. 130. The once controversial relationship between the availability of cheap immigrant labor and post-Civil War urban innovations is introduced again in a subsequent portion of this essay.

preneur's role qua potential industrial innovator is related to the noneconomic roles — and to the uncertainties generated by these noneconomic roles — that he must simultaneously perform outside his manufacturing firm; and second, that the entrepreneurial decision to innovate varies with the importance of noneconomic sanctions and roles vis-à-vis the sanction to acquire wealth and the assignment of status (prestigious roles) to large profit-makers.[58] Or, to employ an earlier terminology, entrepreneurs willing to take the risks of industrial innovation are much more likely to appear in cities of "heterogenetic transformation" than in rural areas or cities of "orthogenetic transformation." Moreover, distinctions between communities whose social environment does or does not make them susceptible to the acceptance and development of innovations can *equally well* be made within the subcultural context of a single nation, as well as within the cultural context of geographically separated countries; e.g., English communities accepting change during the "Industrial Revolution" tended to be pretty much identical with those accepting different changes at considerably earlier dates.[59] This last elaboration bears some ramifications of import for the ensuing locational analysis of U.S. urban-industrial inventions and innovations from 1860 to 1900.

The Location of U.S. Urban-Industrial Inventions and Innovations: 1860–1900

Until this juncture our discussion has dealt explicitly with the attraction that cities as a general class, rather than as specific places, exert upon inventive and innovational activities. And yet throughout the discussion itself, it has been implicit that inventions and innovations do not occur with equal frequency in all types of cities but instead concentrate in cities with important industrial functions, or, more precisely, in cities that are rapidly industrializing and expanding in population. Crude data for selected American cities from 1860 to 1900 would seem to indicate

[58] See related discussions in Leland H. Jenks, "Role Structure of Entrepreneurial Personality," in *Change and the Entrepreneur, op. cit.,* pp. 108–152; Arthur H. Cole, *Business Enterprise in its Social Setting* (Cambridge: Harvard University Press, 1959); Thomas C. Cochran, "Cultural Factors in Economic Growth," *Journal of Economic History,* Vol. 20 (1960), pp. 515–532; and Hagen, *op. cit.*

[59] Margaret T. Hodgen, *Change and History: A Study of the Dated Distributions of Technological Innovations in England* (New York: Viking Fund Publications in Anthropology, No. 18, 1952), p. 96.

that these implications and innuendos are essentially valid (Tables 3.1 through 3.3).

It has been observed that "were it not for the fact that no other statistical material exists [relating directly to inventions] the patent

TABLE 3.1 *Patent and Population Data for Selected U.S. Cities, 1860*

	Population	Patents granted	Patents per 10,000 capita	A Percentage of U.S. population	B Percentage of patents granted	B/A[a]
U.S. Total	31,443,321	4,325[b]	1.37	100.00	100.00	1.00
New York	1,174,799[c]	638	5.43	3.74	14.75	3.96
Philadelphia	565,529	211	3.73	1.80	4.88	2.72
Baltimore	212,418	41	1.93	.68	.95	1.41
Boston	177,840	126	7.08	.57	2.91	5.17
St. Louis	160,773	35	2.17	.51	.81	1.59
Chicago	112,172	39	3.47	.36	.90	2.53
Pittsburgh	77,233[d]	49	6.34	.25	1.13	4.63
San Francisco	56,802	26	4.57	.18	.60	3.33
Detroit	45,619	9	1.97	.15	.21	1.44
Cleveland	43,417	41	9.44	.14	.95	6.89
Los Angeles	4,385	0	0.00	.01	.00	.00
New Orleans	168,675	34	2.01	.54	.79	1.46
Louisville	68,033	11	1.61	.22	.25	1.17
Albany	62,367	31	4.97	.20	.72	3.63
Charleston, S.C.	40,522	4	.98	.13	.09	.72
Mobile	29,258	4	1.36	.09	.09	.99

SOURCES: Compiled and tabulated from *Census of Population: 1960*, Vol. 1, Part A (Washington, D. C.: 1961), p. 1-66; *8th Census of the U.S.: Population of the United States in 1860* (Washington, D. C.: 1864); and *Report of the Commissioner of Patents for the Year 1860*, Vol. 1 (Washington, D. C.: 1861).

[a] In Tables 3.1 through 3.3 B/A is actually arrived at by computing the following compound fraction:

$$\frac{\frac{\text{Local patents granted}}{\text{Local population}/10,000}}{\frac{\text{Total U.S. patents granted}}{\text{U.S. population}/10,000}}$$

[b] Not including patents granted to foreign corporations and nonresidents of the United States.

[c] "New York and its boroughs as constituted under the act of consolidation in 1898." *Census of Population: 1960* (*op. cit.*), p. 1-67.

[d] 49,221 in Pittsburgh as then constituted, plus 28,012 in the subsequently annexed municipality of Allegheny.

INVENTIONS AND INNOVATIONS: 1860–1900   107

TABLE 3.2 *Patent and Population Data for Selected U.S. Cities, 1880*

	Population	Patents granted	Patents per 10,000 capita	A Percentage of U.S. population	B Percentage of patents granted	B/A[a]
U.S. Total	50,155,783	12,638[b]	2.46	100.00	100.00	1.00
New York	1,911,698[c]	1,667	8.71	3.81	13.19	3.54
Philadelphia	847,170	541	6.38	1.69	4.28	2.59
Chicago	503,185	489	9.71	1.00	3.87	3.95
Boston	362,839	419	11.54	.72	3.32	4.69
St. Louis	350,518	173	4.94	.70	1.37	2.01
Baltimore	332,313	195	5.87	.66	1.54	2.38
Pittsburgh	235,071[d]	204	8.67	.47	1.61	3.52
San Francisco	233,959	167	7.13	.47	1.32	2.90
Cleveland	160,146	133	8.30	.32	1.05	3.37
Detroit	116,340	96	8.25	.23	.76	3.35
Los Angeles	11,183	2	1.78	.02	.02	.73
New Orleans	216,090	44	2.03	.43	.35	.82
Louisville	123,758	53	4.28	.25	.42	1.74
Albany	90,758	56	6.17	.18	.44	2.51
Charleston, S.C.	49,984	5	1.00	.10	.04	.40
Mobile	29,132	5	1.71	.06	.04	.69

SOURCES: Compiled and tabulated from *Census of Population: 1960*, Vol. 1, Part A (see Table 3.1), p. 1-66; *10th Census of the U.S., 1880: Statistics of the Population of the United States* (Washington, D. C.: 1883); and *Official Gazette of the United States Patent Office*, Vols. 17 and 18 (Washington, D. C.: 1880 and 1881).

[a] See Table 3.1.
[b] Not including patents granted to foreign corporations and nonresidents of the United States.
[c] "New York and its boroughs as constituted under the act of consolidation in 1898."
[d] 156,389 in Pittsburgh as then constituted, plus 78,682 in the subsequently annexed municipality of Allegheny.

statistics would probably be ruled out of court as useless,"[60] and therefore, before Tables 3.1 through 3.3 are subjected to any further scrutiny and analysis it is necessary to make some critical, constricting, and clarifying remarks concerning the data contained in the *Official Gazette of the United States Patent Office*.

Although by 1860 a statute reaffirmed the established practice of

[60] Jewkes, Sawers, and Stillman, *op. cit.*, p. 105.

TABLE 3.3 *Patent and Population Data for Selected U.S. Cities, 1900*

	Population	Patents granted	Patents per 10,000 capita	A Percentage of U.S. population	B Percentage of patents granted	B/A[a]
U.S. Total	75,994,575	21,315[b]	2.80	100.00	100.00	1.00
New York	3,437,202	2,188	6.36	4.53	10.27	2.27
Chicago	1,698,575	1,476	8.68	2.24	6.92	3.10
Philadelphia	1,293,697	849	6.56	1.70	3.98	2.34
St. Louis	575,238	346	6.01	.76	1.62	2.15
Boston	560,892	430	7.66	.74	2.02	2.74
Baltimore	508,957	236	4.64	.67	1.11	1.66
Pittsburgh[c]	451,512	437	9.67	.59	2.05	3.45
Cleveland	381,768	337	8.82	.50	1.58	3.15
San Francisco	342,782	231	6.73	.45	1.08	2.40
Detroit	285,704	186	6.51	.38	.87	2.33
Los Angeles	102,479	102	9.95	.13	.49	3.55
New Orleans	287,104	79	2.75	.38	.37	.98
Louisville	204,731	73	3.56	.27	.34	1.26
Albany	94,151	32	3.40	.12	.15	1.21
Charleston, S.C.	55,807	3	0.53	.07	.01	.19
Mobile	38,469	10	2.59	.05	.05	.93

SOURCES: Compiled and tabulated from *Census of Population: 1960,* Vol. 1, Part A (see Table 3.1), p. 1-66; *12th Census of the U.S.: Population,* Part 1 (Washington, D. C.: 1901); and *Official Gazette of the United States Patent Office,* Vols. 90, 91, 92, and 93 (Washington, D. C.: 1900 and 1901).

[a] See Table 3.1.

[b] Not including patents granted to foreign corporations and nonresidents of the United States.

[c] 321,616 in Pittsburgh as then constituted, plus 129,869 in the shortly annexed municipality of Allegheny.

forbidding the granting of patents for the discovery of scientific principles, all patents were not inventions (some were no more than "a legal scrap of paper," representing "nothing but foolishness or chicane"),[61] and all inventions did not become patents. From all indications, and for a variety of reasons, the number of inventions that did not become patented increased with the passage of time in the late

[61] Gilfillan, "Inventiveness by Nation: A Note on Statistical Treatment," *op. cit.,* p. 303. Technically speaking, grants of patent gave an individual (inventor or agent) or a corporation exclusive legal rights to the manufacture, use, or sale of an invention for a period of seventeen years.

nineteenth century, and hence Table 3.3 probably conveys a less complete picture of the geographic distribution of inventions for 1900 than the preceding tables do for 1860 and 1880. The repeatedly strict actions of the Supreme Court (dating from the 1880's) in denying patents for lack of inventive quality; the cost of patent procurement; the fear that compulsory revelation of cost-cutting production techniques would lead to imitation and the erasure of market-expansion opportunities; the increasing institutionalization of invention by corporations who were generally concerned, even more so than individuals and small firms, with the maintenance of advantage-compounding secrecy rather than the securance of royalties; the dread of defensive infringement litigation; and the accelerated rate of invention, whereby many devices became obsolete or improved upon before a patent could be obtained, all contributed to the mounting volume of unpatented improvements in industrial technology. Moreover, the value of the U.S. Patent Office data is undermined by the fact that "there is no sound basis to assume that decade after decade the quality of patents has remained constant."[62]

There are yet other cracks in the wall of patent statistics. At any date rates of invention tend to vary from industry to industry, and insofar as individual cities have different nonthreshold manufacturing specialties, as well as different arrays of threshold manufactures,[63] it can be assumed that their over-all rates of patents granted per 10,000 capita will be correspondingly distorted; and, as earlier mentioned, patents within a single industry vary tremendously in their technological and economic impacts. Nonetheless, it may be argued, as others have done before, that when large numbers of similarly dated patents are studied, "the disparate significance of patent-units may resolve itself into compensating errors fluctuating at random about . . . [some] mean 'unit-value.' "[64]

Tables 3.1 through 3.3 are even more severely limited as indicators of innovational activity, because: there is usually a time lag between the granting of a patent and its implementation; the place of invention and innovation need not be identical; there are many patents that never

---

[62] Barkev S. Sanders, "Some Difficulties in Measuring Inventive Activity," in *The Rate and Direction of Inventive Activity: Economic and Social Factors, op. cit.,* p. 76.

[63] Due to variations in size of city, accessibility to regional population (regional market potential), and entrepreneurial perception of opportunity.

[64] Robert K. Merton, "Fluctuations in the Rate of Industrial Invention," *Quarterly Journal of Economics,* Vol. 49 (1935), p. 456.

become innovations (conversely, there are many technological innovations that do not trace their origins to patented inventions); and the scale of innovation can differ considerably from patent to patent. On the positive side, when invention originates within the structure of a manufacturing firm, there is a fair chance that at least experimental implementation (innovation) will occur in order to establish practicability.[65]

Despite the previous and other possible negative comments, scholars continue to employ patent statistics for diverse purposes; and there appears to be no reason why the data, when once conceded to be imperfect and crude, need have their utility completely discounted for this essay.[66]

Generalizations

The considerable shortcomings of the data aside, then some more specific generalizations can be made regarding the distribution of inventive and, by extension, of innovational activity in the final four decades of the nineteenth century.

1. With the exception of Charleston, South Carolina, and Albany, New York, two cities that modestly increased their number of inhabitants but lost relative importance in the U.S. system of cities during the late nineteenth century (see Table 2.4), the absolute number of patents granted increased in the selected cities as population expanded from 1860 to 1900.

2. Among the most rapidly growing metropolises (the first eleven cities in Tables 3.1 through 3.3), there was a general relationship, but not a perfect correlation, between rank in population and rank in number of grants of patent attained. This relationship is confined to the 1880 and 1900 dates. Its absence in 1860 is not unexpected, for in most of the eleven cities the process of circular and cumulative growth described in the previous essay was presumably not yet in full operation. Significantly, Baltimore and St. Louis, the only two cities whose rank in number of patents attained was as much as two rungs below their rank in size in either 1880 or 1900, are both transitional cases, as both

---

[65] Compare William Fellner, "The Influence of Market Structure on Technological Progress," *ibid.*, Vol. 65 (1951), p. 576.

[66] For a defense of the use of patent statistics see Jacob Schmookler, "The Interpretation of Patent Statistics," *Journal of the Patent Office Society* (Feb., 1950), pp. 123–146; and *idem,* "The Utility of Patent Statistics," *ibid.* (June, 1953), pp. 407–412.

are located on the margins of the South, where relatively low inventive rates prevailed in the cities. It is also noteworthy that Baltimore, the city among the top eleven with the lowest 1900 rate of patents per 10,000 capita, registered population gains in the following decade that were less impressive than those of the other ten leaders.[67]

3. Patents were disproportionately concentrated in the swiftly emerging metropolises. The first eleven selected cities in Table 3.3 accounted for 31.99 per cent of the country's patents in 1900, while containing only 12.68 of the population for that year.[68]

4. The rate of invention per 10,000 capita did not evince an especially strong relationship to size among the most rapidly growing metropolises; *but* where all of these quickly expanding centers (Los Angeles not included until 1900) had a rate of patent registration that was consistently well above the national rate, and usually in considerable excess of twice that rate,[69] the per 10,000 capita ratio in those Southern cities that were tumbling down the ranks of the urban hierarchy was, by 1880, either less than, or, in the case of Louisville, not substantially above the national figure.[70] Albany is an ambivalent example, exhibiting

[67] In 1910, when Baltimore's population presumably included the multiplier effects of implemented 1900 patents, the number of people residing in the city exceeded the turn-of-the-century total by just less than 10 per cent (558,485 as compared to 508,957).

[68] Actually, if one considers suburban areas that had to some degree become integrated with their respective central cities by 1900, the amount of inventive effort associated with some of the larger and older metropolises of the Eastern Seaboard was much greater than Table 3.3 would intimate. For example, in 1900, 679 patents were granted to individuals and firms in the New Jersey portion of what later became known as the New York Metropolitan Region, and well over 400 grants were secured by persons and corporations located in Boston's industrial suburbs (tabulated from the *Official Gazette of the United States Patent Office*, Vols. 90, 91, 92, and 93; see Table 3.3).

[69] In 1900, Baltimore was the only one of the first eleven cities whose rate of invention per 10,000 capita was not twice the national average; in 1880 there were no exceptions among the ten quickly growing large centers; and in 1860, Baltimore, St. Louis, and Detroit failed to double the rate for the country as a whole.

[70] Between 1860 and 1910 (again, a date when urban populations would presumably include the multiplier effects of implemented 1900 patents), New Orleans lost its position as the fifth largest city in the country and fell to fourteenth place; Louisville dropped twelve notches in the ranking of American cities, falling from tenth to twenty-second place; Charleston, South Carolina, crashed from the twentieth to the seventy-seventh rank; and, even more dramatically, Mobile plummeted from twenty-fifth to nineteenth position in the hierarchy. See Tables 2.4 and 2.5.

inventive patterns similar to the quickly growing cities in 1860 and 1880, but resembling the urban laggards of the South in 1900. Albany, then, is the exception that proves the rule. For in 1860 the Hudson River port was one of the largest cities in the country and still growing at a respectable rate, increasing its population almost 50 per cent between 1860 and 1880; after that, however, when Erie Canal traffic began to decline, the city's expansion almost ground to a halt, population grew by no more than 3.7 per cent from 1880 to 1900, and Albany's high position in the urban hierarchy was relinquished.[71]

When these four interrelated generalizations are considered in totality, *it becomes evident* that any implication that invention is a locational "accident," a geographic irregularity primarily governed by the residence of the independent inventor, is without foundation; and, more significantly, *that the locational configuration of inventive and innovative activities is some function of both the size and rate of growth of cities.*

The Influence of the Size of Cities and the Size of the Local Manufacturing Sector

If there are any answers to the question of why the size of cities affects the frequency of inventions and innovations, then they are to be found in large part by refining much of what has already been said regarding the urban concentration of the two phenomena.

It has been proposed that industrial invention is dependent upon the supply of inventors and capital (risk-taking entrepreneurs), the demand for inventions created both by "technological disequilibrium" in existing manufactures and a more general awareness of particular technical (production) problems, and by the multiplicative and dovetailing aspects of production improvements ("technological convergence"). Therefore, it may be further argued that as the size of a city expands the quantity of patentable developments should also expand because of

[71] Freight traffic originating on the Erie Canal grew from 2,253,533 short tons in 1860, to an all-time peak of 4,608,651 tons in 1880, and thereafter, with the railroads usurping many of the canal's functions, the total slipped downward to 2,145,876 tons in 1900. *Historical Statistics of the United States: Colonial Times to 1957, op. cit.,* p. 455. It may be hypothesized that with 1880 traffic at a record high, and with the outlook for entrepôt and canal-related manufacturing consequently brightened (Albany manufacturing employment, like Erie Canal traffic, had doubled from 1860 to 1880), local entrepreneurs must have been fairly open-minded toward the allocation of resources to the solution of technological problems.

concomitant increases in the volume of requisite supply-and-demand factors, and the augmented possibilities of "technological convergence" resulting from a larger amount of industrial activity.

At least one basic, but modifiable, flaw exists in this chain of logic. City size is only an indirect mirror of the dimensions of any local manufacturing sector, and on occasion the image it reflects is quite distorted. For example, New Orleans was comparable in size to St. Louis in 1860, to San Francisco in 1880, and to Detroit in 1900 (Tables 3.1 through 3.3), but in each of these instances the Crescent City had a much lower number of persons employed in manufacturing (Table 3.4).[72] These dissimilarities in occupational structure pointing to New Orleans' anachronous role as a mercantile city throughout the period 1860–1900)[73] go a long way in explaining why the city consistently had a lower rate of invention per 10,000 capita than centers of a comparable size. In other words, *the rate of invention in specific units of a given size-class of cities is not entirely dependent upon population, but is partially reliant, in each case, upon the magnitude and relative importance of manufacturing in the urban economy.*

However, while conversion of the patent ratio from a per 10,000 capita base to a per 10,000 manufacturing employees base does bring the inventive rates of all sixteen selected cities into somewhat closer harmony, it does not eradicate all the discrepancies between the eleven emerging metropolises and the five relatively declining cities (Table 3.4). If one ceases to compare rates between cities of the same population class, and instead juxtaposes the figures for cities with similar manufacturing employment totals, then it still appears as if the backsliding centers had a lesser proclivity to generate inventive activity than

---

[72] Note also in Table 3.4, that while both the group of eleven quickly growing cities and the group of five slowly growing cities are listed in order of their 1900 populations, there is not a completely corresponding order in the 1900 figures for manufacturing employment.

[73] Indicatively, in 1870, the first date within the 1860–1900 interval for which occupational statistics are available, New Orleans was the only one of the selected cities where manufacturing employment did not exceed that of trade and transportation combined (Los Angeles and Mobile excluded due to lack of data). Moreover, with the exception of the city's sugar refineries, most of New Orleans' industrial establishments served local consumer and construction markets. See *9th Census of the U.S., 1870*, Vol. 1 (Washington, D. C., 1872), pp. 776–800. The calculations of manufacturing employment in each of the selected cities were adjusted by subtracting the following subcategories from the totals given: clerks and bookkeepers in manufacturing establishments; fishermen and oystermen; lumbermen, raftsmen and woodchoppers; miners; and quarrymen.

TABLE 3.4 *Patent and Manufacturing Employment Data for Selected U.S. Cities, 1860, 1880, and 1900*

	Manufacturing employment			Patents per 10,000 manufacturing employees		
	1860	1880a	1900b	1860	1880	1900
U.S. Total	1,311,246	2,732,595	5,478,301	32.98	46.25	38.91
New Yorkc, d	106,216	281,591	510,774	60.07	59.20	42.84
Chicago	5,360	79,414	297,624	72.76	61.58	49.59
Philadelphia	98,983	185,527	265,558	21.32	29.16	31.97
St. Louis	9,352	41,825	92,450	37.43	41.36	37.43
Boston	19,283	59,213	80,982	65.34	70.76	53.16
Baltimore	17,054	56,338	85,005	24.04	34.61	27.76
Pittsburghe	11,151	43,401	97,872	43.94	47.00	44.65
Cleveland	3,462	21,724	64,220	118.42	61.22	52.48
San Francisco	1,503	28,442	46,019	172.99	58.72	50.20
Detroit	2,350	16,110	51,155	38.30	59.59	36.36
Los Angeles	f	f	8,983	f	f	113.55
New Orleans	5,062	9,504	21,272	67.17	46.30	37.14
Louisville	6,679	17,448	32,819	16.47	30.38	22.24
Albany	5,821	11,785	13,307	53.25	47.52	24.05
Charleston, S.C.	852	2,146	5,295	57.55	23.30	5.67
Mobile	664	704	3,030	60.24	71.02	33.00

SOURCES: Manufacturing employment from *8th Census of the U.S., 1860: Statistics of the United States* (Washington, D. C.: 1866), p. xviii; *10th Census of the U.S., 1880*, Vol. 2, *Statistics of Manufactures* (Washington, D. C.: 1883), pp. xxxv, 379–380; *12th Census of the U.S., 1900*, Vol. 8, *Manufactures*, Part 2, *States and Territories* (Washington, D. C.: 1902); and *Historical Statistics of the United States: Colonial Times to 1957, op. cit.*, p. 409. Patent ratios from grant totals in Tables 3.1 through 3.3.

a Includes females under 15 years of age and males under 16 years of age.

b Includes salaried officials and clerks, a category that was not tallied until the Census of 1890. This inclusion in all probability contributes to the apparent 1880-to-1900 decline in inventiveness per 10,000 manufacturing employees (also see textual comments on the post-1880's trend toward an absolute and relative increase in the number of unpatented inventions).

c "New York and its boroughs as constituted under the act of consolidation in 1898."

d The first group of eleven cities and the second group of five cities are each arranged in order of their 1900 populations.

e Including the municipality of Allegheny, which was annexed to Pittsburgh in 1907. In this table, as well as in Tables 3.1 through 3.3, this inclusion is made because of the great number of patents which were jointly granted to residents and firms of both places.

f Not available.

their vigorously expanding counterparts. This is especially true of the 1880 and 1900 data.[74] To be specific: the number of industrial workers in 1880 New Orleans was slightly larger than that in 1900 Los Angeles, but the patent ratio of the latter was more than twice that of the former (113.55 versus 46.30); although Detroit's manufacturing work force was somewhat smaller than Louisville's in 1880, the Michigan city's patent ratio was almost twice as high (59.59 vs. 30.38); and similarly, 1900 New Orleans is not flattered by its comparison with 1880 Cleveland (37.14 vs. 61.22), 1900 Charleston pales beside 1860 Chicago (5.67 vs. 72.76), and 1900 Louisville was completely outdone by 1880 San Francisco (22.24 vs. 58.72).[75] Comparisons of this sort, of course, inevitably suffer from differences in the state of the economy at the three dates, from the diminishing percentage of inventions that became patented after 1880, and from interurban differences in the composition of manufacturing employment.

Interurban variations and changes in manufacturing structure were almost certainly partially responsible for the divergencies to be found in the inventive rates of the cities rising to, or remaining at, the top of the urban hierarchy. Thus, Philadelphia's abnormally low rates can in part be interpreted as a consequence of the early and prolonged importance of its textile and apparel sectors. The former was a sector that had run much of its inventive course prior to the Civil War, and the latter, one that was associated with relatively few technological improvements after the introduction of the sewing machine. New York City's 1900 rate ought also be viewed in the light of its enormous, invention-poor, clothing industry. At the other end of the spectrum, San Francisco's high 1860 ratio of inventions to industrial workers can be attributed to the local dominance of mining machinery and equipment factories and workshops. Most of the production of these establishments was in response to specific orders, a situation that frequently required the solution of previously unencountered problems.

[74] The observation holds true for the 1860 data (compare 1860 Chicago with 1860 New Orleans, Louisville, and Albany), but only in one of three possible parallels is the difference very striking (Chicago versus Louisville). This may in part be due to the fact that the hypothesized urban-industrial growth process was not yet in full swing, and in part due to the aberrancies that are quite likely to arise when small universes of crude data are analyzed. It is extremely difficult to draw any conclusions regarding 1860 Charleston and Mobile (as well as 1880 Mobile) because of the even smaller number of laborers and patents involved.

[75] Also compare 1900 Albany with 1880 Detroit, and, on less certain grounds, 1900 Mobile with 1860 Cleveland.

One other anomaly of Table 3.4 is crucially relevant to a line of thought to be subsequently introduced in this essay. Baltimore, to repeat, was a city bordering on the South that had rates of invention per 10,000 manufacturing employees in 1900 much like those of its urban sisters in Dixie. Also observe that both the number of industrial workers and the patent ratios for 1860 Baltimore and 1880 Louisville are not far apart; and, despite nearly equal manufacturing employment totals, that the patent ratios for Baltimore and Boston were quite dissimilar in 1860, 1880, and 1900.

Turning now to the effect of city size upon the frequency of innovations, it has been suggested that industrial innovation is conditional upon the presence of an environment where uncertainty can be reduced, upon the availability of imitable successes, upon the potential for interplant "technological disequilibrium," upon the supply of inventions and capital, and upon the demand for innovations, plus information regarding recent technical improvements. Therefore, it can be maintained that the probable incidence of innovations increases with urban size because the greater industrial activity that presumably accompanies population increments swells the quantity of requisite supply-and-demand variables and enhances the probability of "technological disequilibrium" between linked establishments, and because size growth implies an accretion of those qualities that reduce the uncertainty of decision-makers.

Once again, this chain of reasoning must be tempered so as to take into account the imperfect relationship between city size and the magnitude of local manufacturing activities. This qualification implies that cities, such as New Orleans, Charleston, and Mobile, that had low absolute levels of manufacturing employment would have correspondingly low absolute levels of industrial innovation; and, to the extent that low absolute levels of invention reflect low absolute levels of innovation, this implication would seem to be valid. The foundation for such an implication can be shored up by introduction of a variation on the demand-for-innovation theme, namely, Adam Smith's durable precept "that the division of labour is limited by the extent of the market." This is, when a low level of manufacturing prevails in a city, the local market for specialized machine tools and machinery is quite likely to be small, and, consequently, there are few viable opportunities in this innovation-rich sector (few thresholds are fulfilled).[76] Likewise, where the level of urban

---

[76] See Nathan Rosenberg, "Capital Goods, Technology, and Economic Growth," *Oxford Economic Papers*, New Series, Vol. 15 (Nov., 1963), pp. 217–227, especially comments relating to nineteenth-century U.S. conditions.

manufacturing is low, potential innovations in all industries whose outputs are consumed by local factories will be inhibited because of the difficulties of sustaining a market large enough to justify new intraplant divisions of labor.

The observations and conclusions contained in this brief section are wholly compatible with experiments indicating that the larger the size of a city, the greater is the probability that any kind of innovation will be responded to by imitation or adoption,[77] and with Hägerstrand's proposition that the spatial distribution of innovational acceptance is governed by (1) an unevenly distributed readiness to accept, (2) an uneven distribution of information regarding the innovation, and (3) some combination of (1) and (2).[78] They are also only one short step removed from the thoughts of contemporaries, such as Hagen, and earlier scholars, such as Ratzel and Durkheim, who in one form or another have expressed the idea that the greater density of urban population or the larger "scale" of urban society facilitates accumulation of knowledge, and thereby, industrial-technological progress.[79]

The Growth Rate of Cities

Industrial inventions and innovations are bound to the rate of growth of cities by ties of varying complexity. To the extent that rapid urban growth means a quick fulfillment of a succession of manufacturing thresholds, such growth entails a mounting demand for inventions and innovations, a diminishing of uncertainty factors, more earnings to plow back, an accelerated stockpiling of knowledge, and increasing "technological convergence" and "technological disequilibrium," all of which are conducive to industrial inventions and innovations. In contrast, in more slowly growing urban centers, where market expansion and the fulfillment of industrial thresholds proceeds at a correspondingly slow pace, the vital stimuli to technical creation, and implementation thereof, are less operative. Also, rapid urban growth promotes invention and innovation "since it facilitates adding new equipment without scrapping

---

[77] Stuart Carter Dodd, "Diffusion Is Predictable: Testing Probability Models for Laws of Interaction," *American Sociological Review*, Vol. 20 (1955), pp. 392–401.

[78] Torsten Hägerstrand, *Innovationsförloppet ur Korologisk Synpunkt* (Lund: Meddelanden från Lunds Universitets Geografiska Institution, Avhandlingar no. 25, 1953), p. 152; see also Innovation Diffusion as a Spatial Process, a translation by Allan Pred, with postscript (Chicago: University of Chicago Press, 1967).

[79] For example, see Hagen, *op. cit.*, p. 251.

old,"[80] because larger markets encourage imitation and permit partial success to the less skillful inventors and entrepreneurs,[81] and because physical urban expansion (of the late nineteenth-century variety) itself provokes lighting, sewerage, paving, construction, transportation, and other *nonindustrial* problems that frequently require inventive and innovative responses from the local manufacturing sector.

In a related context, the contents of Tables 3.1 through 3.4 can be seen as reaffirming the proposed circular and cumulative model of urban-size growth for major American cities from 1860 to about 1910 or shortly thereafter. If the model is correct in suggesting that manufacturing leads to inventions and innovations, and ultimately to population growth and more manufacturing through the multiplier effects of these technological changes, then the slowly growing cities should have had small or stagnant manufacturing sectors and/or low rates of invention per 10,000 capita. And this was the case for the five relatively declining centers considered here.[82] This interplay between retarded urban growth, weak local manufacturing, and low absolute levels of per capita inventiveness can also be placed in a self-generating framework.

Consider a fairly large late nineteenth-century city that has a low level of manufacturing. Its relatively feeble manufacturing sector is not only synonymous with a small number of patents acquired per 10,000 capita but also with relatively few opportunities for interplant linkages and specialization (division of labor). *Ceteris paribus,* this latter condition is in turn commensurate to a relative absence of external and scale economies, and to relatively high production costs. In many industrial categories high costs per unit of output permit usurpation of at least part of the local market by more efficient threshold and non-

[80] Gilfillan, *The Sociology of Invention, op. cit.,* p. 9.
[81] Compare with remarks of Mansfield, *op. cit.,* p. 755; and Hagen, *op. cit.,* p. 238.
[82] In 1900, New Orleans, Mobile, and Charleston still had less than 10 per cent of their population employed in manufacturing, and Albany's number of industrial workers showed little expansion over 1880. It is true that Louisville had as much as 16 per cent of its 1900 inhabitants in industrial occupations, *but* it was making the largest population gains of the declining group.

While slowly growing cities had small manufacturing sectors, it must be reiterated that not all cities with low levels of manufacturing were slowly growing in the post-Civil War era; i.e., a few newly created rail hubs, such as Denver and Omaha, flourished more on commercial functions than on manufacturing, and their process of rapid size-growth bore considerable resemblance to that of the major Atlantic Coast ports in the early nineteenth century. See final essay.

threshold plants that are located in quickly growing centers with larger manufacturing sectors (plants in centers at the same or higher levels of the urban hierarchy capable of substituting higher transport costs to the city in question for lower production costs). Subnormal control of the local market by the affected industries at best implies slow increases of output, slow accumulation of capital that might be appropriated to invention and innovation, retarded (below potential) multiplier effects, retarded urban growth, a persisting pattern of limited problem awareness, and limited opportunities for "technological disequilibrium" and "technological convergence" vis-à-vis similarly sized cities. As a result of a low metabolic growth rate the hypothetical city fails to maintain its rank in the urban hierarchy, simultaneously falling behind its former peers and being overtaken by once smaller but now more rapidly industrializing cities. By definition then, the new peers have larger and more specialized manufacturing sectors and are more likely to produce and adopt innovations. They will also cut costs, usurp part of the laggard city's slowly expanding markets (a process made easier by falling transportation charges), and outpace it in population growth due, in large measure, to technologically derived multiplier effects. Meanwhile, the problem-dependent nature of technological progress in itself will confine inventive and innovative progress in a great number of manufacturing categories more and more to places where output has already succeeded in shifting to a larger scale by virtue of previous technical advances.[83] Still characterized by a relatively weak manufacturing sector, the city in question will continue to experience low absolute levels of inventiveness per capita.

To accept this oversimplified ideal-typical sequence of events as a total "explanation" would be to indulge in foolhardy economic determinism. Because industrial inventions and innovations in themselves help precipitate urban-size growth, it is almost mandatory to go beyond the circular reasoning of economic factors and to consider some of the social forces that at one and the same time hindered technical progress

---

[83] Fels, in trying to reconcile the "depression" of 1873–1882 with a concomitant rapid increase in real GNP, has proposed that "previous innovation must have made possible a great increase in output that imposed hardship — symptoms of depression — on all parts of the economy unable to adapt to the new conditions" [editor's introduction to Schumpeter, *op. cit.*, p. x]. The gist of the argument here is that slumping cities were among the "parts" unable to adapt, and that, in their case, the negative effects were self-feeding and prolonged beyond the early eighties.

and the growth rate of some cities. The introduction of social factors is all the more warranted if it is recalled that even when patent ratios are computed only for manufacturing employees, instead of for the total urban population, there were still indications of a tendency for backsliding Southern cities to exhibit a relatively low ability to generate inventions in 1880 and 1900.

To repeat, innovativeness and inventiveness are often seen as varying with the norms of a social system, and class-divided societies in particular are viewed as presenting rather strong inhibitions and obstacles to technological originality. Similarly, the effect of an uneven distribution of readiness to accept innovation has already been alluded to, and regional differences of this ilk may be assumed to be at least partially attributable to differences in social structure. (It is noteworthy that in Schumpeter's formal structure the existence in a community of vested interests disliking change is considered to be a major impediment to innovation.)[84]

Although one cannot go so far as to refer to late nineteenth-century Southern cities as centers of orthogenetic transformation, it nonetheless is evident that class lines were comparatively strict, and social mobility was relatively small in New Orleans, Charleston, Mobile, and other urban agglomerations of the former confederacy, and that these conditions, in combination with certain prevailing attitudes and values, must have obstructed the appearance of industrial inventions and innovations.

The inflexibility of the Southern urban class system stemmed largely from the South's rural heritage. Long prior to the Civil War, bondage and the well-demarcated lines between white and Negro were transcribed from the plantation to the agricultural trading cities. And there, "as the institution [slavery] encountered mounting difficulties [mainly due to the intermingling of slaves and Free Negroes] . . . another arrangement [legal segregation] was devised which maintained great social distance within the physical proximity of town life."[85] After the Civil

---

[84] Joseph A. Schumpeter, *Capitalism, Socialism, and Democracy* (2nd edition; New York: Harper Brothers, 1948), pp. 81–110. Also note comments by Brozen, *op. cit.*, p. 243; and Rogers, *op. cit.*, p. 311.

[85] Richard C. Wade, *Slavery in the Cities: The South 1820–1860* (New York: Oxford University Press, 1964), p. 266. As segregation was enforced "the distinction between slave and free Negro was erased; race became more important than legal status; . . . [*ibid.*]."

War urban segregation was maintained, even strengthened, in the face of absolute increases in the cityward movement of Negroes. In fact, as cotton prices fell to just under ten cents per pound in 1876, and continued downward to a low of less than five cents per pound in 1894,[86] the number of Negroes driven off the land was such that their socially immobile ranks began to account for a mounting percentage of the total population in Southern cities (Table 3.5). Moreover, moderately strong class lines also existed within the white segment of Southern urban communities. These lines were built on the family prestige and family name of old local commission merchants, bankers, and cotton factors (groups of people whose economic orientation was toward the rural agricultural sector, and whose social position was embellished through their traditional ties with the romanticized and revered landlord class). Class distinctions among whites were sufficiently defined so that "By implication at least, . . . the average person of lower or middle rank . . . had less drive and desire to climb the class ladder than . . . his northern counterpart."[87]

The restriction of industrial inventions and innovations through the operation of a class system that held relatively little promise for social advancement via achievement was fortified by long-standing attitudes toward manufacturing and things Northern. In the decades preceding the Civil War scorn for the factory had already reached a point where a prominent Southern commercial figure could contend that "agriculture and agricultural improvements make the only permanent additions to a country's greatness . . . ."[88] In response to the humiliation of defeat there was a widespread glorification of the past in the South, an increased truculence toward ideas and practices emanating from the North, and, as one result, an increased denigration of manufacturing. Entrenchment of these attitudes directly subverted innovation and, in all probability, indirectly caused the erection of barriers by discouraging the allocation of scarce capital resources to technological experimentation and implementation. In addition, the intimate bonds between agricultural

---

[86] *Historical Statistics of the United States: Colonial Times to 1957, op. cit.,* pp. 301–302.

[87] Harold F. Kaufman, "Social Class in the Urban South," in Rupert B. Vance and Nicholas J. Demerath, eds., *The Urban South* (Chapel Hill: University of North Carolina Press, 1954), p. 178.

[88] James De Bow, "Some Remarks on Agriculture and Our Agricultural Products," *De Bow's Review,* Vol. 9 (Oct., 1850), p. 393.

TABLE 3.5 *Racial Composition and Patent Data for Selected U.S. Cities, 1860, 1880, and 1900*

	1860		1880		1900	
	White	Negro[a] and other non-white	White	Negro and other non-white	White	Negro and other non-white
New York[b]	1,153,200	21,599	1,877,180	34,518	3,369,898	67,304
Chicago	111,217	955	496,495	6,690	1,667,140	31,435
Philadelphia	543,344	22,185	815,362	34,805	1,229,673	64,024
St. Louis	157,476	3,297	328,191	22,327	539,385	35,853
Boston	175,579	2,261	356,826	6,013	548,083	12,809
Baltimore	184,520	27,898	278,584	53,729	429,218	79,739
Pittsburgh[c]	75,389	1,844	228,912	6,159	430,973	20,539
Cleveland	42,618	799	158,084	2,062	375,664	6,104
San Francisco	55,626	1,176	210,496	23,463	325,378	17,404
Detroit	44,216	1,403	113,475	2,865	281,575	4,129
Los Angeles	3,854	531	10,379	804	98,479	4,397
New Orleans	144,601	24,074	158,367	57,723	208,950	78,158
Louisville	61,213	6,820	102,847	20,911	165,590	39,141
Albany	61,718	649	89,694	1,064	92,962	1,189
Charleston, S.C.	23,106	17,146	22,699	27,285	24,238	31,569
Mobile	20,854	8,404	16,885	12,247	21,402	17,067

investment and social prestige "may have engendered an economic environment that resisted the penetration of 'foreign' finance."[89] Put in a slightly different context, the responses (choice models) evoked when Southern businessmen were exposed to the stimuli of inventive or innovative opportunities frequently were distorted by precedent-taking social values; and therefore, depending on the qualitative and quantitative attributes of the stimuli (information), individual respondents usually, but not invariably, behaved either as unsuccessful adaptors or unsuccessful adopters.[90] In sum, the routinization of behavioral re-

---

[89] Lance E. Davis, "The Investment Market, 1870–1914: The Evolution of a National Market," *Journal of Economic History*, Vol. 25 (1965), p. 392. In terms of the urgency of capital availability to local inventive and innovative efforts, it is quite significant that, at the turn of the century, Southern manufactures were still much less characterized by corporate control than those anywhere else in the country. See George Heberton Evans, Jr., "Geographical Differences in the Use of the Corporation in American Manufacturing in 1899," *ibid.*, Vol. 14 (1954), pp. 113–125.

[90] Or, in Danhof's terminology, as drone and "Fabian" entrepreneurs. See footnote 46.

TABLE 3.5 (continued)

	Patents per 10,000 white population			Increase over corresponding ratios for total white and nonwhite population		
	1860	1880	1900	1860	1880	1900
U.S. Total	1.61	2.91	2.19	.24	.45	.39
New York[b]	5.53	8.88	6.49	.10	.17	.13
Chicago	3.51	9.85	8.85	.04	.14	.17
Philadelphia	3.88	6.64	6.90	.15	.26	.34
St. Louis	2.22	5.27	6.41	.05	.33	.40
Boston	7.18	11.74	7.85	.10	.20	.19
Baltimore	2.22	7.00	5.50	.29	1.13	.86
Pittsburgh[c]	6.50	8.91	10.14	.16	.24	.47
Cleveland	9.62	8.41	8.97	.18	.11	.15
San Francisco	4.67	7.94	7.10	.10	.81	.37
Detroit	2.04	8.46	6.61	.07	.21	.10
Los Angeles	0.00	1.93	10.36	.00	.15	.41
New Orleans	2.35	2.78	3.78	.34	.75	1.03
Louisville	1.80	5.15	4.41	.19	.87	.85
Albany	5.02	6.24	3.44	.05	.07	.04
Charleston, S.C.	1.73	2.20	1.24	.75	1.20	.71
Mobile	1.92	2.96	4.67	.56	1.25	2.08

SOURCES: Racial composition from *8th Census of the U.S.: Population of the United States in 1860, op. cit.; 10th Census of the U.S., 1880: Statistics of the Population of the United States, op. cit.*, pp. 402, 416–424; *12th Census of the U.S.: Population*, Part 1, *op. cit.*, pp. 609–642; and *Historical Statistics of the United States: Colonial Times to 1957, op. cit.*, pp. 10–12. Patent ratios from patent totals in Tables 3.1 through 3.3.

[a] The 1860 Negro population of St. Louis, Baltimore, New Orleans, Louisville, Charleston and Mobile included both slaves and "free colored."

[b] "New York and its boroughs as constituted under the act of consolidation in 1898."

[c] Including the municipality of Allegheny, which was annexed to Pittsburgh in 1907.

sponses within the subculture of the urban South contributed to the repeated vetoing of industrial originality throughout the last half of the nineteenth century.[91]

[91] Even in those few Southern cities that were experiencing growth modest enough to avoid descending the ranks of the urban hierarchy, such as Memphis and Birmingham, the rate of industrial experimentation was significantly below that of centers in other parts of the country where absolute population gains were more striking. In 1900 the number of patents granted per 10,000 capita was 3.64 in Birmingham, and 3.91 in Memphis. Tabulated from the *Official Gazette of the United States Patent Office*, Vols. 90, 91, 92, and 93 (see Table 3.3).

Given the supposed impact of a class structure whose relative inflexibility apparently even permeated the confines of the manufacturing establishment, where relations between employer and employees often resembled those on former plantations, and, given the supposed repercussions of the prevalent values of potential inventors and innovators, it would appear desirable to assign these factors a quantitative expression. Although the assembly of data relevant to values and attitudes would be a Herculean and perhaps impossible task, a crude partial solution is possible with regard to class structure.

If the not unreasonable assumption is made that, because of their social immobility and extremely low level of education, it was virtually impossible for Negroes to perform acts of invention and innovation, then it becomes feasible to examine roughly the degree to which the presence of large Negro populations influenced the low rates of per capita inventiveness in slowly growing Southern cities.[92] Table 3.5, whose patent ratios were arrived at by dividing the number of grants received by the local white population/10,000, instead of the total local population/10,000, reveals that the most significant increases, particularly in 1880 and 1900, were recorded by the four declining Southern centers and Baltimore.[93] A comparison with Table 3.3 also shows New Orleans and Mobile shifting from positions slightly below the national average for patents granted per 10,000 capita to positions, like Louisville's, well above the national average for patents granted per 10,000 white capita. Only Charleston, with its unique Negro majority (and therefore most conservative elite attitudes?), remains below the 1900 national average per 10,000 white capita.

While these observations indicate that large Negro populations unintentionally served as a brake on total per capita inventiveness in Southern cities, it nevertheless is true that the gap between the ratios of these units and their rapidly expanding counterparts is only partially closed by eliminating nonwhites from the computations. Presumably, the remainder is accounted for by discrepancies in the size of local manufacturing sectors, attitudinal differences, and other intangibles.

[92] Of course, this does not mean that Negroes were not employed in urban manufacturing. It is also conceded that many newly arrived European migrants had low levels of social mobility and education. However, as a group they were so heterogeneous in skills and background that there is no sound basis for eliminating them from the patent ratios in Table 3.5.

[93] San Francisco also registered large gains in 1880 due to the peaking of its Chinese population.

In many respects Table 3.5 is most telling and fascinating in its clarification of Baltimore's deviant patterns of invention and growth. The Chesapeake Bay city's concurrent possession of a 1900 patent ratio per 10,000 capita lower than that of any other selected growth leader, of a 1900 patent ratio per 10,000 manufacturing employees below that of any other selected dominant of the urban hierarchy, and of a turn-of-the-century growth rate less impressive than that of the other ten pacesetters, appears less than coincidental when it is noted that the city had the country's largest urban concentration of Negroes. The presence of nearly 80,000 low-status Negroes undoubtedly depressed wages in many of those Baltimorean manufacturing categories employing substantial numbers of unskilled and semiskilled laborers (compare "foundry and machine shop products" with all other categories in Table 3.6), and the availability of extremely cheap labor, in turn, must have encouraged many entrepreneurs to substitute labor inputs for capital goods inputs (innovations), thereby decreasing the probability of technological problem-awareness and inventive responses. The substitution assumption is tenuously confirmed by 1900 statistics for capital invested in "machinery, tools and equipment" per manufacturing employee that attribute a rate of $210.4 per worker to Baltimore, and rates of $341.2, or more, to all other selected cities in Tables 3.1 through 3.4.[94] Insofar as the assumption is accurate, the relatively slow population expansion of Baltimore can be interpreted as a joint consequence of a frequent failure to attain scale and specialization economies (and

---

[94] *12th Census of the U.S.,* Vol. 8, *Manufactures,* Part 2, *States and Territories, op. cit.* Predictably, with the exception of Baltimore, rates in the rapidly growing group of cities ($390.8–$539.4) exceeded those of Albany, Louisville, Mobile, and Charleston ($341.2–$377.7). When questionably adjusted, New Orleans' rate was also low ($371.1). However, these figures ought to be approached with extreme caution, as Census officials warned that the returns regarding capital invested in "machinery, tools and equipment" were "too variable to permit statistical accuracy." They added, "[each] return is, strictly speaking, a return of estimated market value, rather than of capital invested. The amount of the latter is affected by many causes — by depreciation requiring additional investment, by throwing out old machinery and substituting new, by business failures, and by other causes. So that in the case of most of the old and successful manufacturing concerns of the country the total investment in the plant has been very much greater than the present market value, as estimated by assessors." *Ibid.,* Vol. 7, *Manufactures,* Part 1, *United States by Industries,* p. xcix. The perils of the data are compounded by intercity variations in industrial structure, the exclusion of large suburban factories, and the inclusion of "neighborhood and hand" industries.

TABLE 3.6 *Selected Manufacturing Wage Data for Baltimore, Philadelphia, and New York, 1900*

	Baltimore		Philadelphia[a]		New York City[b]	
	Average number of wage-earners[c]	Annual earnings[d]	Average number of wage-earners[c]	Annual earnings[d]	Average number of wage-earners[c]	Annual earnings[d]
All Industries	78,738	$371.1	246,445	$453.8	462,763	$529.5
Furniture, Factory Production	1,627	458.1	2,391	519.0	6,760	576.3
Men's Clothing, Factory Production	9,690	327.6	6,463	510.8	30,406	515.9
Enameling and Enameled Goods	1,136	278.5	22	347.0	1,458	361.4
Fruits and Vegetables, Canning and Preserving[e]	4,360	207.7	f	f	379	313.2
Foundry and Machine Shop Products	3,375	534.9	19,643	569.0	19,560	582.7

SOURCE: *12th Census of the U.S., 1900*, Vol. 8, Manufactures, Part 2, *States and Territories, op. cit.,* pp. 340–342, 620–624, 784–786.

[a] Philadelphia is compared with Baltimore because of its geographic proximity and assumed similarities in the state of its regional economy.

[b] New York City is compared with Baltimore because of its large European immigrant population.

[c] Excluding salaried officials and clerks.

[d] These averages are not entirely comparable because of differences in average number of work-hours per year and other data imperfections.

[e] Affected by seasonality of employment.

[f] Not available.

therefore frequently diminished opportunities for market expansion)[95] and the abbreviated multiplier effects normally associated with low-wage manufacturing.

In this light, Baltimore's location at the perimeter of the South was important not so much because it allowed the partial penetration of

[95] As Alfred Weber and others have pointed out, low wages per man-hour are not necessarily synonymous with low labor costs per unit of output. High labor costs per unit of output, and high total costs per unit of output can obtain when cheap labor is substituted for capital-intensive production techniques, and when this situation occurs there is little opportunity for market area expansion through the substitution of additional transport inputs for production savings.

Southern attitudes and values regarding industrialism but rather because it made the city the nearest, and most accessible, non-Southern urban-migration destination for northward-moving Negroes. Similarly, it is tempting to couple the Mississippi location of St. Louis with its inventiveness rates and population increases from 1900 to 1910. The record, which was not unimpressive but was substandard in relation to most of the other selected growth leaders, may be ascribed to related but much less pronounced migration and attitudinal causes.

Any invocation of geographical variations in class structure and values leads almost inevitably to the terra infirma of regional differences in consumer tastes and preferences. Cultural predilections of this sort are purported to have influenced patterns of innovation in nineteenth-century Europe.[96] However, such a heavy mist lies over the two-way interconnections between regional tastes and innovation that it would be unreasonable to create further obfuscation by attempting to identify a three-way interplay between these two phenomena and the 1860–1900 growth rate of Northern and Southern U.S. cities.

The Circulation of Information

In the last essay's presentation of a theory of circular and cumulative urban-size growth, and in this essay's discussion of the general proclivity of industrial inventions and innovations for urban environments, it has been suggested: (1) that technological progress in late nineteenth-century cities was promoted by the dissemination of ideas, concepts, observations, and other pieces of technical knowledge through a complex network of interpersonal communications and confrontations; and (2) that such a personal circulation of information was critical in an era when technical periodicals were of increasing but limited importance[97]

---

[96] Habakkuk, "The Historical Experience on the Basic Conditions of Economic Progress," *op. cit.*, p. 160.

[97] Again, this is not to imply that diffusion of industrial production technology was wholly independent of the growing volume of trade-journal literature (see qualifications in footnote 3.29), for evidence exists to the contrary. For example, a Carnegie representative addressing the British Iron and Steel Institute in 1881 could state:

While your metallurgists, as well as those of France and Germany, have been devoting their time and talents to the discovery of new processes, we have swallowed the information so generously tendered through the reports of the Institute, and have selfishly devoted ourselves to beating you in output.

Burton J. Hendrick, *The Life of Andrew Carnegie* (Garden City: Doubleday, Doran and Co., 1932), Vol. 2, pp. 309–310.

and mass communications media either unknown or poorly developed, particularly inasmuch as the Usherian formulation of inventive problem solution involves progressive synthesis through multiple exposure to information and other stimuli. In view of these contentions and of the ostensible indications that as cities grow in size and per capita wealth the per capita rate of information flow accelerates even more rapidly,[98] a brief illumination ought to be made of the attributes of interpersonal communication that presumably contribute to the already observed relationship between the size and growth-rate characteristics of urban centers, and their frequency of industrial inventions and innovations.

Hägerstrand and others have shown that: the intensity of interpersonal information flow is greatest at very short distances; "On the average, the density of contacts included in a single person's private-information field[99] must decrease very rapidly with increasing distance";[100] the distance decay of the density of the private-information field may have irregularities due to "differentials of sex, age, income, education, occupation, marital status, political, religious and other affiliations;[101] and the

---

[98] That is to say, the total volume of information flow is an exponential function of a city's size, and the rate at which the circulation of information expands is therefore determined by the urban-size growth rate. See the comparison of information flow estimates for San Francisco, New York, and London with similar data for Addis Ababa, Djakarta, and Tehran in Richard L. Meier, *A Communications Theory of Urban Growth* (Cambridge: The M.I.T. Press, 1962), pp. 131–132.

[99] The private-information field of an individual (or small cohesive group) is usually contrasted with his public-information field, or mass communications sources of information.

[100] Hägerstrand, *op. cit.*, p. 237. This is so because distance acts as a barrier both to the establishment of individual contacts and to the maintenance of already established ties. For other statements regarding human interaction and distance see George Kingsley Zipf, "Some Determinants of the Circulation of Information," *American Journal of Psychology*, Vol. 59 (1946), pp. 401–421; Stuart Carter Dodd, "Testing Message Diffusion in Controlled Experiments: Charting the Distance and Time Factors in the Interactance Hypothesis," *American Sociological Review*, Vol. 18 (1953), pp. 410–416; Gunnar Boalt and Carl-Gunnar Janson, "Distance and Social Relations," *Acta Sociologica*, Vol. 2 (1957), pp. 73–97; Duane F. Marble and John D. Nystuen, "An Approach to the Direct Measurement of Community Mean Information Fields," *Papers and Proceedings of the Regional Science Association*, Vol. 11 (1963), pp. 99–109; and Gunnar Olsson, *Distance and Human Interaction* (Philadelphia: Regional Science Research Institute, 1965).

[101] Stuart Carter Dodd, "The Interactance Hypothesis: A Gravity Model Fitting Physical Masses and Human Groups," *American Sociological Review*, Vol. 15 (1950), p. 246. That is, the configuration of a person's private-information field may be distended or contracted by his motivation to interact with specific

closer two people live to one another, the greater the likelihood that their private-information fields will overlap or be nearly identical.[102] Now, insofar as the efficiency of knowledge diffusion declines outward from the center of a private-information field (or alternatively, from a person or a viable economic unit such as a factory),[103] and insofar as these fields are in many instances occupationally bound,[104] it is logical that the larger the city, the larger the number of intentionally and unintentionally overlapping information fields of laborers and other industrial personnel, the larger the volume of influential short-distance information flows, and the greater the awareness of specific technical problems and existing production process improvements. Recalling that advances in industrial technology usually occur in response to particular problems, and that innovation frequently takes the form of imitating observed success (the "acceptance of a new trait occurs as the result of an accumulation of many experiences with that innovation"),[105] it ultimately follows that the larger the city (local manufacturing sector), the higher the *absolute number* of industrial inventions and innovations.

---

social types or groups. Note Georg Karlsson, *Social Mechanisms* (Glencoe: The Free Press, 1958), pp. 29 ff.

[102] Hägerstrand, *op. cit.*, pp. 238–239. Also see Boalt and Janson, *op. cit.*, pp. 85–86, and Anatol Rapoport, "Spread of Information through a Population with Socio-Structural Bias: I. Assumption of Transitivity," *Bulletin of Mathematical Biophysics*, Vol. 15 (1953), pp. 523–533.

[103] Human ecologists have put the distance and waning potency of diffusion syndrome into such formalistic terms as the following:

> Briefly, suppose a particle (or person or any entity) has a constant amount of energy (or social influence of any sort) which is equally likely to diffuse in any direction. Draw concentric zones of equal widths around the particle .... The space in each zone can be proved geometrically to vary with its distance (radius) from the particle. Since the constant energy was assumed to diffuse evenly, it will become divided into smaller amounts per unit space the further out it goes. The energy per unit space at distance L will be inversely proportional to L, i.e., it will vary as L^{-1}, ...

Dodd, "Diffusion is Predictable: Testing Probability Models for Laws of Interaction," *op. cit.*, pp. 394–395.

[104] Similarity of occupation increases the probability of interaction between pairs of individuals (see, for example, Boalt and Janson, *op. cit.*, p. 95). In his classic article on the sociological character of city life, Wirth, building upon Max Weber and Georg Simmel, pointed out that the multiplication of human interaction within an urban environment causes fleeting personal contacts to be "segmentalized" and utilitarian, and, by extension, specialized according to the individual's roles. Louis Wirth, "Urbanism as a Way of Life," *American Journal of Sociology*, Vol. 44 (1938), pp. 1–24, especially pp. 11–13.

[105] H. Earl Pemberton, "The Spatial Order of Culture Diffusion," *Sociology and Social Research*, Vol. 22 (1938), p. 250. Also note Hägerstrand, *op. cit.*, pp. 266–267.

(The same cannot be said of the *rate* of invention and innovation because of interurban variations in manufacturing composition and the possibility that communications overload and other factors cause per capita levels of problem-awareness and imitation to taper off once city size becomes extremely large.)[106] In this sequence the number of overlapping and interacting information fields is especially important because only some carriers, and some receivers who become carriers, will feed the knowledge into their information fields, while others will retard the circulation by passively retaining the information and failing to forward it to other individuals.

In relating the rate of late nineteenth-century urban growth to this framework, it need only be added that the faster the rate of growth, the quicker the expansion of the local manufacturing sector, the higher the volume of pertinent information in circulation, the faster the rate of circulation accelerates, and the higher the absolute number of acts of technological improvement that will probably materialize.

There are those who might question the applicability of these arguments to the American urban scene in the pre-electric-traction portion of the late nineteenth century. Mandelbaum has contended that the slowness of public horse-drawn transportation, its clustering of services on north-south (downtown) oriented routes, and the scarcity of crosstown carriers, combined to make large sections of 1870 New York City "relatively isolated from one another," and therefore to limit severely "face-to-face contact between its inhabitants."[107] To the extent that horse-drawn public transportation was also oriented to the central business district in the other rapidly growing cities, this contention could be devastating. However, the conditions of "relative isolation" prior to the electric trolley were such as to strengthen, rather than weaken, the circulation of invention- and innovation-generating information. For large U.S. cities as a group, manufacturing was largely

---

[106] See Rashevsky, "A Note on Imitative Behavior and Information," *loc. cit.*

[107] Seymour J. Mandelbaum, *Boss Tweed's New York* (New York: John Wiley & Sons, 1965), pp. 1–39. Mandelbaum also asserts that New York City's manufacturing firms tended to be small in size due to these factors. This would appear to be a gross oversimplification in view of the limited availability and cost of land in the built-up portion of the city (85 per cent of the 1870 population dwelt within two miles of Union Square and 14th Street), the absence of nuisance legislation in the New Jersey portion of the metropolis, the distortion created by the small optimal scale of the clothing industry establishments, and the superior rail facilities and accessibility to distant markets available at sites just west of the Hudson.

concentrated in rail-terminal and port districts proximate to the downtown area, and high-density factory-worker residential areas intermingled with, and surrounded, production units. In short, "relatively isolated" neighborhoods tended to be inhabited by populations that were fairly homogeneous from an occupational standpoint, and therefore the chances for intentional and accidental exposure to related bits of technical information were enhanced.

Although electric traction did begin to break the log-jam of downtown industrial concentration after 1890, many blue-collar workers and technicians continued to live in close proximity to their now more widely dispersed workplaces, and face-to-face contacts remained quite important to technological change. For example: it was reported in the 1900 Census that in specialized communities (industrial concentrations) "the contact of workmen and employers with each other results in a mutual improvement in manufacturing";[108] and the "bar-room of the old Pontchatrain Hotel in Detroit is reputed to have been a hot-house of early automotive technology in the early years of this century."[109]

The Role of Migration

As stated in the previous essay, it is sometimes noted that, because destinations of previous out-migrants and knowledge of job and residential opportunities are two of the most important determinants of individual migration decisions, the volume of migration flowing into a city is a positive function both of urban size and of the city's rate of growth (or rate at which new employment possibilities are created). Therefore, to the extent that in-migrants have an impact on the frequency of industrial inventions and innovations, this impact would also be a positive function of a city's size and rate of growth.

During the late nineteenth century, the spread of information relating to industrial inventions and innovations occurred not only by short-distance radiation outward from urban individuals and production units

---

[108] *12th Census of the U.S.*, Vol. 7, *op. cit.*, p. ccxiii. The statement continued: "Laborers 'talk shop' more or less when not at work, and the devices adopted in one establishment for making the work easier are soon adopted in all. Similarly, it is easy for a manufacturer in such a place to note the experiments with patented improvements carried on in another establishment, and to adopt such improvements just as soon as their value is demonstrated, by paying the royalty demanded."

[109] Wilbur R. Thompson, *A Preface to Urban Economics* (Baltimore: The Johns Hopkins Press, 1965), p. 45.

but also by international, interurban, and rural-to-urban migration. The technological consequences of diffusion by migration were often more spectacular than those of local information dissemination because such diffusion sometimes was synonymous with the introduction of completely new skills, concepts, techniques, and varieties of problem-awareness. Of course, the potential impact of migrants who are carriers of technological skills and information will usually, but not invariably, differ with the form of their arrival. When migrants arrive as isolated individuals or migration units (families) diffusion "is apt to be uncertain and not very rapid."[110] This is so at least partly because change is dependent on repeated experience, while at the same time there is a low probability of a lone, private information field influencing others through multiple exposure. On the other hand, when migrants arrive in numbers from the same place, and/or with the same occupations, as they frequently did in the decades following the Civil War, specialized bits of information are injected into the community from many sources and the probability of invention or innovation is raised considerably. This observation does not mean to convey the idea that more than a limited number of in-migrants were prospective contributors to the technical progress of cities, particularly in the case of foreign immigrants who either came with the values of a traditional society or, if bearing usable information, often had the horizons of their private-information fields constricted by their social status.[111]

Nevertheless, the late nineteenth-century impact of European immigrants upon the technological progress of urban manufacturing cannot be exaggerated, because, through their presence in massive numbers in the rapidly growing cities (as shown in Table 3.7) and their availability for employment in factories (close to 45 per cent of the country's gainfully occupied foreign-born whites were employed in manufacturing in 1900),[112] their influence went beyond the realm of information diffusion. While today's scholars recognize "that the view that unskilled [immigrant] labor 'caused mechanization . . . [is] grossly oversimpli-

---

[110] Warren C. Scoville, "Minority Migrations and the Diffusion of Technology," *Journal of Economic History*, Vol. 11 (1951), p. 350.

[111] Compare with Hagen, *op. cit.*, pp. 242-243.

[112] It is also noteworthy that, throughout the late nineteenth century, foreign-born laborers comprised over 31 per cent of total American manufacturing employment. In some industries, e.g., iron and steel, the figure approached or exceeded 40 per cent. See Charlotte Erickson, *American Industry and the European Immigrant 1860-1885* (Cambridge: Harvard University Press, 1957), p. 191.

TABLE 3.7 *Immigrant Elements of Population in Selected U.S. Cities, 1900*

	Foreign born	% of total population	Persons of foreign parentage[a]	% of total population
U.S. Total	10,460,085	13.7	26,198,939	34.3
New York	1,270,080	37.0	2,643,957	76.9
Chicago	587,112	34.6	1,315,307	77.4
Philadelphia	295,340	22.8	1,293,697	54.9
St. Louis	111,356	19.4	350,777	61.0
Boston	197,129	35.1	404,999	72.2
Baltimore	68,600	13.5	194,223	38.2
Pittsburgh	115,094[b]	25.5	284,246[c]	63.0
Cleveland	124,631	32.6	288,491	75.6
San Francisco	116,885	34.1	257,784	75.2
Detroit	96,503	33.8	221,281	77.5
Los Angeles	19,964	19.5	46,311	45.2
New Orleans	30,325	10.6	108,010	37.6
Louisville	21,427	10.5	77,253	37.7
Albany	17,718	18.8	54,582	58.0
Charleston, S.C.	2,592	4.6	7,921	14.2
Mobile	2,111	5.5	8,049	20.9

SOURCE: *12th Census of the U.S.: Population,* Part 1, *op. cit.,* pp. ciii, cix–cx, clxxxiii–clxxxix.

[a] Includes foreign born and their first-generation offspring born in the United States.

[b] 84,878 in Pittsburgh as then constituted, plus 30,216 in the shortly annexed municipality of Allegheny.

[c] 205,247 in Pittsburgh as then constituted, plus 78,999 in the shortly annexed municipality of Allegheny.

fied,' "[113] it is still felt in some quarters that "Immigration encouraged the American industrialist to buy additional machines, . . . , but machines which would have been the most economic even in the absence of heavy immigration."[114] Or, as previously put, relatively cheap immigrant labor did not stimulate innovation by presenting an opportunity to eliminate more costly skilled labor,[115] but by facilitating operation at

[113] *Ibid.,* p. 124.
[114] Habakkuk, *American and British Technology in the Nineteenth Century, op. cit.,* p. 131.
[115] Although the demand for some craft skills was reduced by the mechanization of output, there was no general obliteration of job opportunities for the skilled. As the industrial adoption of complicated machinery proceeded, there was a growing need for skilled labor in the production of machine tools and machinery itself. As a matter of fact, there already was a slight tendency for cranes and other automated devices to eliminate unskilled jobs.

larger scales of production[116] — scales requiring an increase in the total number of *unskilled and skilled* hands.

Innovations of this sort can also be seen as part of a self-generating process whose tempo was governed by business cycles. To play a variation on a familiar theme, the arrival of large numbers of immigrants precipitated the adoption of technological improvements (innovations), these improved manufacturing techniques led to production economies and market expansion, higher levels of output and multiplier effects (job opportunities). These in turn attracted additional immigrants and promoted further technological improvements (including inventions and innovations arising from "technological disequilibrium," "technological convergence," and the circulation of information). This cycle, as well as the other ideas presented in this section, are consistent with the fact that ten of the first eleven cities in Table 3.7 had a much higher percentage of their 1900 population accounted for by immigrants than slowly growing (low-opportunity) Southern cities. The exception, Baltimore, may be hypothesized to be no exception, for at the onset of the twentieth century it was the slowest growing city in the group of eleven, and its great Negro population, combined with an apparent local preference to substitute cheap labor inputs for capital goods inputs, may well have induced immigrants to turn toward similarly sized cities where opportunities were both more numerous and better paying.

The Diffusion of Industrial Innovations: Suggestions for a Typology

It is apparent from the preceding introduction of migrational influences that the intraurban diffusion of information regarding industrial innovations is only one narrow aspect of the spatial spread of technological advances. There are also patterns of adoption and diffusion that cover extensive areas, and it is self-evident that the geographical sequence of implementation varies from industry to industry, and that, even if social barriers to change are absent, acceptance patterns may differ from one manufacturing activity to another within a single city[117]

---

[116] Habakkuk's following position is quite similar: "The principal effect of immigration was not on the manufacturer's choice of technique but on his ability to give effect to his choice." Habakkuk, *loc. cit.*

[117] Note the evidence for early nineteenth century Philadelphia offered by Sam B. Warner's "Innovation and the Industrialization of Philadelphia 1800–1850," in *The Historian and the City, op. cit.*, pp. 63–69.

(due largely to interindustry variations in the mix and successfulness of adaptive and adoptive entrepreneurs). Economists acknowledge the fact that the diffusion of production technology is generally a slow process whose course meanders singularly in individual industries, and a number of aspatial factors underlying these peculiarities are usually cited. They generally list attitudes toward risk, the intensity of market competition, financial health, labor force adaptability, age of existing equipment, and capital availability among the most crucial determinants of diffusion.[118] However, such contributory explanations are inadequate insofar as they fail to deal with locational variations and spatial attributes.

As an alternative means of differentiating diffusion patterns of industrial innovations, broad manufacturing categories with similar geographic distributions may be sorted into ideal-typical groups, because, presumably, the locational characteristics of each group will dictate the path, and perhaps the speed, of individual innovation diffusions. The groupings that follow are selected with an eye toward their applicability to the state of manufacturing and communications during the late nineteenth century, although it is felt that with some modifications they could be made pertinent to contemporary mass communication systems and levels of production.

In the general case industrial innovations are theoretically diffused over space in three stages:[119] (1) concentration of imitation and adoption in the center(s)[120] of origin; (2) continued densening at the initial agglomeration while irregular (uneven) radial dissemination from that original center results in development of secondary centers; (3) equal relative increases in acceptance and implementation at all agglomerations, and ultimate cessation of diffusion. In particular instances the

[118] Mansfield, *op. cit.*, p. 747; and Brozen, *op. cit.*, p. 240.

[119] After Hägerstrand, *op. cit.*, p. 138; and *idem*, "The Propagation of Innovation Waves," in Philip L. Wagner and Marvin W. Mikesell, eds., *Readings in Cultural Geography* (Chicago: University of Chicago Press, 1962, p. 365. Reprinted from *Lund Studies in Geography*, Series B, Human Geography, Vol. 4 (1952).

[120] Under unusual circumstances parallel research interests, brought about by a common perception of demand and similar levels of technological problem awareness, can result in geographically divorced but nearly identical inventions (potential innovations). This is more likely under present-day conditions of research and development in the United States than it was in the past. See Richard L. Nelson, "Uncertainty, Learning, and the Economics of Parallel Research and Development Efforts," *Review of Economics and Statistics*, Vol. 43 (1961), pp. 351–364, especially pp. 362–363.

process can be arrested prior to the second or third stage, and in some cases the secondary agglomerations are restricted to specific types of locations. The applicability of the general case and its deviations is superficially intimated below for two broad industrial categories. The depiction of geographic patterns of innovation acceptance for these two groups should not be construed as anything more than a tentative suggestion for a more precise and refined typology of the diffusion of industrial innovations. Such an elaboration awaits the appearance of detailed case studies.[121]

Threshold Industries

Threshold industries are market-oriented in the sense that they require a minimum local or regional volume of sales to support a new factory or an addition to existing facilities, although because of adoptive and irrational behavior they may actually appear in a city before the market is of adequate size. Innovations in these industries should diffuse in hops whose distances are more or less in proportion to the threshold population. That is, the higher the threshold, the larger the city in which a sufficient market should be found to permit successful (profit-making) duplication of the innovation, and the longer the average distance between urban units with plants capable of introducing the new technique; and, conversely, the lower the threshold, the smaller the city in which a sufficient market should be found to permit successful duplication of the innovation, and the shorter the average distance between urban units with plants capable of introducing the new technique. In other words, imitation should continue in the initial center only as long as the local or regional market size will permit, and concurrent and subsequent diffusion should be channeled through the urban hierarchy,[122] ceasing at that level where the threshold is no longer fulfilled. Diffusion of this type can be hindered in some areas by social barriers to acceptance, but

---

[121] The difficulties of tracing spatial patterns of industrial innovation diffusions are enormous but not insurmountable. The use of late nineteenth-century manufacturing censuses is possible insofar as the appearance of new establishments reflects innovation. However, the employment of this source, even in the form of now available original schedules, would be severely handicapped by its inability to provide data more frequently than at ten-year intervals. Where available, records of patent royalty payments would appear much more promising.

[122] Diffusion beyond the initial center must occur in threshold industries since, by definition, the curtailment of imitation to the place of origin would involve mounting transportation diseconomies (transport costs to the market).

in general it should be abetted by the general tendency of information to be funneled through the urban hierarchy[123] (a tendency partially ascribable to the effect that the P_1P_2/D relationship has on interurban communications flows),[124] and, occasionally, by social (customer) dissatisfaction with productivity in adequately sized centers whose manufacturer(s) have not as yet adopted the innovation. Variations in diffusion through the urban hierarchy may occur with respect to consumer goods industries due to geographical differences in per capita income (diffusion would cease in larger cities in regions with low income), and with respect to producers' goods industries due to anomalies in the size of local manufacturing sectors (diffusion would come to a halt in relatively large units among those cities that had an abnormally small manufacturing sector). Eccentricities may also come about because of fluctuations in the business cycle, local shortages of capital or entrepreneurial talent, or other intangibles.

A diffusion pattern that hops through the urban hierarchy, rather than radiating outward from the original agglomeration to *all* proximate population clusters,[125] is consistent with the earlier expressed proposition that the spatial distribution of innovational acceptance is governed by (1) an unevenly distributed readiness to accept (an uneven distribution of population thresholds in this case), (2) an uneven distribution

---

[123] Note, for example, Hägerstrand, "The Propagation of Innovation Waves," *op. cit.*, p. 358; and *idem, Innovationsförloppet ur Korologisk Synpunkt, op. cit.*, pp. 234–235.

The pattern of step-wise migration observed by scholars from 1885 to the present implies that "information flows — running in the opposite direction and causally closely related to the migration — largely work their way downward from each hierarchial level." Olsson, *op. cit.*, p. 32. See the pioneering work of Ernest G. Ravenstein, "The Laws of Migration," *Journal of the Royal Statistical Society,* Vol. 48 (1885), pp. 167–235, and Vol. 52 (1889), pp. 241–305; and Torsten Hägerstrand's modern classic, "Migration and Area," *Lund Studies in Geography,* Series B, Human Geography, No. 13 (1957), pp. 27–158. Recent empirical work tends to validate this implication (Olsson, *loc. cit.*). The implication also falls in line with Hägerstrand's references to a hierarchy of information fields, and with Redlich's less rigorous formulations on the movement of ideas outward from metropolises to lower-order centers. Fritz Redlich, "Ideas — Their Migration in Space and Transmittal over Time," *Kyklos,* Vol. 6 (1953), pp. 301–322, especially p. 313.

[124] Zipf, *op. cit.;* and *idem, Human Behavior and the Principle of Least Effort* (Cambridge: Addison-Wesley Press, 1949), pp. 391–392.

[125] Because of irregularities in the movement of ideas, the diffusion of manufacturing innovations need not occur to all proximate settlements even when there is no threshold barrier. See Redlich, *op. cit.*, pp. 311–312, and subsequent discussion.

of information regarding the innovation, and (3), some combination of (1) and (2).[126] According to this terminology, as the cities of the hierarchy grow in size, and the lower ranks become characterized by larger populations, new patterns of acceptance readiness evolve and it should be possible for some threshold industry innovations to permeate those lower echelons.

A special permutation of the diffusion of threshold industry innovations through the urban hierarchy could occur when the particular innovation reduces production costs. Under circumstances when cost reduction led to price reduction it would be conceivable that, because of increased per capita consumption (demand elasticity), the threshold could be met by smaller cities and diffusion could extend to lower levels of the urban hierarchy. However, in the late nineteenth-century United States, the opposite effect usually would have been more likely because of the tendency of cost-reducing innovations to raise, rather than to reduce, threshold levels by requiring larger scales of output and permitting the extension of market areas through the substitution of transport outlays for production outlays.

"Footloose" and Raw-Material-Oriented Industries

"Footloose" and raw-material-oriented industries are diametrically opposite in terms of their respective cost structures, but their patterns of innovation diffusion should be variations on the same theme; i.e., the succession of imitations and adoptions should be curtailed at an early stage and geographically limited.

"Footloose" manufacturers are basically insensitive to transportation costs, are unaffected by threshold or other market considerations, and therefore, from a theoretical standpoint, they may locate as economically in one area or city as in another. To the degree that footloose industries are impervious to transport costs and serve extensive nonlocal as well as local markets, the number of imitations of observed success may be increased almost indefinitely in the initial center, subject only to the accrual of inordinate diseconomies of concentration, or exhaustion

---

[126] Unsymmetrical distributions of readiness and information may be attributed to "barrier effects." For a classification and elaboration of such effects see Robert S. Yuill, *A Simulation Study of Barrier Effects in Spatial Diffusion Problems* (Ann Arbor: Michigan Inter-University Community of Mathematical Geographers, Discussion Paper No. 5, 1965), pp. 4–7. Also note Pemberton, *op. cit.*, p. 251.

of the market. The process whereby diffusion in these industries becomes inert prior to attaining the third general stage[127] is to some extent self-propelling.

The high-value-added nature of footloose manufactures often results in their concentrating at a few relatively close locations within highly industrialized areas,[128] and this propinquity telescopes diffusion temporally by multiplying the rate of exposure to technical changes, reducing uncertainty, stimulating competition, and increasing the demand for information regarding innovation. The success of these urban-industrial concentrations tends to breed further success, as innovation leads to new problem awareness, possible "technological disequilibrium," a greater supply of inventions, and additional rounds of innovation *before* more scattered and distant plants have made the initial innovation.[129] Also, as the innovation gap widens between factories in the original center and a few secondary centers on the one hand, and those production units that did not implement the initial invention on the other, the possibilities of the latter group "catching up" technologically become ever smaller because of tendencies for the relevant information to grow increasingly complex and more difficult to assemble[130] and for the information itself to follow established routes.[131] (In the era prior to the development of modern mass communications, the tendency for information in general to follow routes from one major city to another, without immediately percolating down to lesser centers, must have been well pronounced.)[132] This is particularly true when scale-shifts accompany innovation, and/or the industry becomes increasingly oligopolistic, with the major plants expanding in large metropolises (communications foci).

When diffusion is short-circuited in this manner, with the concen-

---

[127] Compare with Hägerstrand, "The Propagation of Innovation Waves," *op. cit.,* p. 368.

[128] See Allan Pred, "The Concentration of High-Value-Added Manufacturing," *Economic Geography,* Vol. 41 (1965), pp. 108–132.

[129] The last of these points specifically underscores the importance of the time element to *all* diffusion processes.

[130] This is in keeping with Isard's and Tung's earlier mentioned contention that "scale [and urbanization] economies obtain in processing and beneficiating information." Isard and Tung, *op. cit.,* Vol. 11, p. 36.

[131] This latter tendency is clearly demonstrated in Hägerstrand's works.

[132] Inasmuch as the routing of information favors some producers over others, this condition can be seen as another important contributing factor to the late nineteenth-century growth of large cities at the expense of small towns.

trated producers compounding their advantages (setting relatively falling prices and expanding markets),[133] the nucleated accumulation of innovation is, in a sense, illustrative of the obvious "functional relationship between resistance and spatial distribution [diffusion]. The higher the resistance then the more concentrated the distribution."[134] Here, resistance away from the agglomeration(s) can be interpreted as taking the form of an inadequate volume of information and the other supply and demand factors prerequisite to innovation,[135] and of a magnification of the debilitating effect that distance usually has upon diffusion. While the piling up of imitations and adoptions in the initial agglomeration and a limited number of secondary centers may reach considerable proportions, it should be eventually slowed or blocked by the growing percentage of observers and information recipients (existing firms or potential investors) who have had previous contacts and accepted the innovation.[136]

It is even more clear-cut that raw-material-oriented industries should have narrowly circumscribed patterns of innovation diffusion. Not only does the absence of threshold considerations remove most barriers to the number of successful adoptions in the initial area of implementation, but the overbearing importance of transport costs by definition confines production to concentrations (frequently nonurban or small-city) in the proximity of raw material deposits (sources). Thus, the diffusion process is again accelerated in the area of origin by the rate of exposure, the reduction of uncertainty, and the stimulation of local competition — all of which, by promoting further innovation, reinforce local initial advantages and reduce the probability of extensive diffusion. Because an innovation may only spread outward to other exploitable deposits,[137] the diffusion pattern may be somewhat more irregular than in the case of footloose industries. Resistance away from the initial agglomeration therefore takes the form of raw-material scarcity, as well as distance

---

[133] When widespread brand preferences exist, market expansion may occur for an innovating firm without a full adjustment of price to new cost-savings.

[134] Hägerstrand, *Innovationsförloppet ur Korologisk Synpunkt, op. cit.,* p. 274.

[135] Significantly, it was observed in the 1890's that: "Occasionally we find industries confined to a certain locality because of [a] dearth elsewhere of adequate technical knowledge . . . ." Edward A. Ross, "The Location of Industries," *Quarterly Journal of Economics,* Vol. 10 (1896), p. 260.

[136] Compare with Hägerstrand, *op. cit.,* p. 254.

[137] This need not be true indefinitely, as technological improvements can alter the geographic distribution of an industry by reducing the locational attraction of raw materials, as has been the case in the U.S. iron and steel industry.

decay, and the insufficient presence of supply-and-demand factors (the supply of capital has historically loomed very large as a diffusion determinant in raw-material-oriented industries because major innovations often necessitated sizable increases in the scale of plant operations).

Other Industries

While it is not an intention of this essay to delve into the patterns of labor-oriented industries and other more narrowly defined manufacturing categories, it ought to be pointed out that in each instance the spatial sequence of their innovation diffusions would merely combine features of the general case and both the loosely defined groups on the preceding pages. More explicitly, in proceeding toward the termination of their diffusion, innovations would, to varying degrees, tend both to follow the urban hierarchy and to form self-generating agglomerations of imitation and adoption.

Concluding Remarks

Although Hägerstrand has written brilliantly on the spatial aspects of rural innovations and their diffusion, the subject of industrial inventions and innovations has been all but ignored by geographers and location theorists. This disciplinary neglect of invention doubtlessly springs in part from the mistaken assumption that the location of inventive activity is "accidental" and in part from the cost-perspective blinders legitimately worn by location theorists when approaching the distribution of manufacturing. The lack of concern for innovation probably is a manifestation of the traditional tendency to isolate many of the locational aspects of manufacturing and cities, rather than to view industrialization and urbanization as interacting spatial processes.

Because of the past lack of attention to the geographical dimensions of industrial inventions and innovations, much of this essay represents an exploratory journey into essentially uncharted waters. In navigating unfamiliar seas, the related works of economists, sociologists, and historians have served as compass, sextant, and rudder; and, due to the borrowing of concepts from other scholars and disciplines, the course has been one of synthesis, as well as of interpretation and tenuous speculation. But in amalgamating divergent concepts and analyzing patent statistics, in intentionally interdigitating, juxtaposing, and overlapping ideas so as to build up a logical construct and to view the panorama of events from alternative perspectives, the exploration has only begun. The unknown has not been deeply penetrated, for much of what has been accomplished amounts to little more than a geographical embellishment and formalizing of dated arguments, and to a belaboring of what should be obvious—that industrial inventions and innovations have a strong propensity to occur where manufacturing is found.

However, no alibis are offered for this initial probing, for it is necessary if the locational information contained in the publications of the U.S. Patent Office is to be given the further attention it warrants, and if a number of unresolved questions begging additional consideration are to be tackled. The most significant unanswered questions seem to be dynamic in aspect, particularly as the emphasis here has been largely, but not exclusively, on that period of time when the role of manufacturing as an instigative force behind urbanization was most pronounced, and when private information influenced the location of industrial inventions and innovations more than public information. Specifically, one might ask how the progressive institutionalizing and scientizing of invention, the improvement of transport, and the development of mass communications media have each affected the geographic patterns of industrial invention and innovation diffusion. Answers to these questions, and to related problems posed by the work of economists,[138] would presumably contribute to a deeper understanding of the urban growth process, and this is all the more reason to seek them out.

---

[138] One such problem is general verification of the specific hypothesis put forth in the following statement:
    . . . the timing of San Diego's [population] growth was associated with long swings in national growth which left its imprint on the whole of the region of which the city is a part. If the timing was due to national factors, the magnitude of growth was probably due to primarily local factors. It is tempting to view the process in Schumpeterian terms with technological know-how advancing over the long downswing to be implemented with a flood of repercussions during the subsequent upswing.
Eugene Smolensky and Donald Ratajczak, "The Conception of Cities," *Explorations in Entrepreneurial History*, Second Series, Vol. 2 (Winter, 1965), p. 105.

4

The American Mercantile City: 1800-1840

Manufacturing, Growth, and Structure

During the initial decades of the last century, American manufacturing was characterized predominantly by an emphasis on consumer rather than capital goods, by handicraft rather than machine techniques, by household and workshop rather than factory organization, and by rural dispersion rather than concentration in major urban centers. Even in the textile industries, where factories were the most important production units by the 1830's,[1] activity was largely confined to rural waterfall sites and mill towns recently superimposed upon the rural landscape. The factory and industrial capitalism had not as yet become the cornerstones of metropolitan growth. In other words, at a time when the economy of the United States was agricultural, the industrial as well as the agrarian population was preponderantly rural.

Within the framework of these commonplace facts, it is perfectly logical that the magnitude of absolute population growth in rural areas completely overshadowed relative urban advances during the early nineteenth century. Certainly New York, Boston, Philadelphia, and Baltimore thrived commercially and expanded rapidly in size; but while the total 1840 population stood at 17,120,000 and therefore surpassed the

---

[1] By 1831, when U.S. cotton textile production was slightly in excess of $40,000,000, factories accounted for $26,000,000 of the total value of output. In contrast, Gallatin had claimed that roughly two-thirds of the clothing worn by the rural populace in 1810 was the product of domestic family industry. Timothy Pitkin, *A Statistical View of the Commerce of the United States of America* (New Haven: Durrie and Peck, 1835), pp. 472, 482–484.

1800 total by nearly 12 million, the number of inhabitants in "urban places" increased from only 322,000 in 1800 to 1,845,000 in 1840.[2]

Rural dominance, however, was to be of short duration. Subsequent to the financial panic and depression of the late 1830's, a series of developments that had previously been set in motion began to gain the momentum that ultimately shifted the locational spotlight of manufacturing from a rural to an urban proscenium. The railroad network, which consisted of a mere 2,800 miles of disjointed trackage in 1840, mushroomed into a well-articulated system exceeding 30,600 miles in 1860,[3] and began to facilitate the long-distance raw material assembly and finished product distribution that was so vital to urban-industrial growth. In addition, the score of years preceding the Civil War were marked by a perceptible diffusion of uniform production based on interchangeable parts and of the factory system outside the textile industries, a gradual replacement of water-power by steam-driven engines, an increased use of coal rather than wood fuels, a critical expansion of machine tool output, a growing stream of European migrants and a consequent enlargement of the domestic market and labor pool, and an increasing popularity of the joint-stock and limited liability corporation. The panic of 1837 itself was partly instrumental in provoking some of these post-1840 urban-industrial adjustments, as that commercial and financial fiasco terminated the conditions that forced many American merchants to make unnecessarily large imports of foreign factory production.[4] In short, between 1840 and 1860, the principal functions of the country's major cities were still mercantile, but changes were under way that were bringing the phenomena of urban growth and industrial growth into closer association — an association whose culmination has

---

[2] U.S. Bureau of the Census, *Historical Statistics of the United States: Colonial Times to 1957* (Washington, D. C.: 1961), pp. 7, 14. It is quite likely that these figures understate urban population, as the data compiled by the Bureau of the Census refer only to places with a population in excess of 2,500. Cities, particularly in the early stages of economic growth, ought to be defined in functional and structural terms, and not by arbitrary demographic limits.

[3] *Ibid.*, p. 427.

[4] In respect to these conditions Clark commented:

> British mercantile houses had allowed American importers to pyramid credits in England by accepting their bills, with an understanding that before maturity bills signed by other parties might be substituted for those falling due. As this practice stimulated undue purchases of foreign manufactures, it was evidently unfavorable to American industry, and its termination by the panic was a compensating feature of that event.

Victor S. Clark, *History of Manufactures in the United States* (New York: McGraw-Hill, 1929), Vol. 1, p. 380.

permitted us to interpret metropolitan-size growth from 1860 to 1910 as a circular and cumulative process, in which successive manufacturing thresholds were fulfilled and the possibilities of industrial invention and innovation were continuously enhanced.

Because it was prior to the transition period 1840–1860 that manufacturing occupied its most subordinate position in the urban economy, because industrialization and initial advantage were apparently the keys to the growth of the United States' highest order urban centers in the post-Civil War era, and because zones of manufacturing became such an important component in the internal structure of metropolises, a series of economic-geographical questions arises regarding the process of urban growth and role of industry in the American mercantile city during the formative years of the early nineteenth century. What factors militated against the location of additional manufacturing activities in the larger commercial cities? Why were existing industries located in New York, Boston, Philadelphia, and Baltimore? In the absence of a primary stimulus from manufacturing, how did the urban-size growth process function, and how did selective urban growth occur within a rudimentary system of cities? What forces operated in shaping the intraurban locational patterns of specific industries?

These questions are important not only because they promise to clarify subsequent patterns of urban-industrial growth and internal metropolitan structure, but also because they look into the spatial prism of early nineteenth-century manufacturing through the face of urban units, rather than through the face of individual industries, as Clark and others have done. These same broad queries require an expansive canvas upon which to depict their answers. While some of the more subtle strokes can be painted with the delicate brush of primary sources, the grosser splashes of color must derive from the varied palette of secondary classics by economic historians and other students of the early nineteenth century.[5]

[5] Scholars of the stature of Schumpeter and Rostow have insisted that the development of theory to some degree depends on the syntheses and generalizations to be constructed from secondary works. See Joseph A. Schumpeter, "Economic Theory and Entrepreneurial History," in Harvard Research Center in Entrepreneurial History, *Change and the Entrepreneur* (Cambridge: Harvard University Press, 1949), p. 83; and W. W. Rostow, "The Interrelation of Theory and Economic History," *Journal of Economic History,* Vol. 17 (1957), pp. 509–523. Also note the introductory remarks on "Analytical Models in the Study of Social Systems," in Everett E. Hagen, *On the Theory of Social Change: How Economic Growth Begins* (Homewood: The Dorsey Press, Inc., 1962), p. 505.

The Economic Functions of the Mercantile City

Any logical pondering of the above questions is extremely difficult without first establishing some frame of reference, and therefore a sound interpretation requires at least an outlining of both the economic functions of the mercantile city and the relative importance of manufacturing within that city's over-all economy.

A contemporary portrayed New York City as a "mercantile town" with "the character of a general mart for the exchange of foreign and domestic productions."[6] On a smaller scale, the other major Atlantic ports and New Orleans also performed as "hinges" linking the national agricultural economy with Europe through a "network of trade relationships on the continent and on the high seas."[7] (See Tables 4.1 through

TABLE 4.1 *Population of Major U.S. Cities: 1800–1840*

	1840	1800
New York (Manhattan)	312,710	60,515
Baltimore	102,313	26,514
Philadelphia[a]	93,665	41,220
Boston	93,383	24,937
New Orleans	102,193	[b]

SOURCE: U.S. Bureau of the Census, *1960 Census of Population*, Vol. I, Part A.

[a] Not included are the unincorporated Northern Liberties, Spring Garden, Kensington, or Southwark. These suburbs, whose growth was inseparable from that of Philadelphia, had a combined 1840 population slightly in excess of 100,000. The failure to include these later incorporated suburbs, while admittedly detracting from the scale of Philadelphia's early nineteenth-century increase, is justified by similar omissions for New York, Boston, and, to a lesser degree, Baltimore.

[b] Not available. In 1810 New Orleans had a population of 17,242.

4.3 for some indication of the relative importance of the leading mercantile cities.) Dominance of internal trade by the "hinge" cities was almost complete. Until agents became nearly ubiquitous, shop- and storekeepers from throughout the country created "a great concourse of persons at the principal sea-ports, to purchase groceries, woolens, cotton goods, etc."[8] Most of the lighter manufactured merchandise sold in the young

---

[6] John Adams Dix, *Sketch of the Resources of the City of New-York* (New York: G. and C. Carvill, 1827), p. 14.

[7] Jean Gottmann, *Megalopolis* (New York: The Twentieth Century Fund, 1961), p. 103.

[8] Isaac Holmes, *An Account of the United States of America, Derived from Actual Observation, During a Residence of Four Years in that Republic* (London: The Caxton Press, 1823), p. 355.

TABLE 4.2 *Selected Trade Statistics for Leading Mercantile Cities*

	\multicolumn{6}{c}{Exports (millions of dollars)}	
	New York	Boston	Philadelphia	Baltimore	New Orleans	Total U.S.	Selected ports as a % of U.S.
1815	10	5	4	5	5	52	55.8
1820	13	11	5	6	7	69	60.9
1825	35	11	11	4	12	99	73.7
1830	19	7	4	3	15	73	65.8
1835	30	10	3	3	36	121	67.8
1840a	34	10	6	5	34	132	67.9
	\multicolumn{6}{c}{Imports (millions of dollars)}	
1821	23	14	8	4	3	62	83.9
1825	49	15	15	4	4	96	90.6
1830	35	10	8	4	7	70	91.4
1836a	118	25	15	7	15	189	95.2
1840	60	16	8	4	10	107	91.6

SOURCE: Albion (see footnote 11), pp. 390-391. Compiled from *Reports on Commerce and Navigation* issued annually by the Secretary of the Treasury.
a Peak year 1800–1840.

interior river ports of St. Louis and Cincinnati,[9] and in lesser centers west of the Alleghenies, came from New York, Baltimore and Philadelphia, while Boston compensated for its physically restricted hinterland by channeling much of its commerce to Fall River, Lowell, and the smaller rising textile mill towns of the Merrimac Valley and the Maritime Provinces of Canada.[10] Domestic coastal interaction, as well as inland hinterland trade, accounted for a considerable portion of the economic activity and external relations of the mercantile port cities. Indicatively, in 1835, the tonnage, if not the cargo value, of a fraction of arriving coastal vessels surpassed the tonnage of all arriving foreign-trade vessels in New York, Boston, and Philadelphia (the tonnage ratio

[9] Thomas Senior Berry, *Western Prices before 1861: A Study of the Cincinnati Market* (Cambridge: Harvard University Press, 1943), pp. 19, 23, 328-329 ff.; and Richard C. Wade, *The Urban Frontier: Pioneer Life in Early Pittsburgh, Cincinnati, Lexington, Louisville, and St. Louis* (Chicago: The University of Chicago Press, 1964), pp. 54, 62. The difficulty of ascending the Mississippi prior to the introduction of the steam boat, and the city's subsequent tardiness in promoting internal improvements, resulted in New Orleans having relatively restricted sales in the Upper Mississippi Valley. Until 1856 virtually no manufactured goods, domestic or foreign, were shipped northward from New Orleans.

[10] Oscar Handlin, *Boston's Immigrants 1790–1880* (Cambridge: Harvard University Press, 1959), p. 7.

TABLE 4.3 Selected Economic Characteristics of Major U.S. Cities: 1840

	Commercial houses in foreign trade	Commission houses	Capital invested (1000's of dollars)			Construction employment
			Commission houses	Retailing	Manufacturing[a]	
New York (Manhattan)	417	918	45,941.2	14,648.6	11,228.9	4,033
Baltimore	70	108	4,404.5	6,708.6	2,730.0	845
Philadelphia[b]	182	35	1,944.5	15,177.6	5,387.5	713
Boston	142	89	11,676.0	4,184.2	2,770.3	524
New Orleans	8	375	16,490.0	11,018.2	1,774.2	1,001

SOURCE: "Sixth Census of the United States, 1840" (see footnote 66).

[a] These figures are exaggerations since they include all capital invested in the construction sector of the urban economy.

[b] See footnote 12 for remarks on the striking aberrations of the Philadelphia statistics.

of long-distance coastal to foreign-trade arrivals was at least 1.03 to 1.00 for New York, 1.69 to 1.00 for Boston, and 2.45 to 1.00 for Philadelphia).[11]

With the possible exception of Philadelphia (Table 4.3), the wholesaling trading complex and retailing were the two most prominent economic functions of the leading mercantile cities — even in 1840, when the secondary position of manufacturing was likely to be considerably less pronounced than it had been in earlier decades.[12] The dock, the

[11] Robert Greenhalgh Albion, *The Rise of New York Port 1815–1860* (New York: Charles Scribner's Sons, 1939), pp. 394–397. These figures do not by any means give a full measure of the importance of coastal movements since Albion's sources forced him, in each case, to omit the voluminous short-distance arrivals of wood and produce from the same state and the two adjacent states. Some have gone so far as to say: "Over most of the antebellum period the coastwise trade was the most important artery of interregional commerce." See Albert Fishlow, "Antebellum Interregional Trade Reconsidered," *American Economic Review*, Vol. 54 (May, 1964), p. 362.

[12] Although it is generally acknowledged that Philadelphia was relatively the most industrialized of the nation's largest cities in 1840, there are a number of grounds upon which to question the dwarfed position of the city's wholesaling as indicated by Table 4.3. First, our suspicions are aroused by the purported scale of retailing and the incongruously small number of "commission houses" in Philadelphia. It is most unlikely that Philadelphia, with a population equivalent to that of Boston, and one-third that of New York, would have more capital invested in retailing than the latter, and more than three times as much as invested in the former — even if Philadelphia's populous suburbs were brought into the picture. Second, there is considerable confusion regarding the term "commission houses," as it seemingly included auction houses and other firms

wharf, the counting house, and the warehouse were the principal foci of the urban economy; while the merchant middlemen (shipping merchants and importers), and agent middlemen (brokers, auctioneers, commission merchants, and factors), were the city's primary capital accumulators, in many instances cumulatively assessing "a mark-up of 100–150 per cent on the cost of imported merchandise."[13] In acting as generators of urban growth the mercantile element directly or indirectly provided jobs for a large portion of the city's working population. As a striking example, as early as 1800 there were nearly 1,000 persons licensed as carters to transfer merchandise to warehouses and to transship import and export commodities on the streets of New York City,[14] and by 1833 the number of carts operating on the city's thoroughfares was approaching 2,500.[15]

Of course it was in New York, the largest of the mercantile cities, that the wholesaling-trading function was most articulated (Tables 4.2 and 4.3). In 1832, when the value of foreign goods arriving at Manhattan was less than one-half of that imported during the boom of 1836,[16] it could be said that "The amount of merchandise of every description sold [principally on credit] in one year by New York to

---

performing quasi-retailing functions plus establishments that could be placed in the category of "commercial houses in foreign trade." Typically, in New Orleans "one is confronted with a situation in which many business houses advertised as wholesalers or were referred to in that capacity, but actually may have been carrying on considerable retailing business. . . . Occupational functions were very flexible among early wholesale middlemen . . . , and consequently occupational titles must not be accepted without reservation." Harry A. Mitchell, "The Development of New Orleans as a Wholesale Trading Center," *The Louisiana Historical Quarterly*, Vol. 27 (1944), pp. 947, 950. Therefore, as it is known that local census marshals often resolved these ambiguities by making their own arbitrary classificatory decisions, it may be concluded that much of Philadelphia's 1840 wholesaling and auctioning is masked by its abnormal retailing statistics. Perhaps it may also be surmised that similar discrepancies, but of a lesser dimension, exist in the data pertaining to Baltimore.

[13] H. J. Habakkuk, *American and British Technology in the Nineteenth Century* (Cambridge: The University Press, 1962), p. 41. For a thorough discussion of the roles and operations of individuals in the various urban mercantile professions see Fred Mitchell Jones, *Middlemen in the Domestic Trade of the United States: 1800–1860* (Urbana: Illinois Studies in the Social Sciences, 1937).

[14] *Longworth's American Almanac, New-York Register, and City Directory* (New York: Thomas Longworth, 1800), pp. 92–107.

[15] *Niles' Weekly Register*, Vol. 45 (Sept. 21, 1833), p. 56.

[16] According to Albion's compilations the value of foreign goods entering the port of New York in 1832 and 1836 was respectively $53,000,000 and $118,000,000. Albion, *op. cit.*, p. 391.

supply the other cities, towns and villages of the country, from Maine to New Orleans, may probably be estimated at $100,000,000."[17] In that same year of modest activity, New York merchants were involved in an additional $26,000,000 of foreign-export transactions.[18] By 1841, no less than 59.1 per cent of the nation's foreign imports, as well as 43.5 per cent of the nation's total foreign trade, was passing through the control of New York merchants.[19] The road to this position of dominance had been paved by the collective decisions of British manufacturers to dump their accumulated surpluses in the port following the end of the War of 1812, by establishment of regular packet service to Liverpool and other European cities subsequent to 1818, by the construction of the Erie Canal, and by the aggressive action of New York commercial agents in detouring the cotton trade of the South through their harbor.

Table 4.3 crudely reflects the subservient role of manufacturing in the economy of the mercantile city, particularly in New Orleans, where the ratio of investment in the mercantile sectors to investment in industrial activities exceeded fifteen to one, and in New York and Boston, where the ratio was at least on the order of five or six to one — despite the exclusion of "commercial houses in foreign trade" and the inclusion of sizable construction investments in each city's manufacturing category.[20] The low-ebb position of urban manufacturing during the opening decades of the nineteenth century is well reflected by the fact that in

[17] *Niles' Weekly Register*, Vol. 43 (Dec. 8, 1832), p. 241. Since imports for that year only totaled $53,000,000, it may be reasonably assumed that the remaining value of New York City's domestic trade was derived from markups and the merchandising of commodities associated with coastal arrivals and local manufactures.

[18] Albion, *op. cit.*, p. 390. Figures of this sort are only one reason for arguing that Albion's work probably represents the most detailed scholarly account of the economy of a mercantile city during the period in question.

[19] *Ibid.*, pp. 390–391.

[20] If one follows Marburg's rather conservative precedent, and allocates an investment for each "commercial house in foreign trade" equal to the national average invested in "commission houses" ($41,000), then the 1840 ratio of mercantile to local industrial investments was better than seven to one in New York and Boston. If one makes the alternative assumption that average investments in "commercial houses in foreign trade" were on a par with those in local "commission houses," then the ratio for Boston jumps to 12.4:1, and New York's increases more modestly to 7.3:1. See Theodore F. Marburg, "Income Originating in Trade, 1799–1869," in *Trends in the American Economy in the Nineteenth Century* (A Report of the National Bureau of Economic Research; Princeton: Princeton University Press, 1960), p. 318.

1810 only 230 of 13,241 structures enumerated within the municipal boundaries of Philadelphia were classified as "manufacturing buildings,"[21] and by a Baltimorean's 1825 observation that manufacturing had yet "to become a powerful and certain auxiliary in contributing to the wealth, prosperity, and advancement of the city."[22]

Prior to the 1837 panic there were discernible urban-industrial increases, e.g., by the start of the 1830's the annual value of Baltimore's manufacturing was hazarded at "five millions of dollars,"[23] while similar figures for Boston and Philadelphia were correspondingly in the vicinity of $13,400,000[24] and $20,000,000.[25] However, these increments ought not be exaggerated because many of the establishments placed in the manufacturing category either combined production with retailing or wholesaling functions, as in the case of the food-processing industries, or devoted most of their efforts to making repairs.[26] Furthermore, the value added by production, generally regarded as the best measurement and indicator of manufacturing activity, was naturally far less than the annual value of output.[27] The prevailing relatively insignificant status of urban manufacturing well into the 1840–1860 transition period is superficially accentuated by the conspicuous absence of a single industrial capitalist on a roster of New York City's millionaires in the early 1850's.[28]

While the unimposing role of manufacturing in the urban economy doubtlessly had its roots in the eighteenth century, when industrial growth was hampered by British restrictive policies, it seems that some

[21] James Mease, *The Picture of Philadelphia* (Philadelphia: B. and T. Kite, 1811), p. 32. Some small-scale manufacturing probably also occurred in an additional indeterminable number of buildings that were categorized as "workshops."

[22] Jared Sparks, "Baltimore," *North American Review,* Vol. 20 (1825), p. 124.

[23] *Niles' Weekly Register,* Vol. 40 (Aug. 20, 1831), p. 433.

[24] Compiled from Louis McLane, *Report on Manufactures* (Washington, D. C.: House Document No. 308, 22nd Congress, First Session, 1833), Vol. 1, pp. 432–469.

[25] *Niles' Weekly Register,* Vol. 37 (Jan. 30, 1830), p. 379. This source is unclear as to whether the sum given refers to the city or the county of Philadelphia.

[26] For example, many of the coopers in Boston were "fish dealers and exporters," and in 1832, roughly 95 per cent of the value of production in that same city's cabinetmaking industry was comprised of repairs. McLane, *op. cit.,* pp. 435, 441.

[27] When Boston's annual production was valued at approximately $13,400,000, the value added for the city was less than $5,000,000. *Ibid.,* pp. 432–469.

[28] Albion, *op. cit.,* p. 259.

further amplification of the facts is necessary in order to comprehend the inhibited scale of urban-industrial output in an era when population was expanding and supposedly beneficial import-restricting legislation and protective tariffs were in effect. (The Embargo and Non-Intercourse Acts functioned as protective measures between 1808 and 1815, and levies that were imposed on imported manufactures persisted in altered form throughout the period.)[29] Thus, a question posed earlier may be reiterated: What factors militated against the location of additional manufacturing activities in the larger commercial cities?

Restraints on Early Nineteenth-Century Urban Manufacturing

It is reasonable to contend that the limited dimensions of manufacturing in the American mercantile city were attributable to shortages of capital and labor, the state of technology, an expensive and inadequate transport network, and the restricted size of the accessible market.

Factor Shortages

In 1810, Albert Gallatin argued that "the want of a sufficient capital" was one of the "most prominent of those causes" impeding the growth of manufacturers in the United States.[30] Better than forty years later, a Philadelphian could still bemoan a situation where "bank officers, in distributing their loans, have not yet exercised a wise discrimination" in favor of manufacturers.[31] Adequate capital supplies frequently existed, but the problem most often confronting the factory or workshop owner was that of obtaining a portion of those excess mercantile funds. Because it was in the larger cities that the potential investor encountered the widest spectrum of financial outlets and opportunities, the develop-

---

[29] Although the intricacies of the tariff question are not central to the matters under discussion, reference should be made to Taussig's classical assertion that the limited progress in the early nineteenth-century American manufacture of cotton and woolen textiles, iron, and other products was not attributable so much to the tariff as to inventiveness and resources. See F. W. Taussig, *The Tariff History of the United States,* 8th revised edition (New York: Capricorn Books, 1964 [originally published 1892]), pp. 8–67. Also note Clark, *op. cit.,* pp. 283–287, 308–312.

[30] Albert Gallatin, *Report on Manufactures: American State Papers, Finance* (Washington, D. C.: April 17, 1810), Vol. II, Report No. 325, p. 430.

[31] Edwin T. Freedley, *Philadelphia and Its Manufactures: A Hand-book Exhibiting the Development, Variety, and Statistics of the Manufacturing Industry of Philadelphia in 1857* (Philadelphia: Edward Young, 1859), p. 128.

ment of large-scale, capital-intensive urban industries was particularly hampered under the prevailing conditions of investment capital scarcity.

Although merchants became somewhat more sympathetic toward industrial investments during the twenties, for a number of decades the majority still "preferred to speculate in land purchases or to enlarge their spheres of trade rather than to back manufacturing projects."[32] (Mercantile conservatism regarding industrial investments had been briefly interrupted by the War of 1812, when American ports were cut off from British manufacturers; but even this turn of events tended to favor the textile mills of Massachusetts and Paterson rather than the manufacturing of the larger cities, and much capital began to be rechanneled into its normal outlets immediately ensuing the war when English competition was renewed, industrial prices fell while currency problems pushed the general price level upward, and poor harvests in Europe increased the value of American agricultural commodities considerably.) Enlarging the sphere of trade normally meant that mercantile earnings were ploughed back into expanded exporting and wholesaling, or related retailing, banking, and insurance activities. However, as hinterland competition intensified, a growing share of the financial resources available in the major cities was diverted into a less direct path of commercial promotion, namely turnpike, canal, and railroad development. Investment in transportation projects usually took the form of subscription to state-sponsored bonds, was not accompanied by great expectations of direct profit, and was based on the "economic principle . . . that a town must create trade rather than have trade come to the commercial seat of its own accord."[33]

If the merchant's predisposition toward investment in his own sector of the urban economy is almost self-evident, his preference for real

---

[32] Constance McLaughlin Green, "Light Manufactures and the Beginnings of Precision Manufacture," in Harold F. Williamson, ed., *The Growth of the American Economy* (New York: Prentice-Hall, Inc., 1951), p. 195. The attitude that "investment in manufacturing enterprises . . . was a third choice at best" existed among many American merchants from a period at least as early as the 1770's. See Virginia D. Harrington, *The New York Merchant on the Eve of the Revolution* (New York: Columbia University Studies in History, Economics and Public Law, 1935), p. 145.

[33] James Weston Livingood, *The Philadelphia-Baltimore Trade Rivalry 1780–1860* (Harrisburg: The Pennsylvania Historical and Museum Commission, 1947), p. 161. Even the Baltimore and Ohio Railroad, the most celebrated of the private ventures, received considerable funds from the municipal government of Baltimore.

estate and construction speculation over support for manufacturing can be fully appreciated only through the depiction of specific details. A competent chronicler noted that "in New York, Philadelphia, Boston, or Baltimore, the value of building lots is fully as high as it is in Liverpool, Glasgow, etc.; but if we travel about a mile from an American city, the value rapidly decreases; when at two miles, it would not sell for one-quarter as much as land would produce within the same distance of a large town in Great Britain."[34] The combination of a steeply declining gradient of land values outward from the urban core and exuberant population growth provided an alluring capital outlet for the seeker of quick gains. And quick gains there were to be made in profusion. By 1823 there were streets in New York that had front-lot values of $1,000 per foot,[35] and from that year onward the total assessed value of Manhattan's real estate spiraled dizzily from $50,000,000 to over $76,000,000 in 1829, to slightly more than $104,000,000 in 1833, to $253,201,191 in 1836.[36] Real estate in New York had become "by means of hypothecations familiar to the common course of trade, . . . a circulating capital, which is constantly changing its form, and yielding at every conversion a profit to its employers";[37] and in the other mercantile cities the maneuvering of property proceeded with equal fervor. In Boston a single sale could net close to $100,000,[38] or, on a more ambitious scale, areas as large as East Boston or the South Cove could be manipulated with "cupidity";[39] and in Baltimore, long before land values peaked, a meager 19 × 63 foot (unoccupied?) lot could bring $27,200.[40]

[34] Holmes, *op. cit.*, pp. 151–152. The drop in land values outward from the heart of the city was then even pronounced in lesser centers. Within the 1815 corporation limits of Cincinnati, when the city's population was well under 8,000 and real estate values were only a small fraction of those in New York, Philadelphia, Boston, and Baltimore, "four-acre 'outside' lots . . . were selling for from $500 to $1,000 an acre. Lands within a radius of three miles, if fertile and improved, brought between $50 and $150, according to distance and location. Within twelve miles the price ranged from $10 to $30 an acre, whereas more remote sites fetched from $4.00 to $8.00." Berry, *op. cit.*, p. 11.

[35] *Niles' Weekly Register*, Vol. 25 (Dec. 27, 1823), p. 259.

[36] *Niles' Weekly Register*, Vol. 37 (Nov. 7, 1829), p. 164; Vol. 38 (March 27, 1830), p. 85; Vol. 44 (May 11, 1833), p. 163; and Vol. 51 (Nov. 12, 1836), pp. 167, 176.

[37] Dix, *op. cit.*, p. 41.

[38] *Niles' Weekly Register*, Vol. 49 (Oct. 17, 1835), p. 98.

[39] Handlin, *op. cit.*, p. 4.

[40] *Niles' Weekly Register*, Vol. 35 (Sept. 27, 1828), p. 68. Another indication of the magnitude of potential profits may be obtained by again turning to the

Construction and rent profiteering went hand in hand with climbing land values, the former involving the demolishment and replacement of older structures, as well as the perpetual erection of new wharves, warehouses, and dwelling units. An active year could see Philadelphia become richer by 1,300 buildings, or as many as 2,000 houses built in New York at a cost in the vicinity of $5,000,000;[41] while a single Boston project costing about $450,000 could be considered "a small thing compared with others which have been accomplished, or are about to be done!"[42] The temptation to speculate in properties, and to appropriate investments to build upon them, was compounded by the promise of high rental returns held out by an often inadequate supply of living quarters.[43] In addition, the possibility of the manufacturer securing available mercantile capital was further diminished by the siphoning off of funds into land purchases in upstate New York and the developing agricultural areas west of the Alleghenies.

While the prospects of assembling capital sufficient to establish larger industrial enterprises were dimmed, but not made impossible, by the prevalent pattern of investment behavior among the merchant class, relatively small-scale urban manufactories were able to originate or expand on the basis of funds secured from accumulated firm savings, surplus mercantile capital, or even from artisan savings. Industrial capital was its own progenitor to the extent that a Boston participant in the U.S. Treasury Department's 1832 survey of manufacturing could

lower-valued land of the less populous center of Cincinnati. There a lot which was purchased for $2.00 in 1790 was resold for $800 in 1804. "A small slice from the corner went for $2,500 ten years later, $4,000 in 1817, and $6,000 in 1819. The subdivision was sold and repurchased in 1828 for $15,000, and a still smaller piece (only 20 by 26 feet) was leased in 1839 at an annual rental of $2,000 (with an option to renew at a much higher rent)." Berry, *op. cit.*, p. 10.

[41] *Niles' Weekly Register,* Vol. 33 (Jan. 26, 1828), p. 356; and Vol. 14 (June 27, 1818), p. 310. The volume of construction activity fluctuated violently from year to year. In an extreme instance, the number of new buildings erected in New York City slumped off from 1,826 in 1836 to 840 in 1837. *Niles' Weekly Register,* Vol. 58 (May 16, 1840), p. 164.

[42] *Niles' Weekly Register,* Vol. 45 (Nov. 2 and 9, 1833), pp. 148, 165.

[43] Rents in Baltimore at times surpassed the "excessively high" sums paid out in New York (Holmes, *op. cit.*, pp. 268–273), and housing shortages attained the proportions that prevailed during New York's boom of 1825. It was said of the New York crisis "that a furnished house, without a tenant, is not to be found in this great city . . . and that well-dressed families are observed to be occupying houses of which the builders do not appear to have accomplished the work so far as to have fully closed them in by doors and windows." *Niles' Weekly Register,* Vol. 28 (Aug. 27, 1825), p. 415.

state: "... as a general rule, I am inclined to think that few manufacturers rely upon permanent loans from banks or individuals, the capital invested being their own property."[44] Of course, urban industry could perpetuate itself only because it was overwhelmingly comprised of small-scale establishments requiring small-scale monetary injections. Characteristically, when commercial capital was relegated to manufacturing projects it was more likely to be in the form of credits than in the riskier form of direct investment.[45]

The prevailing forms of business organization and proprietorship multiplied the difficulties of initiating large-scale urban manufacturing. Regardless of the increasing number of modern industrial corporations in the thirties, a division between ownership and control was the rare exception rather than the rule, and most urban workshops and factories remained under the aegis of individual owners, a small partnership, or an unchartered joint-stock company.[46] These bases of organization usually imposed a severe limitation on the capital horizons of any specific project. Moreover, the scale of urban-industrial undertakings was further inhibited by the general practice of confining investment solicitations to proximite sources, for "this was the period of the 'parochial point of view,' when the scope of businessmen's decisions was local or regional and when they could not easily change the locus of their activities."[47]

The fiscal predicament of urban manufacturers was complicated additionally by a number of other local and general factors. The volume of traffic moving to the interior from New Orleans and Baltimore was disproportionately small in comparison to the flow of agricultural produce and other commodities down the Mississippi and the Susquehanna, and as a consequence mercantile capital was detoured into purchasing upstream products that otherwise might have been secured by payment in goods.[48] In mercantile city and mill town alike, scanty capital "forced

---

[44] McLane, *op. cit.*, p. 471.

[45] Clark, *op. cit.*, p. 368.

[46] For dated but relevant discussions of corporate enterprise and industrial organization see *ibid.*, pp. 440–463; and G. S. Callender, "The Early Transportation and Banking Enterprises of the States in Relation to the Growth of Corporations," *Quarterly Journal of Economics*, Vol. 17 (Nov., 1902), pp. 111–162.

[47] Julius Rubin, *Canal or Railroad? Imitation and Innovation in the Response to the Erie Canal in Philadelphia, Baltimore, and Boston* (Philadelphia: Transactions of the American Philosophical Society, New Series, Vol. 51, part 7, 1961), p. 14.

[48] In contrast, the constriction of Boston's hinterland released considerable

many factory-owners to put up with poorly constructed machinery that required continual attention and repairs."[49] Such inefficient production conditions doubtlessly reduced profit margins (endowing the capital problem with a self-generating quality), and curtailed the feasibility of expansion through reinvestment. Finally, capital difficulties were occasionally magnified when industrial investment funds were absorbed by the initiation of unprofitable undertakings during short-lived booms.

Until the enormous migrations of the late forties, the problems of capital availability were intensified by the costliness and inelasticity of labor supplies. Economic historians have repeatedly demonstrated that the abundance of cheap and frequently fertile land led to a high output per man in early nineteenth-century American agriculture, and that these productivity conditions exerted a negative (inflationary) effect on industrial wage levels and the quantity of labor available for manufacturing purposes. Although American urban-industrial salaries were high by the standards of English and other European competitors, "even a temporary cessation of work caused employees to scatter widely in search of other employment, and even to leave permanently the occupations in which they previously had been engaged."[50] Nonetheless, this phenomenon does not require us "to suppose that large numbers of industrial workers moved. It is sufficient if 'the abundance of western land drew many thousands of potential wage earners . . . who might otherwise have crowded into the factories.' "[51]

The shortage of labor was particularly acute in Boston where "there were no appreciable numbers of men ready and willing to work at wages low enough to foster the establishment of profitable new enterprises," and "a constant deficiency of labor had seriously hampered the growth of industry until the forties." Between 1837 and 1845 few Boston industries underwent sizable growth "and many actually declined. The prospective manufacturer desiring a site for a new establishment, or the

---

sums for industrial investment. However, as the subsequent pages will indicate, neither the labor situation, nor the state of technology, permitted much of these capital resources to remain within the legal limits of Boston.

[49] Clark, *op. cit.*, p. 370.

[50] *Ibid.*, p. 244. Quite differently, "The temporary suspension of a factory in Great Britain did not mean the dispersion of all available labor for operating it. A plant could resume operation at any time with a full compliment of qualified workmen."

[51] Habakkuk, *op. cit.*, p. 12. Habakkuk quotes from Carter Goodrich and S. Davidson, "The Wage-earner in the Westward Movement," *Political Science Quarterly*, Vol. 51 (1936), p. 115.

capitalist with an 'abundance of money seeking an outlet' found little encouragement. And even those already established who wished to expand were inhibited by the apparently inflexible labor supply."[52] Boston boot and shoe entrepreneurs found it ameliorative to maintain worshops outside of the city where labor was more plentiful, and, similarly, at one time, 75 per cent of the city's hat dealers had the making of their millinery put out to neighboring towns.[53] These conditions persisted in Boston and the other major Atlantic ports despite the waxing flow of migrants being funneled through these cities (especially New York, through whose portals roughly 58,000 individuals entered the country in 1836).[54] The bulk of the alien newcomers were either attracted away from the urban labor market by the lure of possible agricultural prosperity or did not possess the skills requisite to participation in most of the city's handicraft and workshop industries.

The State of Technology

It appears incontrovertible that the state of technology impeded the spatial concentration of manufactures in the mercantile cities; but the extent of this interference, and the manner in which it operated, is in some ways not entirely clear. The muddy waters overlying this problem issue from the fact that industrial-technological innovation is at least a two-stage process requiring entrepreneurs sympathetic to the adoption of production improvements, in addition to the actual occurrence of invention or technical modification. Therefore a given level of locally *adopted technology* need not have been synonymous with the level of *technical knowledge* achieved locally. For example: "During the years 1800–1850 Philadelphia provided for some industries a nourishing environment for technological innovation; for others it passively received new technology which had been introduced and demonstrated elsewhere; in still other industries the city successfully resisted change for several decades."[55]

[52] Handlin, *op. cit.*, pp. 11, 74. Significantly, industrial investments did begin to stay in Boston to a much larger degree when the Irish eventually provided the city with a cornucopia of cheap labor.

[53] McLane, *op. cit.*, pp. 444, 468–469.

[54] A total of 80,972 migrants entered the United States in 1836. Approximate disembarkations at other Atlantic Coast cities were as follows: Baltimore, 6,000; Boston, 3,000; and Philadelphia, 2,000. See U.S. Bureau of the Census, *op. cit.*, p. 62; and Albion, *op. cit.*, p. 418.

[55] Sam B. Warner, Jr., "Innovation and the Industrialization of Philadelphia 1800–1850," in Oscar Handlin and John Burchard, eds., *The Historian and the City* (Cambridge: The M.I.T. Press and Harvard University Press, 1963), p. 64.

Regardless of the presence or absence of resistance to the adoption of innovations, and regardless of the argument propounded by Habakkuk and others to the effect that labor problems acted as an inducement to American manufacturers to implement capital-intensive production techniques, it remains indisputable that by 1840 the machine had not yet superseded the hand tool. In fact, in some of the largest urban-industrial employment categories, such as the manufacture of shoes and ready-made clothing, inventions that would have permitted the substitution of the factory system for workshop and domestic production had not yet appeared by the onset of the forties. Quite revealingly, the available evidence for New York City indicates that, as late as 1840, the total number of machinists, or machine fashioners and operators, probably did not exceed 300.[56]

Another indication of the inability of technology to facilitate concentration is the fact that the limited number of mechanized urban establishments were small in size by modern standards. Establishments were particularly small previous to the War of 1812; e.g., as of 1811 the most imposing, if not the largest, plant in Philadelphia employed "about thirty five workmen."[57] Subsequent decades saw the appearance of larger manufactories in the mercantile cities, but few, if any, provided work for more than 200 individuals. In the early thirties, New York's biggest industrial facilities were apparently the famed Allaire ironworks, which had 200 laborers in its service, and the Harper Brothers' publishing house, with its 17 presses and 140 employees.[58] At the same date, Boston had no industrial unit employing as many as 100 workers,[59] and somewhat later the vast majority of people engaged in manufacturing there "were employed either in establishments of ten or less or were unclassifiable, that is, worked in their homes."[60] An anomalous cotton mill in Baltimore employed 200 persons as early as 1824, but it

---

[56] *Longworth's American Almanac, New-York Register, and City Directory* (New York: Thomas Longworth, 1840). It is apparent from the 37,125 entries, the prevailing size of family, and the total population of Manhattan (Table 4.1) that the completeness of this directory, which lists 103 machinists, in all likelihood exceeds 33 per cent.

[57] Mease, *op. cit.*, p. 76.

[58] McLane, *op. cit.*, Vol. 2, p. 115; and *Niles' Weekly Register,* Vol. 44 (Aug. 17, 1833), p. 404. New York's second largest ironworking firm employed no more than 90 men in 1832, and the total number of workers in nine similar establishments, including the Allaire Works, was only 465. An identical number of foundries in Boston had an even less impressive employment of 320.

[59] McLane, *op. cit.*, Vol. 1, pp. 432–469.

[60] Handlin, *op. cit.*, p. 10.

appears as if the only other operations notable for their scale within the city itself were a coach "factory," which had 80 hands in 1831, and a carpet "factory" with about 90 employees in 1833.[61]

Equally significant, the urban productive units utilizing machinery were usually characterized, in contrast to their counterparts of the late nineteenth century, by a relatively small volume of undifferentiated, unspecialized production. For instance, the "Mars Works" of downtown Philadelphia were described in 1811 as consisting of "an iron foundry, mould-maker's shop, steam engine manufactory, blacksmith's shop, and mill-stone manufactory." These same works were described as producing cast and wrought work "for machinery for mills, for grinding grain or sawing timber; for forges, rolling and slitting mills, sugar mills, apple mills, bark mills, &c. Pans of all dimensions used by sugar boilers, soap boilers, &c. Screws of all sizes . . . , and all kinds of small wheels and machinery for cotton and wool spinning &c."[62] The "Eagle Works," another Philadephia enterprise of the same period, turned out sugar kettles, sugar-mill rollers, sugar-mill pumps, soap boilers, cannon, cylinders for steam engines, other machinery parts, and "iron castings of every description."[63] Likewise, a plant of somewhat later origin in New York was the producer of printing presses and equipment, sawmill machinery, "and machinery generally"; and a Baltimore concern manufactured chemicals, paints, medicines, and other items simultaneously.[64] Athough these multifunctional plants substantiate the contention that the state of technology had not advanced to a point where many individual urban units could turn out uniform products on a mass production scale, it should be reiterated that these same shops and "factories" often contributed to future urban-industrial growth by acting as seedbeds for dovetailing cumulative inventions of eventual widespread applicability.

The most persuasive point in this whole line of reasoning regarding the state of technology and its deleterious effect upon the spatial concen-

---

[61] Sparks, *op. cit.*, p. 128; *Niles' Weekly Register*, Vol. 40 (Aug. 20, 1831), p. 433; and *idem*, Vol. 45 (Oct. 5, 1833), p. 83.

[62] Mease, *op. cit.*, p. 76.

[63] Thomas Scharf and Thompson Westcott, *History of Philadelphia* (Philadelphia: L. H. Evarts and Co., 1884), Vol. 3, p. 2251.

[64] *The Great Metropolis; or Guide to New-York for 1846* (New York: John Doggett, Jr., 1845), p. 117; and J. Leander Bishop, *A History of American Manufactures from 1608 to 1860* (Philadelphia: Edward Young & Co., 1861, 1868), Vol. 2, p. 231.

tration of industry in the mercantile cities is the simple fact that water power, then the most important source of energy used to drive factory machinery, constituted an immobile raw material. Just as the mountain could not be moved to Mohammed, water power could not be moved to the city. The mechanized cotton textile industry could flourish in Waltham, Paterson, or the Schuylkill suburbs of Roxborough, Spring Garden, and Kensington, but not in Boston, New York, or Philadelphia proper.[65] Similarly, factories utilizing water power functioned profitably beside the Patapsco Falls, and at the foot of at least nine other falls within a 30-mile radius of Baltimore, but no large-scale, water-driven machinery operated within the corporate limits of that mercantile center.[66]

Steam power, the only alternative to water power, was not yet suitable to intensive utilization in the country's largest cities. It is true that steam engines were employed as early as 1801 for grinding plaster of Paris in Philadelphia and for sawing lumber in New York City, that New York City printing presses began using steam power in 1823, and that there were isolated cases of steam-driven cotton mills in Philadelphia and Baltimore.[67] However, by 1832 only four of Boston's 95 industrial categories were evidently utilizing steam engines,[68] and six years hence no more than 429 horsepower could be generated by *all* 46 of the city's steam-powered manufactories.[69] The 1838 picture was little different in Baltimore, whose 45 steam-using industrial establishments had a total capacity of 562 horsepower, or in Philadelphia, whose 59 plants with

---

[65] At least two attempts were made to establish a water-powered textile industry on Manhattan in the 1790's, but both were unsuccessful, and in at least one instance failure was ascribed to the inadequacies of the power site. A futile effort was also made to harness Boston's Mill Dam for manufacturing purposes.

[66] There were 34,102 spindles operating in the cotton mills of Baltimore County in 1839, but only 3,600 of these were within the city proper, and they in a solitary steam-powered manufactory which by this time employed only 120 people. The situation was nearly identical in Philadelphia County where only 3,120 of 40,862 spindles fell within the city boundaries — and these too were presumably all steam-driven. *Aggregate Value and Produce, and Number of Persons Employed in Mines, Agriculture, Commerce, Manufactures, &c. Sixth Census of the United States, 1840* (Washington, D. C.: 1841), pp. 169–171, 217.

[67] Levi Woodbury, *Report on Steam Engines* (Washington, D. C.: House Document No. 21, 25th Congress, Third Session, 1838), pp. 160, 210; and Bishop, *op. cit.*, pp. 91, 205, 286, 336.

[68] McLane, *op. cit.*, pp. 432–469.

[69] Woodbury, *op. cit.*, pp. 41–44.

steam engines were capable of generating 477.5 horsepower.[70] Moreover, it is unlikely that the entire horsepower potential of the country's industrially employed steam engines was equivalent to that of 200 contemporary American automobiles.[71]

Cost was the greatest constraint on the adoption of steam power in the mercantile city. The efficiency of steam engines was such that "By 1839, at Easton, Pennsylvania, *a point accessible to coal,* the relative annual cost per horse power for water and steam was $23 and $105."[72] Of course, neither Boston, New York, New Orleans, nor Baltimore possessed immediate accessibility to coal, and therefore the expense of steam power in those cities was compounded by transport outlays for either coal or wood. The volume of coal consumed, as well as the cost of moving it, was such that even the steam engines of Philadelphia were still quite dependent on wood in the thirties, despite the relative ease with which Lehigh Valley anthracites could be procured by an all-water route.[73] Significantly, in 1838, two places with populations much smaller than those of the mercantile cities, but situated directly upon major coal deposits, surpassed their larger urban brethren in the exploitation of steam power. Specifically, Wheeling, whose 1840 population was 7,885, had steam engines that could generate 768 horsepower; and Pittsburgh, with an 1840 population of 21,115, had steam-mechanized factories and workshops with a total capacity of 2,651.5 horsepower (considerably more than Boston, Baltimore, and Philadelphia combined).[74] In the formal terminology of Weberian and neo-Weberian location theory, coal-burning steam engines were highly concentrated in coal-field cities

---

[70] *Ibid.,* pp. 159–167, 210–211. Numerous small-scale industrial users of steam were also to be found in the remainder of Philadelphia County, and immediately outside of Boston and Baltimore. Woodbury's Treasury Department report gave no detailed statistics for New York City.

[71] Woodbury wrote that

The power employed in all steam-engines in the United States is ascertained and estimated at 100,318 horse-power; of this 12,140 only is in engines estimated and not returned. . . . Of this force, 57,019 horse-power is computed to be in steamboats; 6,980 in railroads, and the rest, being 36,319, in other engines [including those used for pumping water and other nonindustrial uses]. *Ibid.,* p. 10.

[72] Clark, *op. cit.,* p. 410. Italics added by the author.

[73] Of the 90 to 100 steam engines operating in Philadelphia County during 1831, approximately 60 were fed by anthracite coal. *Niles' Weekly Register,* Vol. 40 (July 16, 1831), p. 344.

[74] Woodbury, *op. cit.,* pp. 191–194, 224–225; and U.S. Bureau of the Census, *1960 Census of Population* (Washington, D. C.: 1961), Vol. 1, Part A, pp. 1–66, 50–9.

because in most of the industries using such engines the fuel constituted a "dominant weight-losing raw material" (i.e., its weight consumed per ton of product was equal to or greater than the weight of the product plus the weight of any other localized materials), and thereby was almost an automatic locational determinant.

We can therefore conclude that the immobility of water power, the inefficiency of steam power, and the dominant weight-losing character of coal temporarily prevented the development of urban industries whose scale economies would have stimulated further metropolitan growth by facilitating the extension of market areas, i.e., by permitting the substitution of production economies for the transport diseconomies of larger and longer shipments.

The Transportation Network and the Size of Markets

Irrespective of the state of industrial technology, the costs of shipment on the prerailroad transport network were in themselves a formidable obstruction to the growth of anything but light, high value manufacturing in the larger urban centers. The cost of overcoming distance by any means of overland transportation other than fragmentary rail routes must have been staggering to an entrepreneur contemplating market area expansion; for road and turnpike transport, which was often impractical on a year-round basis, varied in cost from 20 to 60 cents per ton-mile. Representatively: during the century's first decade, the cost incurred in hauling a ton of goods nine miles on inland roads was equivalent to that of importing the identical weight from Europe; in spite of a water leg between Albany and New York, the 1817 charge for freighting a ton from Buffalo to Manhattan was $100, or about 25 cents per ton-mile; between 1817 and 1823, average through rates from Philadelphia to Pittsburgh fluctuated between 20 cents per ton-mile and over 46 cents per ton-mile, the former figure prevailing at the end of the 1820–1823 depression; and in the thirties, a charge of one dollar per ton was imposed for moving merchandise within a radius of a few miles from Boston.[75]

Industrial commodities could move with somewhat greater freedom on riverways and on the canals that began to mushroom in the twenties.

---

[75] Livingood, *op. cit.*, p. 88; Israel D. Andrews, *Report . . . on the Trade and Commerce of the British North American Colonies* (Washington, D. C.: Senate Document No. 112, 32nd Congress, First Session, 1853), p. 278; Berry, *op. cit.*, pp. 73–74; and McLane, *op. cit.*, p. 470.

The canals offered ton-mile tariffs that were usually considerably lower, and on occasion, drastically less than turnpike rates. Illustratively, in 1829, the Governor of Massachusetts estimated that the Blackstone Canal permitted vessels to haul goods from New York to Worcester for half the levy charged on overland carriage between Boston and Worcester.[76] However, in 1840 inland waterway transportation still cost five cents per ton-mile and required large blocks of time for lengthy shipments (after completion of the Erie Canal one week was still necessary for shipments to journey from Detroit to New York, and about thirteen days were needed to go by steamer from New Orleans to St. Louis).[77] The temporal dimensions of inland waterway freighting made it quite difficult for urban manufacturers to respond to demand fluctuations in the nonlocal market, and forced such entrepreneurs to manacle capital to goods in transit. Furthermore, transshipment tariffs frequently added significant sums to the cost of movement; e.g., goods shipped over the mongrel water and rail Mainline from Philadelphia to Pittsburgh in 1838 had to be unloaded and reloaded at Columbia, Hollidaysburg, and Johnstown at a cost of roughly $2.50 per ton, or the equivalent of an additional 50 miles of movement.[78] Because of the rapidity with which total transport outlays were multiplied by transfer and overland movement, prospective market and supply areas were confined to a limited radius around river and canal routes. The disadvantages of canal and river transportation were complicated additionally by winter freezing, the desiccation of locks during summer droughts, and sometimes excessively circuitous routes. In short, even if technology had somehow advanced to a late nineteenth-century level, where agglomeration economies could be substituted for these transport diseconomies, the geographical extent of the area in which most urban industrialists could compete with the products of rural mill and domestic manufacture would not have been very great in the prerailroad era.

This last observation is not to be interpreted as meaning that the

[76] Rubin, *op. cit.,* p. 90. As a result of the opening of the Erie Canal, and the substitution of an all water route for an overland and water route, New York to Buffalo freight rates fell to one-tenth of their former level.

[77] *Niles' Weekly Register,* Vol. 29 (Oct. 8, 1825), p. 96; and Clark, *op. cit.,* p. 350.

[78] William H. Dean, Jr., *The Theory of the Geographic Location of Economic Activities* (Ann Arbor: Edwards Brothers, 1838), p. 45. Testimony by an engineer before the Pennsylvania House of Representatives complained of the repeated delays and the high incidence of lost and damaged goods caused by the transshipments. Rubin, *op. cit.,* p. 18.

manufacturing potential of each of the four infant metropolises on the Atlantic seaboard and New Orleans was equally handicapped by the prerailroad transport network. New Orleans was singularly beset with obstacles to upstream navigation (so much so that her northward shipments, most of which were confined to Louisiana and Mississippi plantations, "never exceeded one-half the volume that came downstream"),[79] and this circumstance was a primary contributor to the inordinately small scale of manufacturing in the Crescent City (Table 4.3). Baltimore, although plagued by similar difficulties in ascending the Susquehanna and its roundabout route to the North and Europe, could tap the National Road, as well as the limited trackage of the B&O Railroad, and was admirably situated for coastwise shipping to the South and exporting to the West Indies. Philadelphia, whose early nineteenth-century hinterland situation is often somewhat overly maligned, had an especially good road and turnpike system to the west, and later, by virtue of the Schuylkill Navigation, could draw more cheaply on the rich but areally limited agricultural and anthracite resources of southeastern Pennsylvania.[80] Most important, the completion and opening of the Erie Canal in 1825 dramatically expanded New York's hinterland and conferred upon some of its manufacturers competitive advantages that did not exist in other ports.

On the one hand, the Erie Canal merely reinforced New York's existing transport advantages — by its nearness to the sea as compared to Baltimore and Philadelphia, its proximity to the South as compared with Boston, its magnificent harbor, and its access to the valleys of the Hudson and the Connecticut.[81] But, on the other hand, the canal repre-

[79] Mitchell, *op. cit.*, p. 941.

[80] From 1836 to 1840, the earliest dates for which comparisons are feasible, the total volume of traffic on the Schuylkill Navigation ranged between 520,000 and 621,000 tons, most of which was coal that moved through the hands of Philadelphia merchants to other coastal destinations [Chester Lloyd Jones, *The Economic History of the Anthracite-Tidewater Canals* (Philadelphia: University of Pennsylvania, Publications in Political Economy and Public Law, 1908), pp. 150, 132], while the total volume of shipments on *all* New York State canals vacillated between 1,171,000 tons and 1,435,000 tons. Albion, *op. cit.*, p. 411. Philadelphia's position is somewhat further flattered if it is realized that during this same period more than half the traffic of the Lehigh Canal (155,300–281,800 tons), again mostly anthracite, either terminated or originated at its docks and wharves. Jones, *ibid.*, pp. 27, 29. Tonnage figures are, of course, questionable substitutes for value-of-shipment statistics.

[81] For a more detailed discussion of the relative situational merits of New York, Baltimore, Boston, and Philadelphia, see Robert G. Albion, "New York

sented a major initial line of penetration and its construction brought with it an "ideal-typical sequence" of transport developments; i.e., market area expansion possibilities were compounded by the establishment of feeder routes and the occurrence of "hinterland piracy."[82] In other words, it may be argued that the relatively large volume of capital invested in New York City manufacturing in 1840 (Table 4.3) was partly ascribable to the spatial lengthening of production made possible by the Erie Canal. However, even "Clinton's Big Ditch" could neither negate the previously mentioned shortcomings of inland waterway transportation nor overcome factor shortages and the state of technology, thus to promote manufacturing from its secondary position in this most important of the mercantile cities.

Inasmuch as the broader transportation network had virtually no effect on finished product distribution within the contiguously built-up area of each city, a final word ought to be injected regarding the ramifications of local market size, and by indirect extension, aggregate market or population accessibility (potential). The number of inhabitants in each of the mercantile cities under consideration was not very impressive by modern metropolitan standards (Table 4.1), and their accessibility to population was meager, even if 1860 is used as a gauge (Map 4.1). At the same time, the evidence discussed in an earlier chapter seems to indicate that, under conditions of mechanized industrial technology, urban manufacturing diversity is to some degree a function of population and market or population accessibility. This implies that large-scale industrial diversity would not have been feasible in the presence of a technology considerably more advanced than that which prevailed in the major urban centers of 1840. If, because of the inadequate local market population and a low index of accessibility to population, a number of large-scale manufactures could not survive, the mercantile city was nonetheless more diversified industrially than its similarly sized counterparts of more than a century hence.[83] This

---

Port and Its Disappointed Rivals," *Journal of Economic and Business History*, Vol. 3 (Aug., 1931), pp. 602–629.

[82] See Edward J. Taaffe, Richard L. Morrill, and Peter R. Gould, "Transport Expansion in Underdeveloped Countries," *Geographical Review*, Vol. 53 (1963), pp. 503–505. Also note Allan Pred, *The External Relations of Cities during 'Industrial Revolution'* (Chicago: University of Chicago, Department of Geography, Research Paper No. 76, 1962), pp. 42–43.

[83] In 1832, Boston had 95 distinct industrial categories, many of which, as already indicated, produced a wide range of products. It is difficult to conceive of a contemporary U.S. city of comparable size (about 65,000) having as diversified an industrial structure.

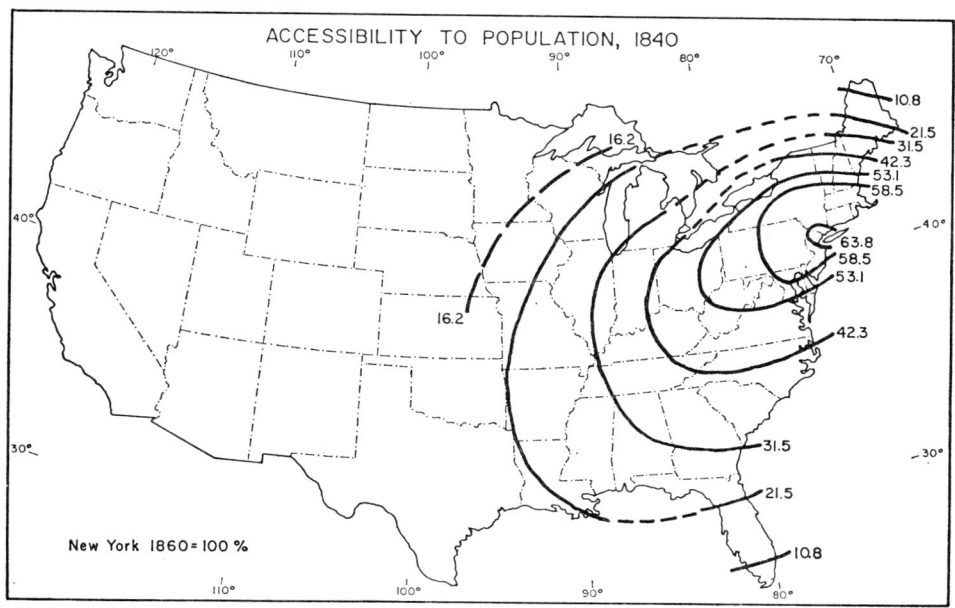

MAP 4.1 Accessibility to population: 1840. Adapted from John Q. Stewart and William Warntz, "Macrogeography and Social Science," *Geographical Review,* Vol. 48 (1958), p. 181; and John Q. Stewart, "Empirical Mathematical Rules Concerning the Distribution and Equilibrium of Population," *Geographical Review,* Vol. 37 (1947), p. 479.

was so because small-scale handicraft and unmechanized production units had low threshold requirements. It should be emphasized however, that the aggregate output of these low-threshold units was not only stunted by the absolute size of the local market and by the other restraining factors already elaborated upon but also by the generally low purchasing power of much of the urban population.

The Manufactures of the Mercantile City

The subsidiary role of manufacturing in the mercantile city is entirely logical within the framework of the restraints and obstacles depicted on the preceding pages. But it is certainly obvious that the presence of obstructions failed to eliminate manufacturing completely from the urban scene, and therefore the question remains: Why were existing industries located in New York, Boston, Philadelphia, and Baltimore?

In 1827 it was observed that "the city of New York has no manufactures, excepting such as are altogether independent of local facilities [raw materials], and such as are likely to grow wherever there are large accumulations of men and means."[84] One can be more explicit and concurrently substantiate the appropriateness of the term "mercantile city" by demonstrating that an overwhelming portion, perhaps virtually all, of the industrial activities located within the confines of New York, Boston, Philadelphia, and Baltimore were either directly or indirectly linked to the mercantile functions of those cities.

Entrepôt Manufactures

The most direct and significant linkages were those that existed between the mercantile city's foreign and domestic commerce and the entrepôt manufacture of consumers' goods. Those merchants who were less hesitant than their colleagues to invest in industrial ventures had, from an early date, "tended to confine their interests and capital to enterprises which combined a mercantile and manufacturing interest, or to those which grew naturally out of their course of trade."[85] The preference for processing import and export commodities with which the merchant class was already familiar was in most instances founded on the security derived from dealing with already known markets and previously established distribution channels. From a purely theoretical viewpoint, entrepôt manufacturing was also rational because it eliminated the additional set of terminal costs that would have been incurred if the particular raw materials were processed at some other point than that where a break in bulk and/or a change of ownership made transshipment almost mandatory.

The apparently modest pre-eminence of entrepôt manufactures in New York in 1810 serves as one indication of prevailing conditions in the other mercantile cities during the period 1800–1840. Ten years after the turn of the nineteenth century, sugar refining, tanning and leather processing, and tobacco milling numbered among Manhattan's most prominent industries, with a combined output approaching or perhaps surpassing $800,000 per annum.[86] The American sugar refin-

---

[84] Dix, *op. cit.*, p. 44.

[85] Harrington, *op. cit.*, pp. 145–146.

[86] *Third Census of the United States, 1810: A Series of Tables of the Several Branches of American Manufactures* (Washington, D. C., 1811), pp. 34–38. The possible relevance of this figure is undermined by the incompleteness and inaccuracy of the Census of 1810, as well as by the drawbacks inherent in using value of production as a measure for industrial comparisons.

ing industry reputedly traces its origins to New York in 1730; and, one century later, Philadelphia, Baltimore, and Boston were important competitors (as of 1813, there were 11 sugar refineries in New York, 11 in Philadelphia, 8 in Baltimore, 3 in Boston, and only 38 in the entire country).[87] Characteristically, at the end of the period, the industry was undergoing technical changes that would later permit it to operate on a truly large scale; e.g., in the late 1830's one New York firm increased its daily output to 12,000 pounds by introducing steam power, and shortly thereafter, in the early 1840's, centrifugals were installed in New York plants to separate sugar from molasses.[88] Although similar scale shifts were not incipient in the New York tanning and tobacco processing industries, a growing trade in hides and tobacco had embellished the importance of these two manufactures. (Over 700 people were employed in New York's tanneries and related leather-working establishments in 1840, and by the forties the city was well on its way to becoming "the largest emporium of foreign hides in the world.")[89] More significantly, the inability of high raw-material assembly costs to interfere with the port location of trade-linked or entrepôt industries is dramatized by the perpetuation and expansion of urban tanning in an era when it was necessary to consume between five and eleven tons of oak or hemlock bark to produce one ton of leather.[90]

A more complete, if somewhat imperfect, image of the stature of entrepôt industries in a mercantile city can be derived for Boston from

[87] Bishop, *op. cit.*, pp. 359–360. The 1840 census, the most comprehensive and reliable manufacturing inventory to that date, indicated that the value of Philadelphia's sugar processing production ($585,000) overshadowed the city's reported output of machinery and related products ($379,500). *Sixth Census of the United States, 1840, op. cit.*, p. 169. Even if concessions are made with respect to possible data deficiencies and differences in the value added ratio of the two industries, there remains little room for disputing sugar refining's position of relative importance within Philadelphia's total manufacturing structure.

[88] Bishop, *op. cit.*, Vol. 3, p. 150; and Clark, *op. cit.*, p. 491.

[89] *Sixth Census of the United States, 1840, op. cit.*, p. 128; and Bishop, *op. cit.*, Vol. 2, p. 425. Tobacco processing and tanning were also still among the leading industries of Baltimore and Philadelphia in 1840.

[90] Adna F. Weber, *Report on the Growth of Industry in New York* (Albany: New York State Department of Labor, 1904), Second Annual Report, Part 5, p. 274. In other words, contrary to the basic precepts of industrial location theory, the dominant weight-losing character of the bark did not confine production completely to forested areas. Admittedly, a good number of persons and workshops assigned to the tanning classification must have practiced currying, or the combing, smoothing, and dressing of leather already tanned in the Catskills and elsewhere.

McLane's 1832 "Report on Manufactures."[91] According to this document, entrepôt manufactures accounted for a minimum of 20 per cent of both Boston's industrial value added and employment (Table 4.4).

TABLE 4.4 *The Structure of Boston's Manufacturing: 1832*

Industry group[a]	Number of establishments	Number employed	%	Value added	%
Entrepôt	201	1,794	20.8	$ 974,774[b]	20.0
Commerce-serving	232	2,599	30.2	1,355,125	27.8
Local Market	561	4,214	49.0	2,553,385	52.2
Construction Materials	55	400	4.7	286,935	5.8
Other[c]	506	3,814	44.3	2,266,450	46.4
Total	994	8,607[d]	100.0	4,883,284[b]	100.0

SOURCE: McLane (see footnotes 24 and 91), pp. 432–469.

[a] As implied in the text discussion of tailoring, industries fitting the criteria for two groups were classified entirely into the more appropriate alternative.

[b] Incomplete data, minor omissions.

[c] This category particularly, and therefore the total, is exaggerated by the unavoidable inclusion of retailing and repairing functions.

[d] Slightly over 40 per cent of this total (3,460) was comprised of boys under 16 years of age, and women and girls.

The magnitude of this percentage would be considerably augmented if it were somehow possible to sort out value added and employment associated with retailing in non-entrepôt categories that either combined retailing and manufacturing functions, as did the "shoe and boot making" industry (Table 4.5), or coupled production and repairing activities, as did the "cabinetmaking" industry. Because all clothes-making establishments were assigned to the "local" group in Table 4.4, an even more impressive percentage increase could be gained if it were possible to segregate that portion of the tailoring industry (Table 4.5) which

---

[91] McLane, *op. cit.*, pp. 432–471. The statistical and descriptive materials presented on these forty pages provide unquestionably the most detailed account available of urban manufacturing in a mercantile environment. The source is not, however, without flaws and idiosyncrasies. Many of the data are in rounded figures, and occasional estimates were inserted where firms or individuals refused to comply with the request for information. With reference to the latter shortcoming, the marshal reported in somewhat comic fashion that

> This class of manufacturing [millinery] has been found difficult to estimate, as women are not generally accountants, and therefore it is not easy for them to answer the questions proposed. Many of them decline giving any answers, apparently from the apprehension that their statements may be considered absurd; others refuse, for the usual woman's reason, "because." This estimate here given is believed to be rather within the actual amount, than to exceed it.

TABLE 4.5 Selected Characteristics of Boston's Leading Industries: 1832

Industry	Number of establishments	Number employed	Cost of domestic raw materials	Cost of foreign raw materials	Value of production	Value added
Printing and Publishing	91	1,309	$583,700	$65,100	$1,426,300	$777,500
Tailoring	100	1,700[b]	400,000	1,500,000	2,600,000	700,000
Shipbuilding and Repairing[a]	102	795[b]	542,440[b]	500,850[b]	1,436,125[b]	392,835[b]
Iron Foundries	9	320	700,000	20,000	1,100,000	380,000
Boot and Shoemaking[c]	200	500[b]	200,000	20,000	500,000	280,000
Baking	40	126	187,775	2,550	400,000	209,675
Distilling	20	80	190,000	1,000,000	1,371,000	181,000
Subtotal	562	4,830	2,803,915	3,108,500	8,833,425	2,921,010
Total for All Industries	994	8,607	4,099,820	4,459,941	13,321,595[d]	4,883,284[d]
Subtotal/Total	56.5	56	68.4	69.7	66.3	59.8

SOURCE: McLane (see footnotes 24 and 91), pp. 432–469.
[a] Includes the independent production of sails, masts, pumps and blocks, etc.
[b] Estimated.
[c] Some establishments with repairing and retailing functions included.
[d] Incomplete data, minor omissions.

catered to the Boston market from that which made "slop clothing for navy and merchant ships."[92] Classificatory problems aside, the most noteworthy aspects of Boston's entrepôt production were the dimensions of its distilling (similarly important in New York, Philadelphia, and Baltimore) and the exotic variety of raw materials used. Strikingly, the umbrella and cane industry alone required imported ivory, silks, buckhorn, linen, rattan, ebony, and boxwood.

Several other manufactures, thus far unmentioned, were also directly associated with the primary trading function of the mercantile cities. One of these, flour milling, was especially well articulated in Baltimore and its vicinity, and, until the Erie Canal commenced operation, the inhabitants of the Chesapeake Bay city boasted that theirs was "the largest flour market in the world."[93] More important, and almost ironically, the largest single industry growing out of urban commercial activity, the integrated power-driven cotton textile industry, was located in Boston's hinterland and the suburbs of Baltimore and Philadelphia, but with the exception of the aforementioned anomalous steam-powered plants, *not in the city proper*.[94] Francis C. Lowell, P. T. Jackson, Nathan Appleton, and many of the other individuals backing the early cotton-spinning and weaving factories in New England, southeastern Pennsylvania, the Baltimore area, and Paterson, had been urban merchants. As active participants in the trade of Boston, Philadelphia, Baltimore, and New York, a number of merchants were acquainted with the market, made familiar to them through the wholesaling of English dry goods, and/or with the raw-material sources, made intimate to them through the re-export of cotton. Because face-to-face contacts were so vital within the context of an essentially primitive communications system, merchant capital was rarely risked in nonlocal industrial projects; and as textile factories were anchored to immobile water-power sources,

[92] McLane, *op. cit.*, p. 465. The information provided for most other industries is sufficient enough to remove any problems of distinction between local and nonlocal markets.

[93] Sparks, *op. cit.*, p. 123. Naturally, much of the wheat arriving from the interior had already been transformed into flour.

[94] In 1840, the city of Philadelphia employed as many as 474 laborers in its cotton textile industry — a larger number than was to be found in any of the other mercantile cities. However, the majority of these workers were apparently associated with dyeing and printing establishments, rather than with integrated spinning and weaving mills. *Sixth Census of the United States, 1840, op. cit.*, p. 169.

it may be conjectured that large-scale integrated cotton spinning and weaving would have initially emerged as a major industry in the mercantile city if an alternative economical energy source had existed (although admittedly, Boston then contained little, if any, space for large factories).

Commerce-serving Manufactures

In addition to the entrepôt industries, a second group of manufactures was directly linked to the commerce of the mercantile city. Shipbuilding, printing, coopery, and other industries had grown in the larger Atlantic ports in response to the demand created by local commercial activities. Periodic increases in the volume of trade required corresponding increments in vessel carrying capacity, and therefore during prosperous years shipbuilding thrived on a noteworthy scale in New York, Baltimore, Philadelphia, and Boston. (Output was also encouraged after the War of 1812 by the termination of European restrictions on the purchase of American-built ships.) Although New York outdistanced its rival ports in vessel construction (Table 4.6), Baltimore

TABLE 4.6 *Selected Shipbuilding Statistics for Leading Mercantile Cities (in thousands of tons)*

	New York	Boston	Philadelphia	Baltimore	U.S. Total
1833[a]	22	16	3	8	161[b]
1837	20	6	3	5	122
1841	16	15	5	7	118

SOURCE: Albion (see footnote 11), p. 406. Compiled from *Reports on Commerce and Navigation* issued annually by the Secretary of the Treasury.

[a] First year for which statistics are available on a port-by-port basis.

[b] Virtually none of the total for all three years was accounted for by New Orleans.

was renowned for the grace of her slender schooners and larger "clippers," and Philadelphia was respected for the shape, speed, and quality of her products, despite a slump of the city's yards during the thirties.[95] Boston's commitment to shipbuilding (Table 4.5) was supplemented by launchings and repairs at Medford (five miles north of the city), where 23 ships and 8 brigs were completed in 1832 and part of 1833,

[95] In 1828, when construction was more active, Philadelphia shipyards created 11 ships, 5 brigs, 5 schooners, 15 sloops, and 1 steamboat, or a total of 6,516 tons. *Niles' Weekly Register*, Vol. 36 (July 18, 1829), p. 334.

and at Charlestown (eventually incorporated into Boston), where 100 men were involved in the industry during 1832.[96]

The shipbuilding market functioned in such a manner that it was essentially obligatory for some production to coincide with the major centers of consumption, even though it was frequently necessary at the leading ports to assemble live oak, white pine, and pitch pine timbers from distant points in the Carolinas, Georgia, Florida, and Maine. Advertisements for individual vessels were usually placed in the local newspapers when the planking stage of construction was reached in the urban shipyards, for most purchasing merchants "preferred to order vessels from builders who were known to them, and whose yard they could visit" in order to dictate structural specifications, ensure quality, and cut costs.[97] Significantly, when New York displaced Philadelphia as the nation's leading commercial metropolis after the War of 1812, it also surpassed the latter city to become the foremost shipbuilding center.

A similar exchange of positions occurred concomitantly in the printing industries, whose size, aside from book publishing, was basically a function of the local demand for newspaper advertising, handbills, business papers, printed blanks, and legal forms. The leading daily newspapers in early nineteenth-century New York carried such banners as *The New York Gazette and General Advertiser, The Commercial Advertiser, The Mercantile Advertiser,* and *The Public Advertiser,* and thereby emphasized the relationship between the printing industries and the primary mercantile functions of the city. The publication of *Niles' Weekly Register* in Baltimore and the appearance elsewhere of lesser known, more short-lived periodicals, such as Philadelphia's *Archives of Useful Knowledge,* were other manifestations of the strong bonds between commerce and urban printing. If numbers employed can be accepted as a valid indicator, then printing and publishing, with over 2,000 workers, was New York City's single most important industry

---

[96] *Niles' Weekly Register,* Vol. 45 (Oct. 26, 1833), p. 130; and McLane, *op. cit.,* pp. 316–317. It is very difficult to assess the total number of people linked with shipbuilding at any given date in any of the mercantile cities. Problems arise because some occupations, such as glazing and painting, involved part-time work in the shipyards, and therefore defy the clear-cut assignments that are possible with sailmaking, sparmaking, and other trades.

[97] John G. B. Hutchins, *The American Maritime Industries and Public Policy, 1789–1914* (Cambridge: Harvard University Press, 1941), p. 194.

in 1840.[98] If the preferable but usually impractical value-added gauge is used, then the same indications of primacy are obtained from the most nearly complete set of data available, for the value added by Boston's printing and publishing industries[99] in 1832 was greater than that of any other manufacturing class (Table 4.5).

The assembly of barrels, boxes, kegs, casks, and other items of cooperage was a less-imposing but still-important industrial servant to commerce. Despite the absence of census materials, we do know there were already upward of 150 coopers on Manhattan in 1800, and at least 220 similar craftsmen in Boston as of 1832.[100] The localization of the coopering industry in the mercantile city derived largely from the handcuffing of much of its output to uniquely specified orders, and the producer's need to avoid the unnecessary transportation costs normally associated with shipping space-consuming empty containers.

Remaining Manufactures

An overwhelming percentage of the manufacturing in the major urban centers that neither fell into the entrepôt category nor responded directly to commercial demands was at least obliquely related to the mercantile aspect of those cities. In more specific terms, the production of construction materials, such as glass, nails, paint, "paper hangings," and plaster of Paris, and the manufacture of beer, baked goods, furniture, clothing, carriages, and other consumer goods, was ubiquitous to New York, Boston, Philadelphia, and Baltimore because of the aggregate demand precipitated by the local mercantile population and the classes serving that population. The evidence that can be ferreted out would seem to indicate that these local-market and threshold manufactures were larger as a group than the entrepôt and commerce-serving

---

[98] Census statistics that may not have been complete indicated 1840 employment in the printing and publishing trades as follows: New York, 2,029; Philadelphia, 904; Boston, 437 (compare Table 4.5); and Baltimore, 279. *Sixth Census of the United States, 1840, op. cit.*, pp. 54, 129, 169, 217.

[99] Includes lithography, engraving, copperplate printing, type founding, stereotyping, bookbinding, and the production of blankbooks, newspapers, books, pamphlets, and miscellaneous printed items.

[100] *Longworth's American Almanac, New-York Register, and City Directory, 1800, op. cit.;* and McLane, *op. cit.*, pp. 434–435. Presumably, there were additional individuals listed or enumerated as carpenters who indulged in coopery on a part-time basis.

industries. However, the local-market industry figures for Boston in Table 4.4 should be interpreted with caution. There is little, if any, reason for doubting the magnitude of the construction material industries in that table,[101] but the same cannot be said of the residue of the local market group. We have already alluded to the unavoidable inclusion of some retailing and repairing in this balance, as well as to the classificatory problems associated with tailoring. Furthermore, testimony from the Philadelphia record suggests additional obfuscation of retailing by the four furniture industries subsumed under the table's local-market residue.[102]

Certainly, some of the remaining urban manufactures were not embraced firmly by the broad local-market category, or by the entrepôt and commerce-serving groups. The machinery and locomotive plants of downtown Philadelphia spring immediately to mind as refractory anomalies. However, closer examination reveals that these deviant examples are not as unruly as their initial impressions might imply. Unless the Census for 1840 is grossly inaccurate on the point, there were less than 400 people employed in Philadelphia's machine-making shops and factories at that time.[103] A portion of this small number was occupied in the manufacture of machinery for cotton and woolen textile mills, much of which was distributed to a market within a few miles of the city. While other machinery industries and locomotive production did not necessarily cater to such a blatantly local market, they originated for the most part rather late in the 1800–1840 period under consideration. For example: the famed Baldwin Locomotive Works did not go into full operation until 1833–34; the Norris Locomotive Works were established in 1834, "in a small shop, employing but six men"; and the Southwark Foundry, a relatively large producer of "heavy ma-

---

[101] The dimensions of construction material production obviously must have oscillated with the rate at which new buildings were put up. In an active year (such as the one Philadelphia had in 1827, when an estimated 40 million bricks were consumed locally), the numbers of workers and value added involved elsewhere in the building material industries almost certainly surpassed the corresponding figures for 1832 Boston. *Niles' Weekly Register,* Vol. 35 (Sept. 6, 1828), p. 19.

[102] According to one account: "In 1840 there were but few Furniture stores in Philadelphia, and they mostly small ones; keeping samples of the styles of goods, but relying mainly on orders from their customers to supply work for their employees." Freedley, *op. cit.,* p. 272.

[103] The census reported 337 males working in the machinery industries of Philadelphia. *Sixth Census of the United States, 1840, op. cit.,* p. 169.

chinery," originated no earlier than 1836.[104] In short, the late arrival and magnitude of these and other apparent exceptions present insufficient cause to refute the premise that manufacturing in the mercantile city was basically an adjunct of the city's dominant commercial functions.

A Model of Urban-Size Growth for the American Mercantile City: 1800–1840

Basic Structure of the Model

In a sense, all that has been said regarding the economic functions of the mercantile city, the constraints on early nineteenth-century manufactures and the composition of those manufactures, has served both as a means of explaining why the circular and cumulative process of urban-size growth did not operate as it did in the post-Civil War era and as a suggestive overture to the third of our initially stated problems. To wit: In the absence of a primary stimulus from manufacturing, how did the urban-size growth process function, and how did selective urban growth occur within a rudimentary system of cities?

If the depiction of the mercantile city's economic functions is combined with the generally accepted interconnection between city growth and the structure of urban activities, then the expansion of major American cities from 1800 to 1840 can once again be interpreted through a descriptive model of circular and cumulative causation. An interpretation of this sort was presaged by an extremely astute and perceptive 1837 commentator in these words: "Cities continue to grow, not because their situation is intrinsically the most advantageous, but because they have already acquired a certain growth, which of itself contains within it the elements of further increase."[105]

Exposition of the 1800–1840 model requires a reiteration of preconditions similar to those cited in the urban-size growth model for periods of rapid industrialization. Therefore imagine a mercantile city that is indiscriminately located in space and unengaged in market-area or hinterland-competition with other cities (though it does exchange local specialities with other urban centers). Assumption of these nearly

[104] Freedley, *op. cit.*, pp. 306, 309, 434.
[105] Nathan Hale, "Poussin on American Rail-roads," *North American Review*, Vol. 44 (1837), p. 438.

aspatial and monopolistic conditions permits concentration on the growth process itself and postpones consideration of the interplay of other developments and the growth of some cities at the expense of others.

Further imagine the occurrence in this city of a *successful* scale increase in at least one subsector of its middleman wholesaling-trading complex (foreign export of hinterland commodities, re-export of carrying-trade commodities, coastal and internal redistribution of hinterland production, or hinterland and coastal distribution of foreign imports). This commercial expansion, which may assume the form either of growth within existing mercantile houses or the creation of new business units, eventually elicits an ideal-typical sequence of events whose causation is circular and cumulative (Figure 4.1).

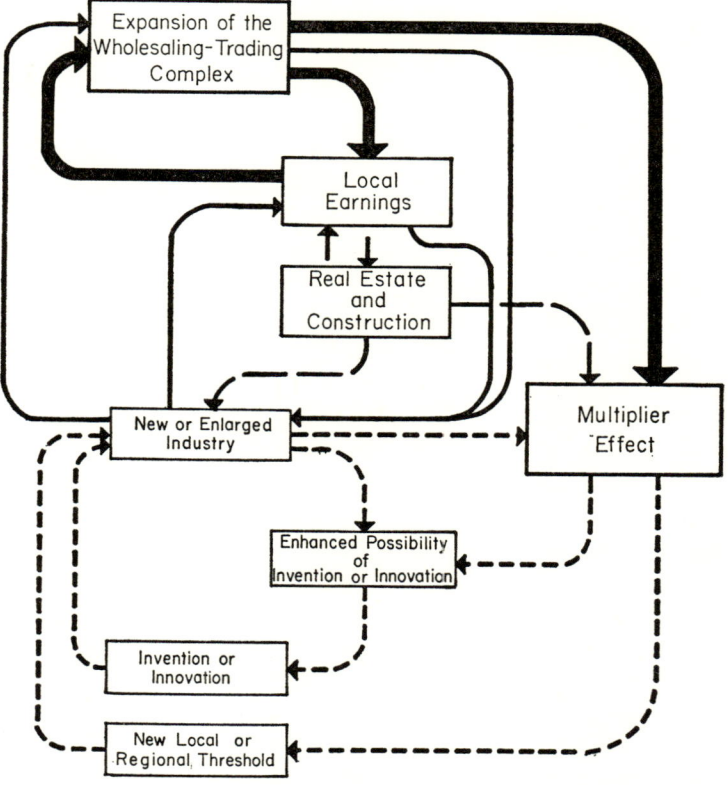

FIGURE 4.1 The circular and cumulative process of urban-size growth for the American mercantile city, 1800–1840.

New mercantile functions give birth to an initial employment multiplier; that is, new local demand created by the trading establishments will call into being additional job opportunities for draymen, stevedores, weighers, bank and insurance company employees, boarding-house operators,[106] and people in other miscellaneous occupations. The combined effect of new mercantile employment and an initial multiplier will be an increase in population (or growth in urban size), and the probable attainment of one or more new local retailing, service, professional, and commerce-serving and local-market industrial thresholds that in turn will further augment the city's population through the job opportunity-migration mechanism.[107] Certain types of new mercantile functions will also add to the industrial working force by precipitating new or expanded entrepôt manufactures. The new or enlarged manufacturing, whether of the entrepôt, commerce-serving, or local-market variety, will generate a secondary multiplier effect[108] and touch off a subsidiary, low-metabolic version of the 1860–1910 growth process in which successive *low* manufacturing thresholds are fulfilled and the possibilities of industrial invention and innovation will be continuously enhanced. (At this stage, the manufacturing threshold and invention-innovation cycles would be incapable of sustaining themselves independently without constant prodding from commercial sources.)

This succession of events soon grinds to a halt if its circuit is not completed and its battery recharged repeatedly by reinvestments derived from the earnings of the new or expanded mercantile functions and other already existing profit-making enterprises within the wholesaling-trading complex. However, each reinvestment in commerce, or scale increase in at least one subsector of the wholesaling-trading complex, will bring forth another initial multiplier and the presumable achievement of thresholds in other sectors of the urban economy, consequently making the growth process perpetual and self-generating unless, or until, some exogenous disruptive force(s) appear.

---

[106] Numerous boarding-houses and hostelries were necessary to accommodate hinterland purchasers and representatives, as well as foreign business agents. Note the comments by Holmes, *op. cit.*, p. 355.

[107] As remarked in a previous chapter, knowledge of the labor market and destinations of previous migrants are two of the most important determinants of individual migration decisions.

[108] Recall the argument that *all* manufacturing entails some multiplier effect. Naturally, the limited scale of new or enlarged early nineteenth-century urban manufacturing operations imply extremely modest multipliers.

But circular and cumulative size growth in the mercantile city is not without additional complexities, for the process is invigorated and accelerated by developments within two other sectors. First, some mercantile earnings will be diverted into real estate speculation and construction, diversions in themselves encouraged by a mounting population. Such investment will cause a multiplier of its own (new jobs for painters, carpenters, roofers, plasterers, and other construction workers, plus further labor opportunities in the building-service manufactures), and contribute to threshold-fulfillment in retailing, local-market manufacturing, and other unrelated sectors. Moreover, a portion of real estate and construction winnings will more than likely spur growth by finding their way back into the wholesaling-trading complex and setting off another round of earnings and multiplier effects. Second, an indeterminate fraction of industrial profits would also be expected to wend its way back to the wholesaling-trading complex, further rejuvenating the circular growth process. The entrepôt manufactures already mentioned will stimulate growth similarly by participating directly in commercial expansion. (Note the arrows in Figure 4.1 that go uninterruptedly from the box marked "expansion of the wholesaling-trading complex" to the box labeled "new or enlarged industry," and vice versa.) The feedback chains from real estate and construction, and from manufacturing, with their progressively compounded consequences, will be reiterated until detoured or obstructed; and the functioning of the entire model will be reinforced by the increasing attractiveness that the city's growing scale and array of mercantile establishments exert upon foreigners and hinterland dwellers seeking a market outlet or purchasing source.

Clarification and Expansion of the Model

Certainly there is no need to repeat the threshold and multiplier arguments espoused in connection with the urban-size growth model for the post-Civil War era. Nevertheless, as it stands, the growth model for the American mercantile city is plagued with the ineluctable deficiencies associated with ideal-typical theories applying to the past and consequently requires more illumination. At the very least, the 1800–1840 model ought to be clarified through some expansive and qualifying remarks regarding its operation, a suggestion of the means by which the circular and cumulative process metamorphosed between 1840 and 1860, and a terse juxtapositional comparison with related generalizations pertaining to "stages" of urban economic growth.

We commence, then, with an enumeration of some amplifications and modifications.

1. Although the model depicts the impetus for growth as coming almost entirely from the city's export base (or more precisely in this instance, the volume and value of hinterland, foreign, and local goods being exported and *re-exported* from the city), it is compatible with the arguments, introduced in the discussion of interacting industrialization and urbanization later in the nineteenth century, that emphasized that the role of "basic" activities ought not be blown up out of proportion. The tenability and consistency of this position becomes clear if it is reasserted that the importance of exports diminishes as the economic unit (city or metropolis) grows in area and population.[109] According to one appraisal for contemporary small U.S. metropolitan areas (50,-000–100,000 population), "as much as one-half" of their economic activity may be devoted "to producing [or merchandising] goods" consumed outside of their respective borders.[110] Given the limited purchasing power of the local market in like-sized American mercantile cities, plus the concentration of almost 90 per cent of the country's 1840 population in rural areas, it is not unreasonable to assume that the percentage of the urban economy then involved in exporting and re-exporting exceeded the estimate for present-day centers.

2. The model does not take into account the presence of English and continental capital (loans and investments) within the mercantile city's wholesaling-trading complex. The presence of foreign capital appears to have had ambivalent consequences upon the rate of urban-size growth. On the one hand, foreign participation in the urban economy presumably meant a departure of some locally derived profits and perhaps a deceleration of growth. On the other hand, the injection of European funds was no different from the reinvestment of local earnings insofar as it: engendered a multiplier effect; had the added virtue of embellishing the local circulation of capital by providing resources (even if only on a temporary basis) that were not otherwise available; and, by enhancing the scale and/or variety of mercantile establishments,

---

[109] Expressed in alternative terms, ". . . a larger city would have a greater proportion of its employed persons furnishing goods and services for each other than would a small city." Victor Roterus and Wesley Calef, "Notes on the Basic-Nonbasic Employment Ratio," *Economic Geography*, Vol. 31 (Jan., 1955), p. 18.

[110] Wilbur R. Thompson, *A Preface to Urban Economics* (Baltimore: The Johns Hopkins Press, 1965), p. 27.

served to advance the attraction of the city to those seeking market outlets or purchasing sources. The positive repercussions of these latter scale increases and localization economies would seem to outweigh the former, or any other, negative ramification.

3. With the passage of time, and particularly after the War of 1812, an increasing inland rural population and tariff conditions caused the wholesaling-trading complex of Boston, Baltimore, and Philadelphia to become more and more oriented toward domestic commerce (observe the importing and exporting statistics for the three cities in Table 4.2), including the redistribution of foreign imports entering at New York. In other words, the circular and cumulative growth process in these cities grew more dependent upon internal and coastal trade but *no less reliant* upon foreign commerce. In contrast, New York's imports and exports, as well as domestic trade, expanded over the long run; and, entirely within the logic of the model, the population of the Hudson River metropolis grew more rapidly than that of Boston, Baltimore, or Philadelphia (Table 4.1). Uniquely, New Orleans extended her international trade without making comparable progress in her strictly domestic commerce (large shipments of cotton from New Orleans to New York were controlled by New York merchants). The comparatively lethargic growth of New Orleans' upstream and coastal shipping should have restricted entrepôt activities. This meant, theoretically, that the subsidiary industrial cycles of the model should have functioned at a pace even more greatly retarded than that of the Atlantic Coast mercantile cities — a contention in accordance with the fact of the city's abnormally low commitment to manufacturing.

4. Unlike the situation some decades later, the trend of average wages per urban worker between 1800 and 1840 apparently did not permit the evolution of progressively larger multiplier effects. On the contrary, there appears to have been a downward oscillation of urban wages in the early nineteenth century, which implies a corresponding decrease in the multiplier tied to most increments in the wholesaling-trading complexes of cities in general, if not in New York, Boston, Philadelphia, and Baltimore specifically.[111]

---

[111] Daily wages for nonfarm labor in the United States fell supposedly from $1.00 in 1800, to $0.75 in 1830, and then climbed back to $0.85 by 1840. Gross statistics of this type fail to give any indication of across-the-board trends in individual cities. See Stanley Lebergott, "Wage Trends, 1800–1900," in *Trends in the American Economy in the Nineteenth Century, op. cit.,* pp. 462–464, 482–484.

The first and third of the preceding qualifications open the door to a tentative formulation of the structural changes that occurred in the mercantile city's circular and cumulative growth process during the score of years from 1840 to 1860. The difference between the 1800–1840 and post-1860 models lies quite obviously in the threshold and invention-innovation cycles originating with each manufacturing addition or enlargement. In the former model the industrial components are a subordinate host of the wholesaling-trading complex, but in the latter model they constitute an essentially independent, self-generating system. The arbitrarily delimited interval separating the two phases of urban growth saw an increase in foreign trade and, more significantly, a tremendous speeding up in the development of interior trade. The continued peopling of the Middle West and the maturation of the railroad network encouraged entrepreneurs, particularly in the 1850's, to widen their spheres of operation through the establishment of new manufacturing.[112] Therefore it may be suggested that, as domestic trade became increasingly important (as market accessibility increased), the urban-size growth process was slowly transformed by greater manufacturing allocations,[113] a related growing capacity of the industrial threshold and invention-innovation cycles to contribute to their self-sustenance, and the emergence of some wholesaling activities that were subservient to manufacturing. *Once the appearance of truly large-scale urban factories commences and the reversal of the wholesaling-manufacturing relationship begins to be widespread* (with most wholesaling becoming a major element of the industrial multiplier), *then the industrial threshold*

---

[112] As Fishlow has pointed out: "One could write an independent history of manufactures and railroads in the 1840's, one could not do the same for western expansion and railroads in the 1850's." Albert Fishlow, *American Railroads and the Transformation of the Ante-Bellum Economy* (Cambridge: Harvard University Press, 1965), p. 261. It must be stressed that despite the greater ease with which less highly valued manufactured goods could now move over both trunk lines and feeder lines from the Great Lakes, competition from imported products and other factors limited the impact of the railroad on urban manufacturing until the post-Civil War era.

[113] This is consistent with North's following contention regarding *regional* growth:
> With the growth of population and income, indigenous savings [from export activities] will increase. Both indigenous savings and the reinvested capital can pour back into the export industries [the wholesaling-trading complex in our case] only up to a point, and then accumulated capital will tend to overflow into other activity.

Douglass C. North, "Location Theory and Regional Economic Growth," *Journal of Political Economy*, Vol. 63 (June, 1955), p. 255.

and invention-innovation sequences may be viewed as having begun to spin off on their own. Such suggestions beg future inquiry and should be interpreted as comprising no more than the roughest sketch.

Whether or not it is entirely satisfactory, the proposed metamorphosis, by allowing urban growth to function as a *continuous process,* manages to avoid a major pitfall found in most traditional and contemporary writings on city growth. Urban growth, like the growth of any geographic unit, moves forward, with inconsistent speed and occasional retreats, through an unbroken continuum. Yet the German political economists of the late nineteenth and early twentieth centuries, whose work was popularized in the United States by Gras,[114] wrote at great length[115] on the evolution of the economy's locational structure in terms of successive "village," "town," and "metropolitan" periods[116] (distinguishing the three urban units on the basis of imprecise functional and size criteria),[117] without introducing concepts or hypotheses governing the evolution from one phase to another.

The more elegant growth theories formulated during the last few years have also failed to provide a fast and certain binder between the different phases of the urban economy's evolution. In a very recent publication Smolensky and Ratajczak borrow from Lösch, by asserting that urbanism "originates because of economies of specialization in performing what would otherwise be ubiquitous economic activities" on a uniform rural plain, and suggest "that the forces initiating growth in a city will usually follow each other in time in a particular sequence" of three stages: "elemental settlement," "conforming city," and "urban agglomerate."[118] Logically, it is implied that each of the stages, which

---

[114] See N. S. B. Gras, *An Introduction to Economic History* (New York: Harper and Brothers, 1922), p. 49 ff.

[115] The work of Schmoller, Bücher, Roscher, Schäffle, and others was concerned largely with the European experience and paid little attention to the emerging American pattern. For a concise review of some of their efforts see Walter Isard, *Location and Space-Economy* (New York: The Technology Press and John Wiley & Sons, Inc., 1956), pp. 26–30. The school of thought, as distinguished from Lösch's later innovations, probably culminated with Hans Ritschl's "Reine und historische Dynamik des Standortes der Erzeugungsweige," [*Schmollers Jahrbuch,* Vol. 51 (1927), pp. 813–870].

[116] Gras partitioned the "metropolitan" period into four subdivisions: "organizing the market," "industrial development," "development of transportation," and "development of financial organization."

[117] For example, Gras drew the line between "town" and "metropolis" as "chiefly a matter of size." Gras, *op. cit.,* p. 181.

[118] Eugene Smolensky and David Ratajczak, "The Conception of Cities,"

are unfortunate jargonistic substitutions for the village-town-metropolis sequence, "should be evident in the industrial and occupational distribution of the labor force"[119] of the city; but the mechanisms of transition are described inadequately. For example: "An elemental settlement becomes a *conforming city* when a factor specific to that site (topological or otherwise), giving an absolute cost advantage to entrepreneurs locating in that town, becomes economically relevant to profit-maximizing entrepreneurs."[120] Admittedly, criticism for this shortcoming should not be carried to extremes, for the authors' empirical efforts are concentrated on the "elemental settlement," and, by their own confession, "The hypothesis that cities grow to standard metropolitan statistical area size pass through three stages remains to be demonstrated."[121]

In another typical effort, Thompson has proposed four consecutive stages of urban development, and although his succession is relatively successful in connoting continuity, it falls short of identifying an evolutionary *process,* as evidenced by this synopsis:

> We might identify, first, the *Stage of Export Specialization* in which the local economy is the lengthened shadow of a single dominant industry or even a single firm. This initial stage gives way with growth and size to the *Stage of the Export Complex* in which local production broadens to other products and/or deepens by extending forward or backward in the stages of production, by adding local suppliers and/or consumers of intermediate products. Next, the *Stage of Economic Maturation* (Local Service Sector Puberty) follows, in which the principal expansion of local activity is in the direction of replacing imports with new "own use" production; the local economy fills out in range and quality of both business and consumer services. Fourth, the *Stage of Regional Metropolis* is reached, when the local economy becomes a node connecting and controlling neighboring cities, once rivals and now satellites, and the export of services becomes a major economic function.[122]

Explorations in Entrepreneurial History, Second Series, Vol. 2 (Winter, 1965), pp. 90–131; the longer phrases cited are from pp. 90–91.

[119] *Ibid.,* p. 92.
[120] *Ibid.,* p. 91.
[121] *Ibid.,* p. 128.

[122] In addition, there may or may not be a *Stage of Technical Professional Virtuosity,* in which "national eminence in some specialized skill or economic function is achieved. This stage may succeed or precede the status of regional metropolis." Thompson, *op. cit.,* pp. 15–16. Thompson's "summary and loose synthesis ... draws liberally ... from innumerable sources." Surely, as these words infer, the Smolensky-Ratajczak and Thompson examples do not exhaust the modern literature on urban growth, but they are representative, and unlike most other items they focus on the growth of cities as opposed to vaguer "regions."

The Selective Growth of American Mercantile Cities

Again paraphrasing the terminology of an earlier chapter, if the circular and cumulative process of urban-size growth just outlined functioned flawlessly, and if all cities were isolated units not in market-area or hinterland competition with one another, then every mercantile city would expand indefinitely, or at least as long as available natural resources allowed. However, between 1800 and 1840 four mercantile hubs on the Atlantic Coast grew more rapidly than, and at the expense of, virtually every other competing port between Maine and Florida (Table 4.7 and Map 4.2).[123] While New York, Boston, Baltimore, and Philadelphia reaffirmed and fortified their supremacy in the urban hierarchy, other coastal centers grew modestly (e.g., Norfolk, Virginia), and some stultified or declined for a period (e.g., New London, Connecticut, and Charleston, South Carolina). Manifestly, then, the circular and cumulative process does not unwind nearly equivalently for all mercantile centers in an interacting system of cities, even within the context of a densening and spreading space economy. As with the post-1860 model, a number of ambivalent forces simultaneously disturb the circuit of cumulative growth in some instances and stimulate the emergence of multifunctional metropolises in others.

Transport and Route Developments

Inasmuch as "Every factor that alters the significance of a route . . . alters the importance of commercial nodes [cities]";[124] it is reasonable first to consider the impact of canal construction, other internal improvements, and related route developments on the selective growth of American mercantile cities.

The intermediate phases of the "ideal-typical sequence" of transport developments in underdeveloped countries proposed by Taafe, Morrill, and Gould serve as excellent point of departure. According to these geographers:

> With the emergence of major lines [canals, turnpikes] of penetration [see B, Figure 4.2], hinterland transportation costs are reduced for certain

[123] The ascendancy of the four mercantile cities would appear even more striking if the population of Brooklyn (47,613 in 1840) were added to New York City's (Manhattan's) total, and if the inhabitants of Philadelphia's, Boston's, and Baltimore's subsequently incorporated suburbs were added to the numbers of those municipalities.

[124] Dean, *op. cit.*, p. 39.

TABLE 4.7 Relative Decline of Selected Atlantic Coast Ports: 1800–1840

	Population 1800	Population 1840	Ratio to Boston 1800	Ratio to Boston 1840	Ratio to N.Y.C. 1800	Ratio to N.Y.C. 1840
Beverly, Mass.	3,881	4,689	1: 6.4	1:19.9	1:15.6	1: 66.7
Gloucester, Mass.	5,313	6,350	1: 4.7	1:14.7	1:11.4	1: 49.2
Milford, Conn.	2,417	2,455	1:10.3	1:38.0	1:25.0	1:127.4
New London, Conn.	5,150	5,519	1: 4.8	1:16.9	1:11.8	1: 56.7
Newburyport, Mass.	5,946	7,161	1: 4.2	1:13.0	1:10.2	1: 43.7
Newport, R.I.	6,739	8,333	1: 3.7	1:11.2	1: 9.0	1: 37.5
Portsmouth, N.H.	5,339	7,887	1: 4.7	1:11.8	1:11.3	1: 39.6
Salem, Mass.	9,457	15,082	1: 2.6	1: 6.2	1: 6.4	1: 20.7

	Population 1800	Population 1840	Ratio to N.Y.C. 1800	Ratio to N.Y.C. 1840	Ratio to Balt. 1800	Ratio to Balt. 1840	Ratio to Phila.[a] 1800	Ratio to Phila.[a] 1840
Annapolis, Md.	2,260[b]	2,792	1:54.7[c]	1:112.0	1:27.8[c]	1:36.6	1:28.2[c]	1:33.5
Charleston, S.C.	18,824	29,261[d]	1: 3.2	1: 10.7	1: 1.4	1: 3.5	1: 2.2	1: 3.2
New Bern, N.C.	2,467[e]	3,690	1:24.5	1: 84.7	1:10.7	1:27.7	1:16.7	1:25.4
Norfolk, Va.	6,926	10,920	1: 8.7	1: 28.6	1: 3.8	1: 9.4	1: 6.0	1: 8.6
Savannah, Ga.	5,146	11,214	1:11.8	1: 27.9	1: 5.2	1: 9.1	1: 8.0	1: 8.4
Trenton, N.J.	3,002[f]	4,035	1:32.1g	1: 77.5	1:15.5g	1:25.4	1:17.9g	1:23.2

SOURCE: Bureau of the Census, *1960 Census of Population*, Vol. 1, Part A.
[a] Not including the unincorporated Northern Liberties, Spring Garden, Kensington, or Southwark.
[b] 1820 population. No earlier figure available.
[c] Ratio for 1820 populations.
[d] Charleston actually had lost population since 1830, when it had 30,289 inhabitants.
[e] In 1800, New Bern was both the largest port and urban place in North Carolina.
[f] 1810 population. No earlier figure available.
[g] Ratio for 1810 populations.

188 AMERICAN MERCANTILE CITY

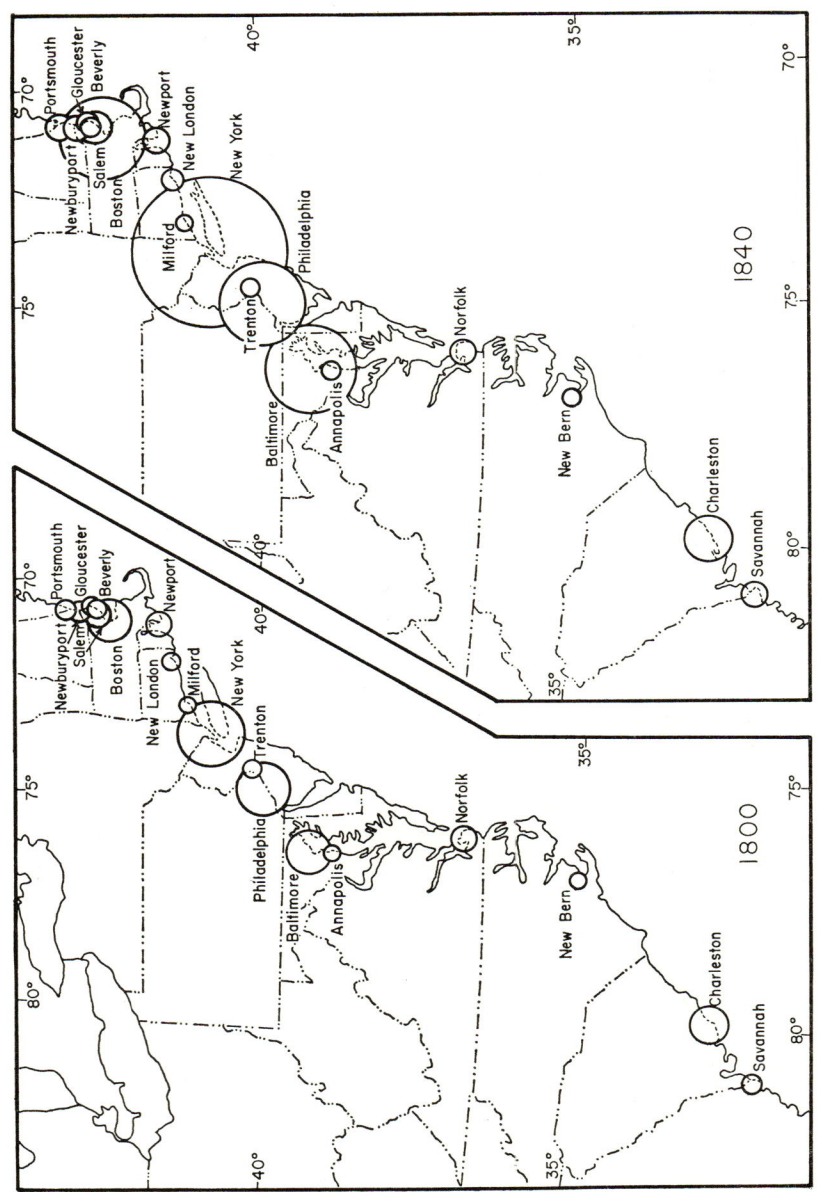

MAP 4.2 The population of selected Atlantic Coast ports: 1800 and 1840. See Table 4.7.

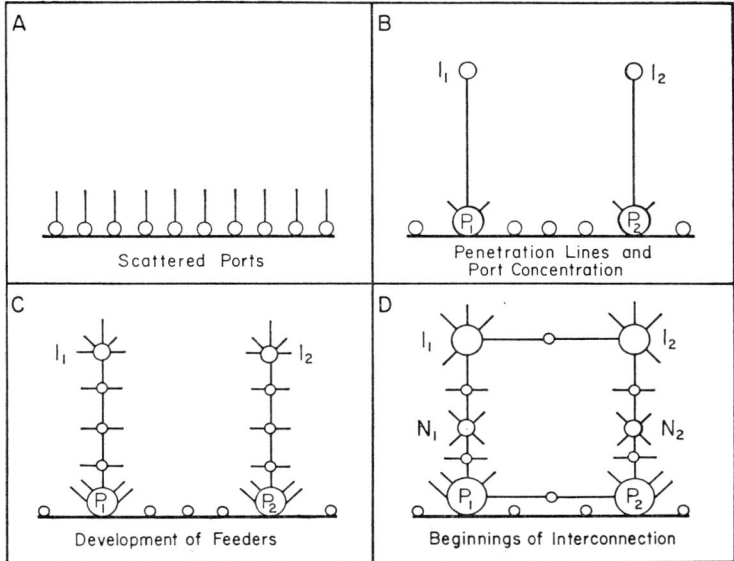

FIGURE 4.2 Initial phases of an ideal-typical sequence of transport developments, after Taafe, Morrill, and Gould.

ports. Markets expand at the port and at the interior center. Port concentration then begins, as illustrated by circles P_1 and P_2. Feeder routes begin to focus on the major ports and interior centers (C). These feeder routes give rise to a sort of hinterland piracy that permits the major port to enlarge its hinterland at the expense of adjacent smaller ports. Small nodes begin to develop along the main lines of penetration, and as feeder [river and branch canal] development continues (D), certain of the nodes, exemplified by N_1 and N_2, become focal points for feeder networks of their own.[125] Interior concentration then begins, and N_1 and N_2 pirate the hinterlands of the smaller nodes on each side [thus embellishing the market outlets and commodity sources of the major ports or mercantile cities].[126]

[125] This would partially account for the rapid post-1825 rise of Rochester, Cincinnati, and other lesser, interior river ports not considered in this study.

[126] Taafe, Morrill, and Gould, *op. cit.*, pp. 503–505. The Taafe-Morrill-Gould model, with its underlying implicit assumption of an unexploited interior, is in much closer conformity with reality than theories which begin with a population distributed evenly on a uniform rural plain. Having been driven into a corner by the latter presupposition, Smolensky and Ratajczak (*op. cit.*, p. 101), are forced to modify their Löschian model by arguing that the "advantages of water-transport and proximity to the transport net outside the region [country] shift the larger cities from the center of the region [country] to . . . points of the periphery . . ."

Theoretically, this procession of events, by distending the market and supply hinterlands of a limited number of port cities ["primary nodes"] and providing for the pirating of hinterlands from other urban places, contributes to locational variations in the rate at which the circular and cumulative growth process progresses. In other words, *each increment in the nodality of a center at the coastal terminus of a penetration line encourages expansion of its wholesaling-trading complex, soon elicits an initial multiplier, fulfillment of thresholds in other sectors of the economy, real estate speculation and construction, and still greater inducements to investment in wholesaling-trading activities, the result of which is population growth at the expense of nonterminus ports.* The interplay between the evolution of the transport network and urban-size growth also proves to be self-compounding, for

> As population increases in an area [hinterland of a mercantile city terminus], the demand for transportation is intensified; as new transport lines are built into the area, a greater population increase is encouraged [magnifying the market outlets and commodity sources of the terminus city], which in turn, calls for still more transportation.[127]

The magnitude of coastal shipping movements between the leading mercantile cities, which is really not taken into account by the Taafe-Morrill-Gould model, *would presumably parallel their respective population increments.* That is, commodity flows between pairs of major termini would be governed by some variant of the interactance hypothesis (P_1P_2/D), as well, of course, as by their complementarity, the ability of their hinterland specialities to absorb transportation costs, and their respective accessibility to the market as a whole (market potential).[128] Because increases in the coasting trade subsector of the wholesaling-trading complex would bring their own multipliers and rounds of growth, the chain reaction of population expansion initiated by improved interior connections would gather momentum and heighten

---

[127] *Ibid.,* p. 528. This is consistent with Ohlin's contention that the "improvement of transport relations through a local concentration of economic activity where they are already good tends to concentrate population and production [or trade] still further." Bertil Ohlin, *Interregional and International Trade* (Cambridge: Harvard University Press, 1933), p. 203. Also note related remarks by Dean, *op. cit.,* p. 41; and Smolensky and Ratajczak, *op. cit.,* p. 92.

[128] For related conceptual discussions see Edward L. Ullman, "The Role of Transportation and the Bases for Interaction," in William L. Thomas, Jr. (ed.), *Man's Role in Changing the Face of the Earth* (Chicago: The University of Chicago Press, 1956), pp. 862–880; and Allan Pred, "Toward a Typology of Manufacturing Flows," *Geographical Review,* Vol. 54 (1964), pp. 65–84.

growth-rate discrepancies between the principal mercantile cities and the lesser ports. As coastal trading routes (such as those between New York and the South and between Boston and the coastal settlements of Maine and the Canadian Maritime Provinces) tend to solidify and embed themselves, they would bring a similar train of consequences, channeling traffic and stimulating urban population growth in much the same fashion as major lines of penetration — a condition whose ramifications should not be minimized in view of the tremendous importance of the coasting trade in the pre-Civil War decades.

The reference in the Taafe-Morrill-Gould model to the reduction of hinterland transportation costs for a few selected ports following the emergence of major routes of penetration is conspicuously applicable to the United States in the early nineteenth century. "Previous to the construction of the [Erie] canal, the cost of transportation from Lake Erie to tide-water was such as nearly to prevent all movement of merchandise."[129] In the more general case, inland waterway freight rates fell from eight cents per ton-mile on the abbreviated river routes of the pre-Canal era, to five cents per ton-mile by 1840. Cheaper transport outlays to and from the major ports were also made possible by freight-mileage and time-in-transit reductions. For example, after completion of the Ohio Canal from Cleveland to Portsmouth in 1832, the freighting distance from New York to Louisville was lowered to approximately 1,000 miles, or over 500 miles shorter than demanded by the pre-Erie Canal route.

The disconnected, uncoordinated railroad fragments constructed during the thirties, and radiating outward from Baltimore, Philadelphia, Boston, and the Jersey shore opposite Manhattan (Map 4.3), were so late in origin, and carried so little traffic, that their 1840 significance ought not be viewed as anything more than that of secondary reinforcing stimuli to the circular and cumulative growth of centers already favored by superior inland waterway, coastal shipping, and turnpike systems. (This statement might be qualified for Baltimore, whose completed portion of the B&O Railroad carried 54,573 tons eastward and 45,878 tons westward in 1839.)[130] The discriminatory influence of the

[129] Andrews, *op. cit.*, p. 278.
[130] Milton Reizenstein, "The Economic History of the Baltimore and Ohio Railroad," *Johns Hopkins University Studies in Historical and Political Science*, Vol. 15 (1897), p. 361. Approximately 80 per cent of the eastward bound freight (mostly flour) terminated in Baltimore. The 1839 volume of traffic, which had grown from 5,931 tons in 1831, was not matched again until 1844.

192   AMERICAN MERCANTILE CITY

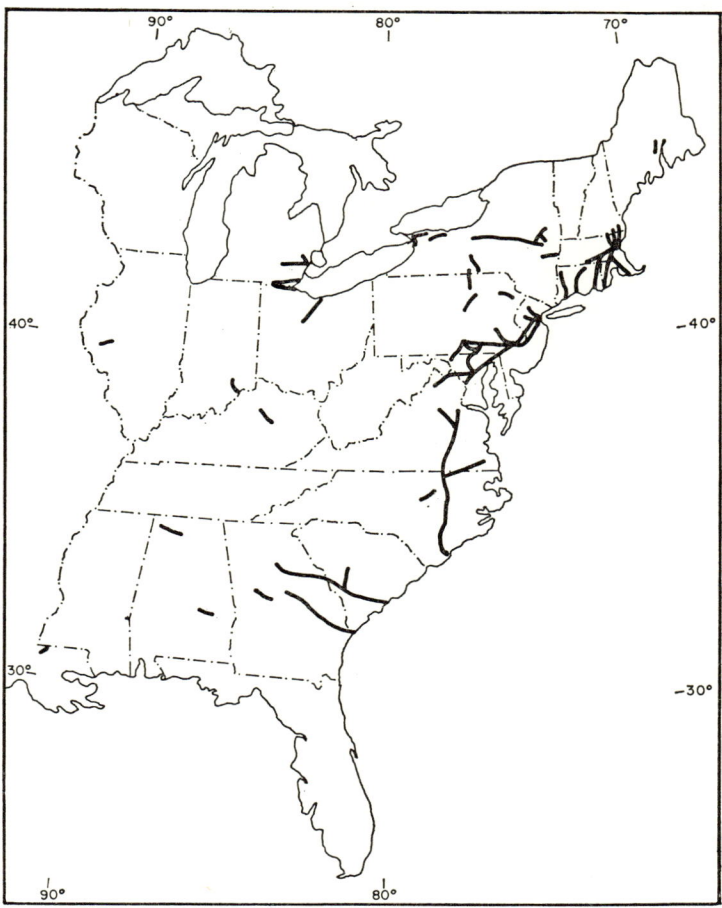

MAP 4.3   Railroads operating in 1840.

immature railroads was discernible to at least one contemporary, who wrote: "The effect of railroads, . . . is to stimulate the growth of towns, and especially of large towns."[131]

Any consideration of transport and route developments cannot close without some allusion to the role of site and situation. The outmoded, but perhaps overly suppressed, environmental determinists were prone to explain the distribution and development of urban settlement along

[131] George Tucker, *Progress of the United States in Population and Wealth* (New York: Press of Hunt's Merchants Magazine, 1843), p. 134.

the Atlantic Seaboard "largely by reason of waterway facilities,"[132] physical barriers, and site qualities (depth of harbor, protection from wind and sea, etc.). It may well be that future transportation patterns were dictated by the presence of superior locations on Chesapeake Bay, and on the Hudson and Delaware rivers; that Charleston suffered both from the absence of a river connection with the Piedmont, and from physical obstacles to the operation of the ill-fated Santee Canal;[133] and that the hazards of Ocracoke Bar strangulated the commercial aspirations of New Bern, North Carolina. But: "Geographic superiority relative to other points [only] furnishes a potentiality, ..."[134] A port city such as Norfolk, possessor of a fine harbor, near the gateway to Chesapeake Bay, blessed with an enviable central position for the coasting trade, master of the James-Kanawha route to the interior, and endowed totally, in the opinion of some, "with advantages second only to those of New York,"[135] *did not* blossom during the 1800–1840 era. In short, site and situation cannot of themselves clarify urban expansion and are unsuited to identifying the *processes* that underlie the selective growth of cities.

Relative Accessibility and Other Selective Growth Factors

Relative accessibility, or the accessibility of a city to the population or market of the country as a whole, is one step removed from site and situation in its influence upon selective urban growth. In fact, if one chose to go beyond concrete hinterland criteria, the population and/or market potential (accessibility) attributes of a given place could be included in its situational dossier. Whatever the choice, *transport and route developments tend to work more to the advantage of points with high accessibility as contrasted to points with low accessibility.* Again, this stems partly from definition, for the lower the accessibility of an area, the lower its aggregate population, income, and output, and the more dispersed its market outlets and commodity sources for mercantile cities. Furthermore, in serving a regional market of given sales volume

[132] Ellen Churchill Semple, *American History and its Geographical Conditions* (Boston: Houghton Mifflin Company, 1903), p. 252.
[133] For greater details on this theme, see Ulrich Bonnell Phillips, *A History of Transportation in the Eastern Cotton Belt to 1880* (New York: Columbia University Press, 1908).
[134] Dean, *op. cit.*, p. 38.
[135] Albion, *op. cit.*, p. 375.

or in assembling a given quantity of hinterland production for coastal or foreign distribution, the low-accessibility mercantile cities would almost certainly have longer average shipments, and proportionately greater allocations for transport, than rival high-accessibility cities.

In this light, the early nineteenth-century growth of Boston becomes somewhat clearer, despite the meager geographical extent of its hinterland in comparison with those of New York, Philadelphia, Baltimore, and some of the lesser Southern ports. Boston, its lopsided location to the contrary, had an accessibility to population not far below that of New York, and far in excess of sputtering Southern cities (Map 4.1). If, in accordance with Boston's down-East trade, the Canadian Maritime Provinces were included in the calculations of population potential, then the city's accessibility to population would be realistically augmented and its expansion made more logical.

Behavioral variables and tradition were also responsible for geographic variations in the urban-size growth process. Rubin has demonstrated effectively that dissimilar collective responses to the Erie Canal by merchants in Philadelphia, Baltimore, and Boston can be traced to "divergencies in the history and traditions of the three regions which produced differences in the attitudes that the decision-making groups brought to the common problem." More specifically, these differences in attitude toward uncertainty and delay "most account for . . . [the] remarkable differences in behavior" in choosing between canal and railroad projects, and between immediate action and procrastination.[136] If the relative lethargy of Philadelphia merchants contrasted with the aggressiveness and assiduity of their Baltimore counterparts, then, by extension, it is easily contended that local entrepreneurial values and attitudes elsewhere caused more drastic slowdowns in the orderly march of investments, multipliers, new threshold levels, earnings, and more investments. Unquestionably, the rise of Southern ports was to some degree inhibited by: the individualism and conservatism operating against joint undertakings and new investments; the presence of "little desire to possess a carrying trade";[137] the disinterest that permitted the abandonment of coastal and foreign exports of cotton and other products to nonlocal agents; and the tradition of directing savings into slaveholding.[138] (In 1840, when human bondage did not exist in New York,

---

[136] Rubin, *op. cit.*, p. 9.
[137] Phillips, *op. cit.*, p. 1.
[138] For comments on the growth-retarding effects of investment in slaves see

Boston, or Philadelphia, and when 3.1 per cent of Baltimore's inhabitants were enslaved, the percentage of the local population accounted for by slaves was 34.0 in Norfolk, 41.7 in Savannah, and 53.6 in Charleston.)[139] The negative effect of large-scale slaveholding upon the growth rate of Southern ports was made two pronged by the negligible purchasing power of the slave population; i.e., their numbers could not make the normal contribution to threshold fulfillments and thereby retarded the entire circular and cumulative process.

Last, and by no means least, the accumulation of agglomeration (localization and urbanization) economies for the wholesaling-trading complexes of the leading mercantile cities hastened the relative decline of smaller rival ports. The greater variety of middlemen and higher frequency of auctions associated with the widening rainbow of mercantile establishments in the largest centers were not alone responsible for increasing the attraction exerted upon foreigners and hinterland dwellers who might otherwise have opted for lesser coastal cities when seeking a market outlet or purchasing source. Extension of credit, reduction of risk, and other services attainable from banking and insurance institutions augmented the lure of the major ports, and also encouraged hinterland aggrandizement (selective urban growth) because these identical services could not mature fully where the aggregate scale of wholesaling and trading activities was relatively small. Localization economies of this type proved self-enlarging by acting simultaneously as external economies for hinterland production,[140] consequently yielding a greater volume of commodities to be channeled through the economy-providing mercantile city, and ultimately stimulating additional agglomeration benefits. One of the forms agglomeration economies presumably took following the augmentation of market and supply areas was a greater division of labor on the waterfront and the division of fixed waterfront maintenance and improvement costs over an increased volume of trade. To sum, in other words, *the agglomeration economies arising from*

John E. Moes, "The Absorption of Capital in Slave Labor in the Ante-Bellum South and Economic Growth," *American Journal of Economics and Sociology*, Vol. 20 (Oct. 1961), pp. 535–541; and Alfred H. Conrad and John R. Meyer, *The Economics of Slavery and Other Studies in Econometric History* (Chicago: Aldine Publishing Company, 1964). The reservations of Conrad and Meyer would not seem to hold for an urban environment.

[139] *Sixth Census or Enumeration of the Inhabitants of the United States* (Washington, D. C.: 1841).

[140] North has emphasized "the role of the nodal center in providing external economies for the export industries" of its hinterland. North, *op. cit.*, p. 257.

increases in the scale and array of the mercantile functions of a few cities favored the propagation of fresh agglomeration economies, further expansion of the wholesaling-trading complex, and, through the mechanism of hinterland usurpation, arrested the development of less diversified and inefficient ports.

The Intraurban Location of Manufacturing

Until this juncture in all three essays, the changing internal geography of the city has been forced to play second fiddle to the growth of the city as a point in space. But, as was remarked in the introduction, it is quite plain that as cities grow in population, acquiring new functions and expanding old activities, their physical extent and internal arrangement undergo transformation and metamorphosis. The following treatment of alterations in the spatial organization of the mercantile city is not meant to be exhaustive, but instead to point to the possibilities of gaining a fuller understanding of the complex interrelationships between nineteenth- and early twentieth-century urban-size growth, the dynamics of urban morphology, and, by extension, the present-day configuration of central cities.

The mercantile city was an extremely compact entity. In 1840, the area occupied by the developed portions of Philadelphia[141] and Baltimore did not exceed ten square miles; the built-up area of Boston was confined within a two-mile radius from City Hall; and New York's 312,000 souls occupied scarcely one-fourth of Manhattan and were for the most part compressed within the area south of 14th Street (Maps 4.4 and 4.5).[142] In some quarters, residential population densities approached or exceeded those encountered in modern high-rise housing projects. Source materials pertaining to New York capture some of the disorder juxtaposed with congestion: the odorous, overcrowded wooden piers — jammed with carts, drays, and wheelbarrows, with sailors, merchants, clerks, laborers, and carters — decaying and sagging amidst the *"pépinière de navires"* or "forest of masts"; or the dirty, squalid streets,

[141] Including the residential areas of the immediately contiguous suburbs of the Northern Liberties, Kensington, Spring Garden, Southwark, and Moyamensing.

[142] In 1845, Manhattan still contained over 4,000 acres of improved farmland. Most of this land was either devoted to the raising of potatoes, corn, and oats, or to the pasturing of over 7,100 dairy cattle. *Census for the State of New York, for 1845* (Albany: 1846).

trafficked by scampering pigs, and flanked by hastily erected, frequently flimsy, wooden structures of two to six stories that contrasted starkly with the attractive brick residences of the small fashionable areas proximate to the Battery and Washington Square.[143]

Despite the superficial prevalence of chaos, all evidence indicates that the morphology of the mercantile city was already characterized by "discrete districts segregated by function."[144] Because some spatial order existed in the mercantile city, it may be assumed that land costs, stage of transportation, "communication economies," and interindustry linkages had begun to exert some influence on the intraurban location of manufacturing. However, it is only through investigating and interpreting the patterns of specific representative industries that the validity of these assumptions may be verified, and that other locational forces may be identified. Consequently, the subsequent pages are devoted to an exploration of the shipbuilding, printing and publishing, and baking industries of New York City between 1800 and 1840.

Shipbuilding in New York

Although shipbuilding in New York probably dates back to 1614, it was not until the termination of the eighteenth century that the city began to emerge as a vessel construction center of some consequence. Because shipbuilding is a capital-goods industry, output thereafter fluctuated with the parade of booms, recessions, and depressions. But four or five decades, later, the "east River represented the greatest concentration of shipbuilding activity in the country [Table 4.6]," and in design, materials, and workmanship, the products of New York "could scarcely be equalled in the world."[145] However, in spite of the scope of production of ships, brigs, schooners, sloops, steamers, tugs, and canal boats, the industry in 1840 remained essentially a highly competitive handicraft nearly devoid of opportunities for scale economies.

Critical to the intraurban distribution of shipbuilding was the fact that shipyards were comparatively extensive consumers of water-front

[143] For greater detail see the text and massive collection of lithographic sources in I. N. Phelps Stokes, *The Iconography of Manhattan Island* (New York: Robert H. Dodd, 1918), Vols. 1 and 3; and the collection of primary written materials in Bayrd Still, *Mirror for Gotham* (New York: New York University Press, 1956).

[144] James E. Vance, Jr., "Labor-Shed, Employment Field, and Dynamic Analysis in Urban Geography," *Economic Geography*, Vol. 36 (1960), p. 192.

[145] Albion, *op. cit.*, p. 287.

198   AMERICAN MERCANTILE CITY

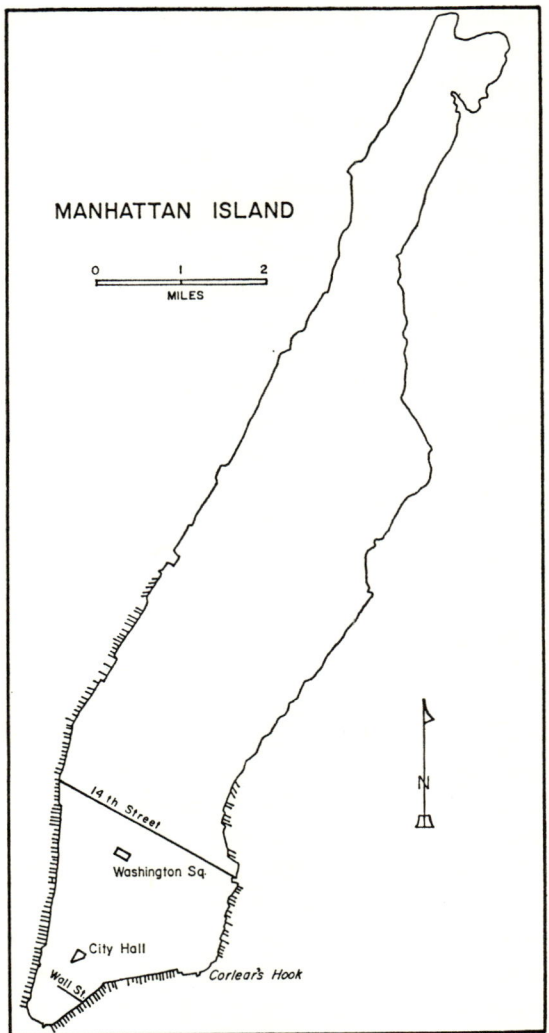

MAP 4.4   Contemporary reference map for Map 4.5.

space, with moderately sized firms occupying at least 140,000 square feet.[146] An extensive land user of this kind was incapable of competing for the expensive acreage of the northward-expanding business district and its hectic waterfront; and so it was that New York's shipyards constantly migrated toward the periphery of the built-up area, initially

[146] Bishop, *op. cit.*, p. 143.

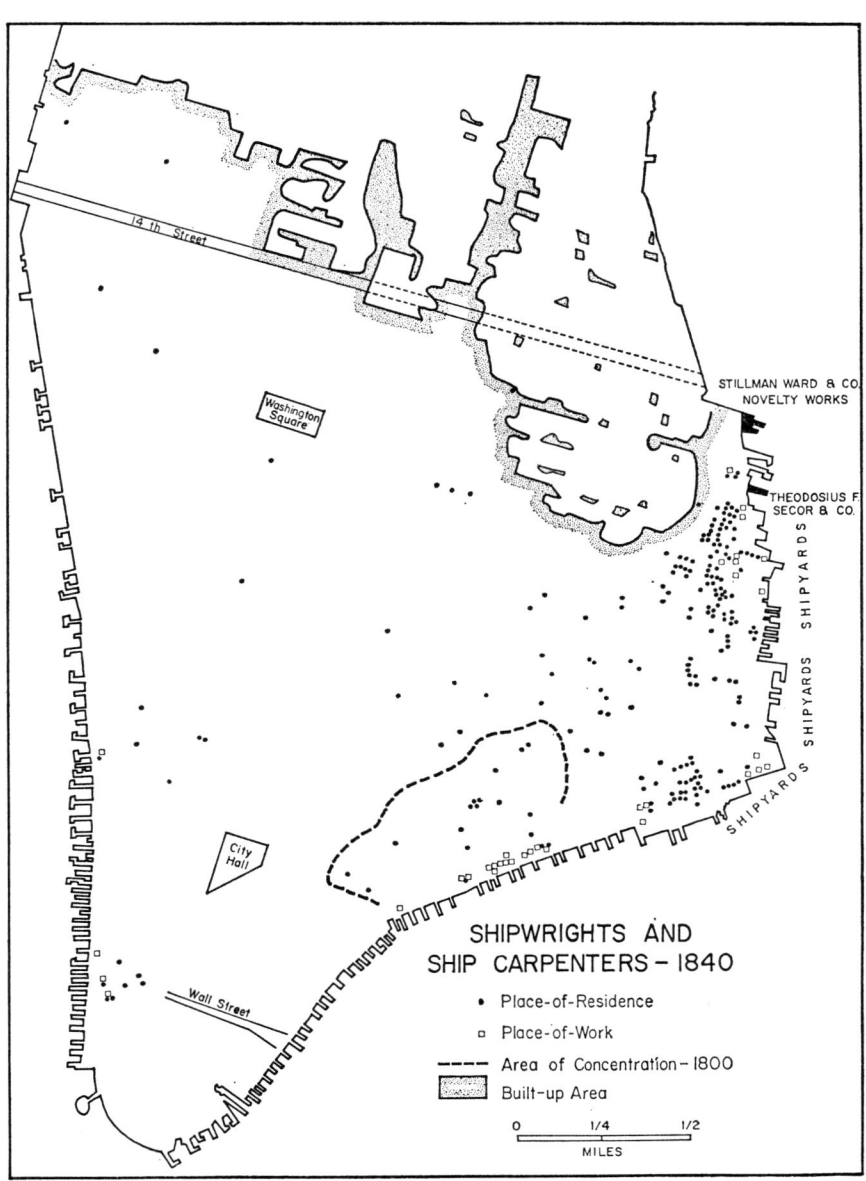

MAP 4.5 The location of New York's shipwrights and ship carpenters in 1840. The delineated area of concentration for 1800 encompasses approximately 87 per cent of the city's known shipwrights and ship carpenters at that date. The area to the east of the 1800 area of concentration was filled subsequent to the turn of the century. For comments on the completeness of this and all ensuing figures see footnote 56 and Table 4.8. Base map constructed from J. Calvin Smith's *Map of the City of New York* (New York: Tanner and Disturnell, 1840).

concentrating three-quarters of a mile north of Wall Street, shifting shortly after 1800 to Corlear's Hook, and by the 1830's focusing on the scant mile separating Corlear's Hook and the then-popular bathing beach north of Twelfth Street (Maps 4.4 and 4.5).[147] Land values at the margins of the business district are known to have increased thirtyfold within a score of years,[148] eventually becoming so formidable that wealthy mercantile families as well as the shipyards were forced to migrate uptown.[149] Ultimately, the oppressive cost of land combined with high wage scales, increases in raw-material costs, and a changeover to iron-hulled vessels to drive shipbuilding out of Manhattan after the Civil War.[150]

Localization economies and interindustry linkages were instrumental in the intraurban clustering of New York shipbuilding throughout the period 1800–1840. Production demands at most of the yards were sporadic and, of necessity, individual shipbuilders maintained a flexible working force consisting of permanent hands and individuals from a small floating army of craftsmen.[151] As this shipyard labor force was comprised of a variety of specialized artisans — shipwrights, ship carpenters, shipjoiners, riggers, caulkers, shipsmiths, painters, glaziers,

---

[147] The area of shipbuilding concentration in 1800 was adjacent to the residential cluster of shipwrights and ship carpenters outlined in Map 4.5. The artisans still employed in the old nucleus in 1840 were generally involved in ship repairing rather than ship construction. The 1840 place-of-residence and place-of-work data plotted in Map 4.5 are based on *Longworth's American Almanac, New-York Register, and City Directory, and therefore are incomplete* (see footnote 56).

[148] John Lambert, *Travels through Canada, and the United States of North America* (London: Baldwin, Cradock, and Joy, 1816), Vol. 2, p. 55. Also note the earlier cited statistics on Manhattan's land values between 1823 and 1836.

[149] Population in the Second Ward (which ran from the East River to Broadway, and included large portions of Pearl Street and other major commercial thoroughfares) declined from a peak of 9,315 in 1825, to 6,394 in 1840. In like fashion, the First Ward (encompassing Wall Street and the Battery) lost almost 1,500 inhabitants between 1820 and 1840. See table in Robert Ernst, *Immigrant Life in New York City 1825–1863* (New York: King's Crown Press, 1949), p. 191.

[150] For greater elaboration and details concerning the intraurban shifts of specific yards, see John H. Morrison, *History of New York Shipyards* (New York: Wm. F. Sametz & Co., 1909); and Henry Hall, "Report on the Shipbuilding Industry of the United States," in *Report of the Tenth Census* (Washington, D. C.: 1884), Vol. 8, pp. 115–116.

[151] Many of those who drifted from yard to yard, spending no more than a few days on each job, were "journeymen who had completed their apprenticeship and were learning the techniques of the various master craftsmen." *Ibid.*, p. 82, and Albion, *op. cit.*, p. 302.

sawyers, etc. — whose daily mobility was minimized by the stage of urban transportation, it was almost inevitable that employers and employees should nucleate in a restricted section where day-to-day adjustments could be carried out efficiently. The so-called "Dry Dock" quarters, stretching from Corlear's Hook to Twelfth Street, and inland as far as Avenue C (about one-quarter of a mile from the East River), developed as just such an agglomeration of shipyards with their complement of laborers and newly arrived artisan migrants from smaller ports.

The "Dry Dock" section was also the scene of numerous intermeshing industrial activities that were intricately linked with shipbuilding itself.[152] Only the larger yards incorporated mastmaking and sailmaking into their operations, and consequently there were a number of independent sail lofts and spar-making establishments located in the area. The construction of engines and other machinery was the province of self-governed "iron works," and some of these firms, such as the Stillman Ward & Co. Novelty Works and Theodosius F. Secor & Co. were as conspicuous on the waterfront as the shipyards themselves (Map 4.5), and eventually provided thousands of jobs.[153] Coppersmiths and brassfounders operated workshops whose entire output of fastenings, fittings, and sheathing was destined for the shipyards; steam-driven sawmills, whose maintenance was beyond the capital resources of individual shipbuilders, provided considerable labor economies to a large segment of the vessel-building community; and, at least one "Dry Dock" canvas manufacturer attempted to compete with the cotton duck of nearby Paterson (which by 1840 was the world's leading producer of that fabric). In addition, there were pump and blockmakers, manufacturers of tools for shipwrights and ship carpenters, and fabricators of lifeboats, capstans, and windlasses.[154]

The variety of goods and services provided by this array of ancillary manufacturing made it almost obligatory for individual shipyard entrepreneurs to locate within their proximity, and this condition in turn

[152] When Manhattan shipbuilding experienced an upswing in 1831, the press was moved to wax enthusiastic, "The change is felt in thousands of workshops in this vast metropolis." *Niles' Weekly Register,* Vol. 41 (Sept. 10, 1831), pp. 18–19.

[153] In 1847, just prior to New York's last great shipbuilding boom, approximately 3,400 people were employed in the four principal iron works of the "Dry Dock" (Albion, *op. cit.,* p. 151). Much of this employment was attributable to the unspecialized production of machine tools, sugar refining machinery, and other items.

[154] *Longworth's American Almanac, New-York Register, and City Directory,* 1840, *op. cit.*

reinforced the tendency of the entire shipbuilding industry to concentrate on a small portion of the waterfront.[155] Expressed alternatively, any shipbuilding (as opposed to ship-repairing) firm that chose to locate outside the "Dry Dock" would have been confronted with considerable diseconomies arising from the difficulties of assembling inputs and making daily labor-supply adjustments.

Finally, physical rather than economic conditions explain the shipbuilding industry's preference for the East River over the North (Hudson) River. Minutes from an 1813 meeting of the city's Common Council indicate that it was "much more hazardous to Vessels to lie at Wharves in the winter at the North, than the East Side."[156] Year-round construction activity was impeded on the Hudson waterfront because its gale winds, tides, and floating ice were highly troublesome to the relatively slight vessels of the early nineteenth century.

The Printing and Publishing Trades of New York

The first four decades of the nineteenth century saw a rapid growth of New York's printing and publishing that paralleled its commercial and demographic expansion. Growth took place in the form of increased employment (over 2,000 by 1840), and increased productivity. The latter was made possible by technical innovations and a greater specialization of production units. During this brief period in New York,

> The lever was substituted for the screw to secure the necessary pressure whereby 250 impressions an hour became possible in place of fifty before; presses were made of iron instead of wood, and it was possible to print a sheet three times as large as before with no increase of labor; composition rollers were substituted for balls to spread the ink upon the type; and, . . . the revolving impression cylinder was substituted for the platen, whereby 1,000 impressions per hour became possible with a single cylinder and 2,000 with two cylinders.[157]

In addition, New York was the scene of the first application of steam power to a newspaper press (1835), and of the invention of the type-

---

[155] Interindustry linkages were also responsible for the nucleating of local-market and entrepôt leather trades. There was a high degree of spatial association between Manhattan's tanners, curriers, and patent leather and morocco workers, and her abounding numbers of boot- and shoemakers, trunk makers, pocketbook makers, and harness makers.

[156] *Minutes of the Common Council of the City of New York 1784–1831* (New York: 1917), Vol. 7, May 24, 1813, p. 478.

[157] Weber, *op. cit.,* p. 168.

casting machine (1838). The precipitous expansion of the daily press, which increased its circulation from less than 9,000 in 1808 to 87,000 in 1840,[158] and the multiplying volume of commercial and legal printing was also facilitated by a division of labor in which inkmaking, binding, engraving, typefounding, stereotyping, and lithographic operations were frequently transferred from partially integrated workshops to self-contained establishments.

Despite this tremendous growth and reorganization, the printing and publishing trades, in contrast to the shipbuilding industry, remained locationally stable (Map 4.6). The capability of the industry to remain highly concentrated and anchored in the emerging business district from 1800 to 1840 is ascribable essentially to three elementary conditions. First, it is commonplace knowledge that the printing and publishing trades are extremely intensive utilizers of space, and are therefore not affected adversely by the spiraling land costs of a growing business district. Second, the industry has traditionally nucleated in the commercial core of American cities in order to realize "communication economies," or external economies that are the consequence of personal confrontations between producer and consumer prior to the actual process of manufacturing.[159] Last, because job printing is characterized by periodic and ephemeral demand, success is often dependent upon propinquity to the market, and the market of New York was composed basically of the mercantile, financial, legal, and municipal government functions sandwiched between Wall Street and City Hall.

The very magnitude of New York's printing and publishing encouraged the development of at least one interindustrial linkage. This associated industry, the manufacture of printing presses and other printing equipment, had at least one establishment that was too extensive a user of land to tolerate the high rents of the district proximate to Wall Street. The largest of the firms in this industry, R. H. Hoe & Co., Inc., began producing in 1805, and by 1847 was the world's chief manufacturer of newspaper presses. Hoe & Co. maintained its offices on Gold

[158] Chauncey M. Depew, *One Hundred Years of American Commerce 1795–1895* (New York: D. O. Haynes and Co., 1895), Vol. 1, p. 317.

[159] The term "communication-oriented" was first used in reference to New York City's printing trades by Edgar M. Hoover and Raymond Vernon in *Anatomy of a Metropolis* (Cambridge: Harvard University Press, 1959), pp. 62–73. However, the concept has long been familiar to students of New York manufacturing. For example, see Edward Ewing Pratt, *Industrial Causes of Congestion of Population in New York City* (New York: Columbia University Studies in History, Economics and Public Law, 1911), pp. 76 and 94.

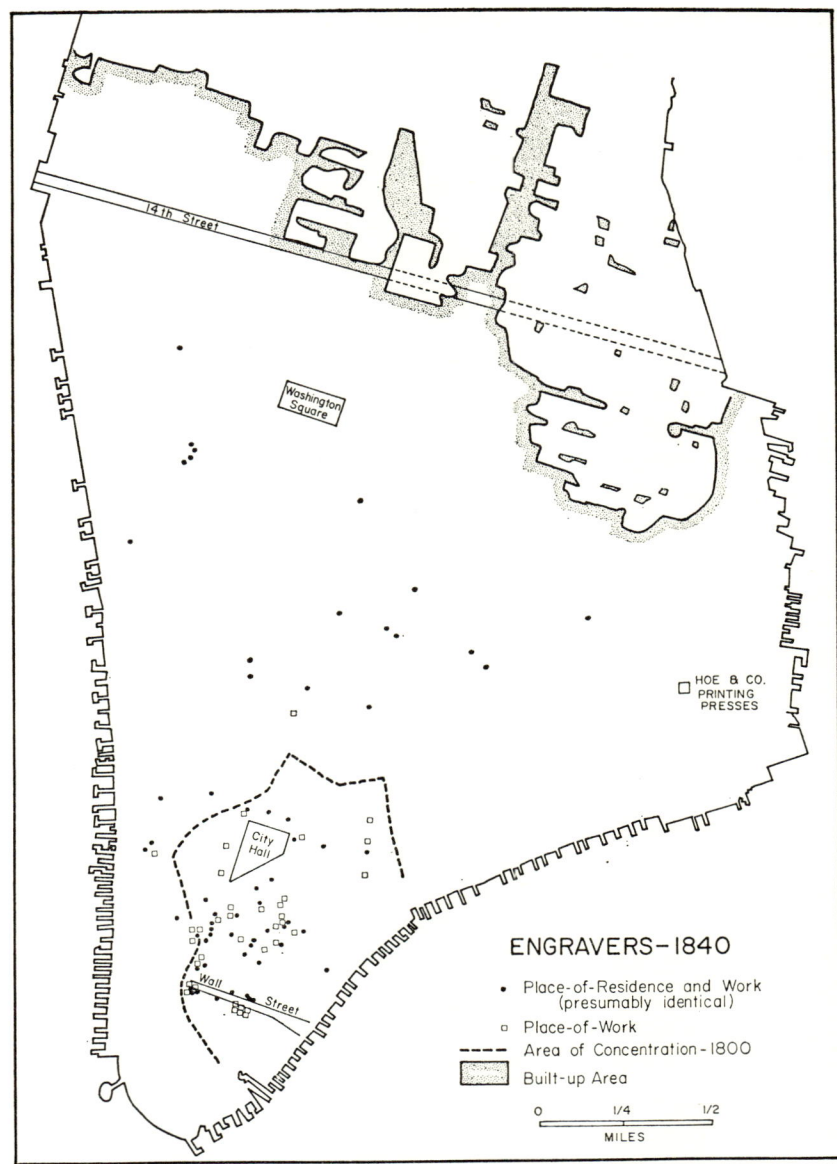

MAP 4.6 The 1840 location of engravers in New York. The delimited area of concentration for 1800 encompasses approximately 96 per cent of those known to have been employed in *all* printing trades at that date. Once again, the area to the east of the 1800 area of concentration was filled in the years intervening between 1800 and 1840.

Street in the heart of the business district, but its plant, or knot of integrated workshops, was on the margins of the "Dry Dock" area (Map 4.6).

Baking in New York

The scattered pattern of New York's bakeries in 1840 (Map 4.7), is at one and the same time a reflection of the stage of transportation, the state of technology, and the dynamic applications of central place theory.

It has always been imperative for profit-making bread retailing establishments to locate within the range or maximum journey-to-shop distance of their threshold population. The baking technology of the early nineteenth century precluded factory production, and, simultaneously, the highly perishable nature of bread, and the fact that it is bulkier than its constituent raw materials, necessitated short-distance product movements and a unification of bread retailing and manufacturing establishments. Thus, the intraurban location of baked goods production in 1840 was a function of the journey-to-shop. Inasmuch as the journey-to-shop was usually a pedestrian journey, there was little locational choice for the typical one-man, one-oven bakery, and a dispersed distribution resulted. Of course, the form of the journey-to-shop did not have the same effect on the location of all establishments that combined manufacturing and retailing functions. On the contrary, the workshop-stores of industries with luxury and speciality products had a proclivity to cluster because of their high thresholds and the preference of consumers to shop for such goods before purchasing (e.g., by 1820, or earlier, New York's Greenwich Street was lined with cabinetmaking and furniture shops).

The tendency toward dispersion was reinforced by the baker's need to market his products as goods of extreme convenience, in order to overcome the stiff competition offered by household baking.[160] In an attempt to counteract this competition, New York bakers made it a common practice to offer home delivery and to have peddlers hawk their output on the streets.[161] The almost uniform intraurban distribution of

---

[160] It has been maintained that "most bread baking was a home activity" in the midnineteenth century urban centers of the United States. See William G. Panschar, *Baking in America — Economic Development* (Evanston: Northwestern University Press, 1956), Vol. 1, p. 34.

[161] R. S. Guernsey, *New York City and Vicinity during the War of 1812–'15* (New York: Charles L. Woodward, 1889), Vol. 1, p. 47.

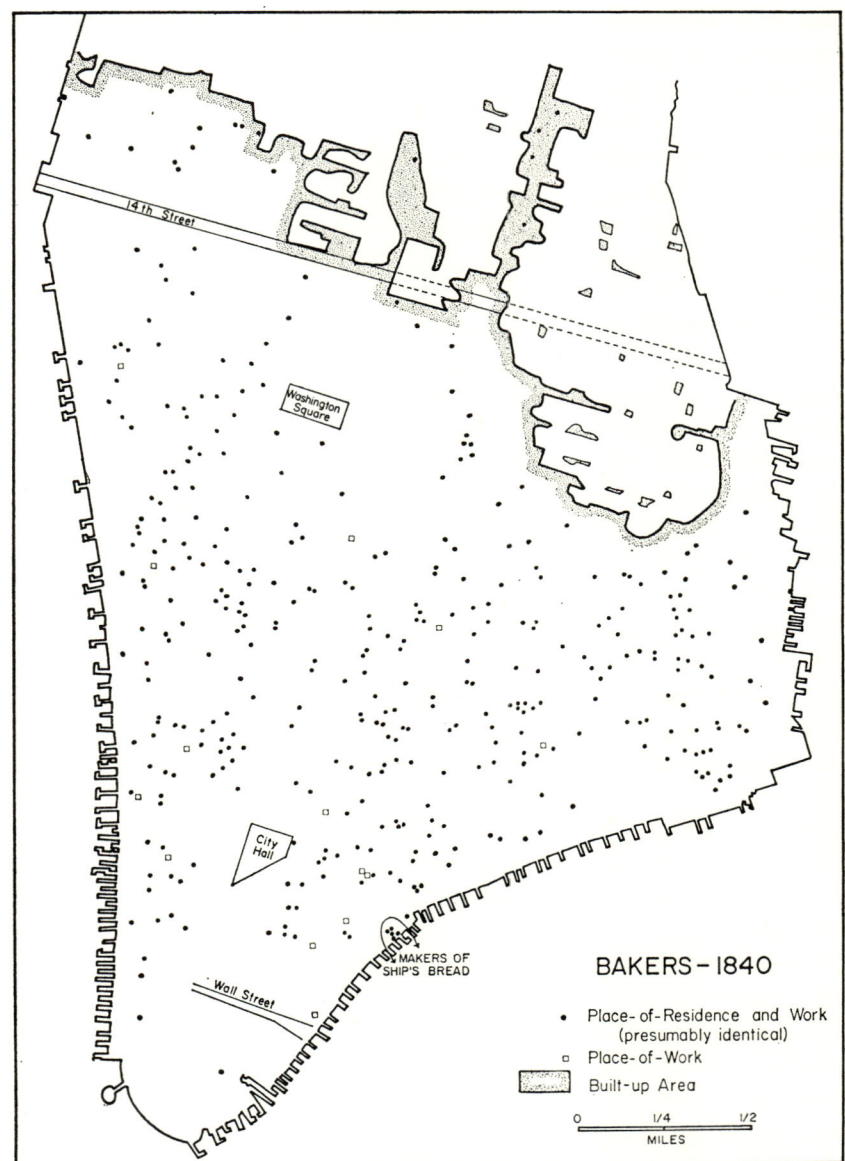

MAP 4.7 The 1840 location of bakers in New York.

baked goods manufacture could only be somewhat modified in the future when increases of consumer range were facilitated by changes in the prevailing mode of urban circulation, when factory production became feasible, and when wage levels and the general standard of living had been improved.

In contrast to the pattern of domestically consumed bakery products, the few shops fashioning ship's bread were extremely concentrated (Map 4.7). Scattering was unnecessary because ship's bread was a durable biscuit or cracker product, involving "little more than the baking of a flour and water mixture without the attendant problems of fermentation and perishability."[162] Also, because the product had a specialized water-front market, the most logical system of distribution for the producer was clustered wholesaling rather than diffused retailing.

The Journey-to-Work

The influence of the stage of transportation upon journey-to-work patterns is inseparable from the question of intraurban industrial location in the mercantile city. Plants, workshops, and shipyards were forced to remain in the heavily built-up area of cities as long as the stage of transportation limited the distance that could separate place-of-work from place-of-residence. As urban transportation facilities improved, the labor-shed, or area from which an establishment could draw its working force, was enlarged and the intraurban locational mobility of manufacturing was enhanced.[163]

As late as 1840, most of New York's industrial workers, being handicraft artisans, had a place-of-work that was identical with, or in close proximity to, their place-of-residence.[164] Lowly paid tailors, journeyman shoemakers,[165] milliners, and piecework dressmakers were by no means

[162] Panschar, *op. cit.*, p. 29.

[163] See Vance, *op. cit.*, pp. 200–205, for a descriptive model of the process through which the labor-shed and the employment field, or area to which laborers from a given locale disperse, are expanded with advances in the stage of urban transportation. Also note Allan Pred, "The Intrametropolitan Location of American Manufacturing," *Annals of the Association of American Geographers*, Vol. 54 (1964), pp. 165–180; and Kate K. Liepmann, *The Journey to Work* (New York: Oxford University Press, 1944), especially pp. 1–11.

[164] Circumstances were no different in the other mercantile cities. In Boston, as of 1845, the majority of industrial workers labored in their homes or toiled in small neighborhood workshops. Handlin, *op. cit.*, p. 10. In the Philadelphia area, the number of weavers working in their homes alone totaled 1,500 in 1827. Bishop, *op. cit.*, Vol. 3, pp. 316–317.

[165] A journalist in the New York *Daily Tribune* (Sept. 9, 1845), reported:
We have been in more than fifty cellers . . . , each inhabited by a shoemaker and his family. The floor is made of rough plank laid loosely down, the ceiling is not quite so high as a tall man. . . . In this . . . often live the man

the only individuals who slept and earned a living in the same quarters. Even some of the most prosperous members of the nonindustrial mercantile class still preferred to utilize their homes for business purposes, or, at least, to dwell within walking distance of their offices. Long working hours and the stage of urban transportation militated against a lengthy journey-to-work, and on occasion the employer was forced to assuage the conflict between housing availability and journey-to-work restrictions by providing a room for his employee above or behind the workshop. In at least one instance, a shipyard owner took the extreme measure of erecting a "hotel" to accommodate his shipwrights and apprentices.[166]

However, significant alterations in the propensity to commute and in the average length of commutation did occur during the forty years that elapsed subsequent to 1800. Local passenger transportation was nonexistent in New York at the turn of the century, although private hackney coaches had been introduced in 1786.[167] In the absence of any cheap service on prescribed routes, it appears that a journey-to-work was highly exceptional and that virtually nobody divorced his place-of-work from his place-of-residence by more than a mile (Table 4.8). Moreover, among the extremely small number of commuters, there were few who ventured more than a quarter of a mile. Predictably, in the era of handicraft manufacturing, most pedestrian commutation was oriented toward the shipyards, cooperages, and sugar refineries that were within a block or two of the waterfront (Map 4.8).

Although most commuters continued to walk to work in 1840, the narrow spectrum of journey-to-work patterns had been broadened slowly by: the inauguration of regular service by a twelve-passenger vehicle on Broadway in 1827; the introduction of the larger omnibus in 1831; the inception of faster, more efficient operations on the horse-drawn New York and Harlem Railroad in 1832; the intensification of ferry traffic between Manhattan and Brooklyn;[168] and the multiplication

---

with his work-bench, his wife and five or six children of all ages, and perhaps a palsied grandfather or grandmother and often both.
Cited in Ernst, *op. cit.*, p. 79.

[166] G. W. Sheldon, "The Old Ship-Builders of New York," *Harper's Magazine*, Vol. 65 (1882), p. 234.

[167] Stokes, *op. cit.*, Vol. 1, p. 373.

[168] By 1838 there were 15 ferries making daily crossings between Manhattan and Brooklyn and Williamsburg. There were also ferries in operation to Staten Island, Jersey City, and Hoboken. Woodbury, *op. cit.*, p. 98.

TABLE 4.8   Selected Journey-to-Work Data Pertaining to New York City: 1800 and 1840

	Miscellaneous occupations 1800	Machinists 1840	Bakers 1840	Printers 1840	Engravers 1840
Commuters	115	22	14	74	35
Total Known Employment	a	103	386	313	94
Commuters as a Percentage of Known Employment		21.4%	3.6%	23.6%	37.2%
Mean of Distance Traveled by Commuters (miles)[b]	.27	.33	.43	.66	.99
Journey-to-work Frequencies at Quarter-mile Intervals[b]					
0–.25 miles	74	10	8	15	5
.26–.50	22	8	2	14	4
.51–.75	11	2	1	11	7
.76–1.00	8	2	1	12	2
1.01–1.25			1	14	5
1.26–1.50				3	4
1.51–1.75			1	3	2
1.76–2.00				1	3
2.01–2.25				1	3

SOURCES: 1800 and 1840 editions of *Longworth's American Almanac, New-York Register, and City Directory, op. cit.* Longworth's 1800 directory may have approached 80 per cent coverage since it contained 10,200 entries at a time when the average household in New York contained approximately five members and the city's population barely surpassed 60,000. For comments regarding the thoroughness of the 1840 directory, see footnote 56.

[a] A figure for total employment is not given, as it did not prove possible to tally all the noncommuting industrial artisans listed in the 1800 directory.

[b] In order to maintain a consistent basis of comparison, distances between place-of-work and place-of-residence were determined on a straight line basis.

of omnibus routes running from Wall Street and the lower parts of the city toward the "Dry Dock" and 14th Street.[169] Out of these transportation developments there evolved further moderate increases in the relative importance of commuting and significant changes in the average length of the journey-to-work. It may be conservatively estimated that 23 per cent of New York's industrial workers were employed outside of

[169] In 1833 the omnibus companies were running 76 coaches. By 1845 there were no less than 12 omnibus lines, with 251 vehicles and 1,594 horses, operating on Manhattan. See *Niles' Weekly Register,* Vol. 45 (Sept. 21, 1833), p. 56; and *The Great Metropolis; or Guide to New-York for 1846, op. cit.,* pp. 114–115.

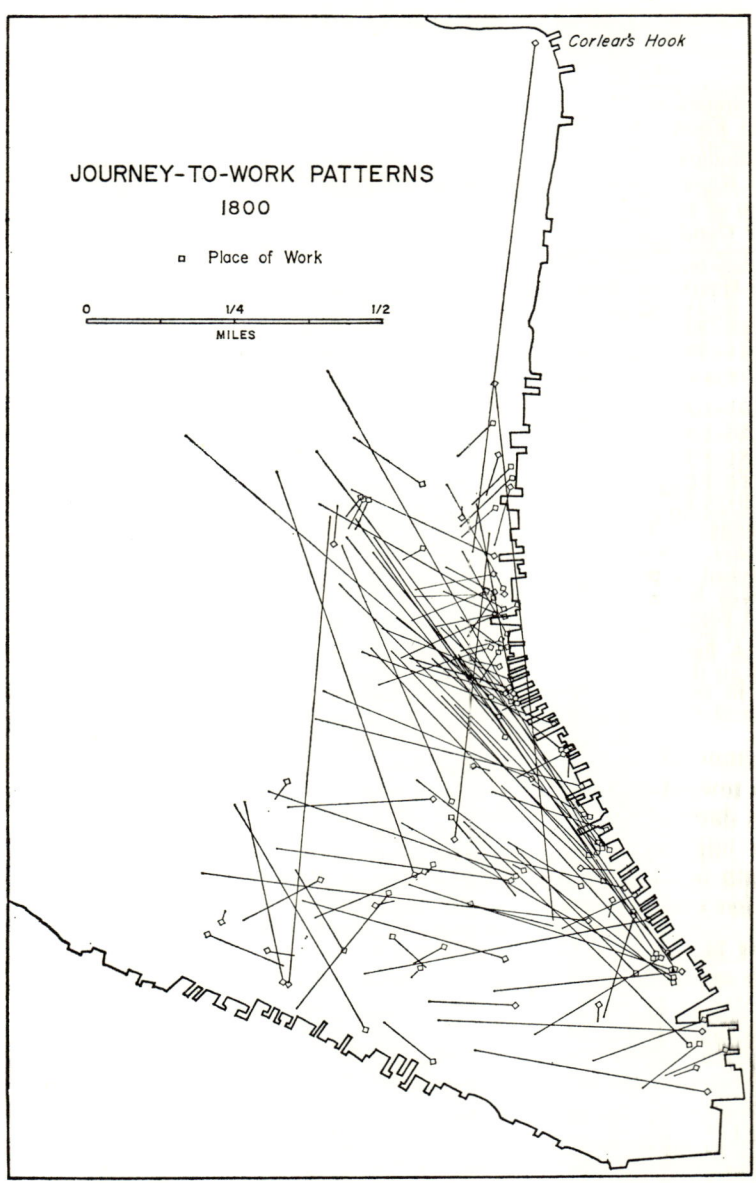

MAP 4.8 Known journey-to-work patterns in miscellaneous industrial occupations (New York, 1800). Base map constructed from the City Surveyor's *Plan of the City of New York* (November, 1803), and altered from other original maps in the archives of the New York Historical Society.

their homes in 1840;[170] and it is apparent from Table 4.8 that there were some people traversing over two miles in reaching their jobs. (The maximum length of the journey-to-work was bound by the operating speeds of the omnibuses and the horse-drawn railroad. Property owners in the core of the business district frequently petitioned the city regarding the congestion caused by the omnibuses,[171] whose crawl in that area probably did not reach two miles per hour. Even the more rapid railroad had difficulty in covering over five miles an hour under the best of conditions, and speeds in excess of that figure were prohibited by statute south of 14th Street.)[172] Admittedly, some of the increase in the propensity to commute may also have been attributable to the small but perceptible growth in importance of larger production units; but, the impact of transportation improvements on the mean length of the journey-to-work is less open to question because the longer journeys were consistently parallel with the north-south orientation of the omnibus routes and the New York and Harlem Railroad (e.g., see the pattern for engravers in Map 4.9).

In 1837, the daily volume of New York omnibus passenger traffic was about 25,000, largely comprised of merchants, and the use of this means of urban transport by others was presumably inhibited by the prevailing 12 and one-half cent one-way fare.[173] Taking the $1.75 per diem wage of the shipwright[174] as representative of the industrial

[170] The 1840 edition of Longworth's directory explicitly states that where they are not identical, work address and home address are listed sequentially. However, there is no way of determining how successful the compilers of the directory were in acquiring the information necessary to make dual entries. Nonetheless, the job types upon which the estimate is based account for over 2,500 entries in the 1840 directory.

[171] *Minutes of the Common Council of the City of New York 1784–1831, op. cit.*, Vol. 17 (March 31, 1828, and Feb. 9, 1829), pp. 80, 620, and Vol. 18 (May 11, 1829, June 1, 1829, and April 19, 1830), pp. 64, 107–108, 665.

[172] *Laws of the State of New York, 1832*, as cited in James Carman, *The Street Surface Railway Franchises of New York City* (New York: Columbia University Studies in History, Economics and Public Law, 1919), p. 19.

[173] Stokes, *op. cit.*, Vol. 3, p. 531. A 12 and one-half cent fare was also current in Philadelphia during the 1830's. In Boston, as late as 1850, "Those who could not afford to pay twenty cents per day to go back and forth to the environs, necessarily sought accommodations within short distance of their daily fifteen-hour drudgery in the mill or at the wharf." See Frederic W. Speirs, "The Street Railway System of Philadelphia, Its History and Present Conditions." *Johns Hopkins Studies in Historical and Political Science*, Vol. 15 (1897), p. 96; and Handlin, *op. cit.*, p. 91.

[174] Albion, *op. cit.*, p. 302.

212 AMERICAN MERCANTILE CITY

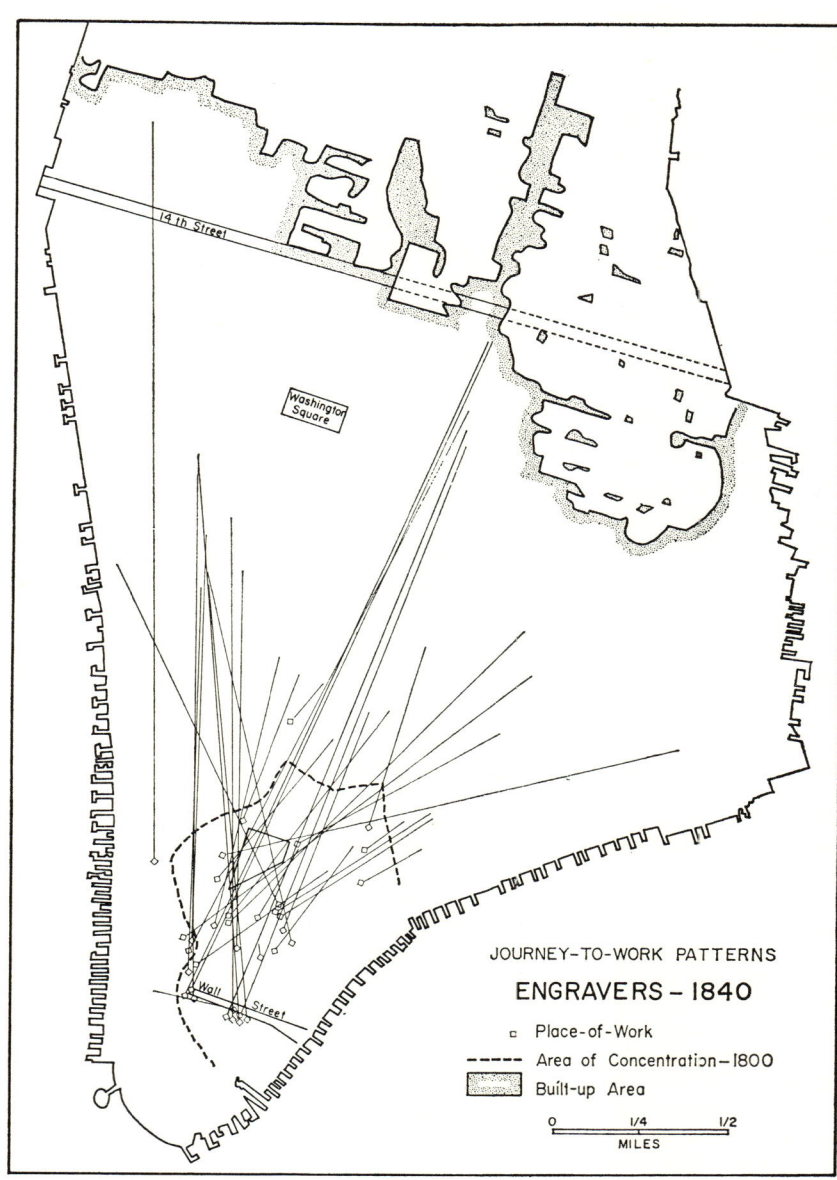

MAP 4.9 Journey-to-work patterns of New York's engravers in 1840.

laborer's earning power,[175] it is clear that a daily allocation of 25 cents for omnibus fares was excessive and beyond the means of much of the working force. With the price of commutation high, it was only the better-paid and prosperous artisans, such as printers and engravers,[176] who could afford a long journey-to-work. In other words, the cost of improved urban transportation diminished its effect on the intraurban location of manufacturing, for firms could not wander beyond the built-up area as long as an inequality existed between the level of omnibus fares and the level of industrial wages.

Conclusions and Reservations

The economy and morphologic structure of the modern multimillion metropolis are the products of profoundly complex evolutionary processes. Comprehension of individual metropolitan units, and of the entire contemporary system of cities, demands more than a model of the interacting spatial processes of urbanization and industrialization for the post-1860 decades. An understanding of the kaleidoscopic growth of urban functions and forms since the Civil War requires an analysis of conditions prior to the 1840's and "the first upsurge in the process of industrialization in the American system."[177] With that objective in mind, this portion of the book has interpreted the character of industrial location and urban size growth in the nascent metropolises of the Eastern Seaboard.

This investigation of the growth and manufacturing of the mercantile city has yielded five themes of substance. First, the scale of individual production units and the aggregate output of manufacturing in New

[175] Wages paid to shipwrights were actually higher than those paid to most other handicraft artisans and workshop hands. In 1840, the average annual income of nonagricultural workers (exclusive of commerce) in New York State was $323. Richard A. Easterlin, "Interregional Differences in Per Capita Income, Population, and Total Income," in *Trends in the American Economy in the Nineteenth Century, op. cit.,* p. 97.

[176] New York printers were generally viewed as "men of property." Lambert, *op. cit.,* p. 79.

[177] Conrad and Meyer, "Income Growth and Structural Change: The United States in the Nineteenth Century," in *op. cit.,* pp. 123–124. As a closing gesture of emphasis regarding the character of the 1800–1840 period, it should be underscored that the share of manufacturing in the total commodity output of the United States was approximately 17 per cent in 1839 (Robert E. Gallman, "Commodity Output, 1839–1899," in *Trends in the American Economy in the Nineteenth Century, op. cit.,* p. 26).

York, Boston, Philadelphia, and Baltimore was obstructed by: factor shortages of capital and labor; the immobility of waterpower and the state of technology; an expensive and inadequate transport network; and an accessible market of restricted proportions. Second, the limited manufacturing functions of the mercantile city were intimately associated with the city's commercial functions. That is, urban industries, almost without exception, either processed import and export commodities that could be distributed through established channels to known markets; or provided printed materials, ships, and other capital goods and services vital to the perpetuation of trade with Europe, coastal points, and the interior hinterland; or catered to the household and construction demands of the local mercantile population and the classes serving that population. Third, with industry in a subordinate position in the urban economy, the size of the mercantile city grew (theoretically) by a circular and cumulative process in which each increment in the wholesaling-trading complex produced a succession of initial multiplier effects, threshold fulfillments (population increases), secondary multipliers (deriving mostly from new endeavors in the construction and manufacturing sectors), and, through the reinvestment of earnings, new increments in the wholesaling-trading complex. Fourth, transport and route developments, differences in relative accessibility, geographical variations in tradition and entrepreneurial behavior, and the accumulation of agglomeration economies led to the growth of some mercantile port cities at the expense of others. Finally, some structural order was manifest in the compact mercantile city, and the intraurban permutations of industrial location were already fettered by the manner in which the stage of transportation affected both the journey-to-work and the journey-to-shop, by the cost of land, and by the need of some firms to realize "communication economies" or to take advantage of interindustry linkages.

The exposition of any one of these themes is subject to a number of criticisms. The factors circumscribing the growth of manufacturing in mercantile cities have not been exhausted, e.g., the competitive advantages of foreign manufactures and related consumer preferences have gone unmentioned; the empirical evidence presented in support of the apparent relationship between mercantile and manufacturing functions is far from definitive; the circular and cumulative size-growth model and the ensuing arguments on selective urban growth are, by virtue of the evidence's thinness, somewhat speculative; and only three intraurban industrial location patterns have been depicted and interpreted in detail. In addition, the effects of Anglo-French hostilities, the impact of the War of 1812, tariff policies, and fluctuations of the national economy (or its regional components)[178] have been either superficially touched upon or totally ignored; and the quite different, but relevant case of New Orleans is given cursory treatment. Irrespective of these and other shortcomings, the 1800–1840 period comprised a formative prelude to the urban-industrial growth of the future, and therefore, to reiterate, the conclusions derived from investigating these forty years are crucial to a comprehension of the broader long-range questions of metropolitan growth and internal metropolitan structure.

[178] An attempt has recently been made to explore statistically the relationships between urbanization rates and early nineteenth-century regional development patterns. See Jeffrey G. Williamson, "Antebellum Urbanization in the American Northeast," *Journal of Economic History,* Vol. 25 (1965), pp. 592–608.

Index

Abramovitz, Moses, 86
Adaptive locational behavior, *see* Entrepreneurial behavior
Addis Ababa, Ethiopia, 128
Adoptive locational behavior, *see* Entrepreneurial behavior
Agglomeration economies, 13, 14, 16, 43–45, 59–71, 78, 100, 164, 195–196, 214
Agricultural implement and machinery industry, 18, 63, 65, 68, 70
Agricultural location theory, 5
Albany, N.Y., 24, 46, 59, 74, 110, 111–112, 115, 118, 125, 163
Albion, Robert Greenhalgh, 1, 148–151, 158, 165, 193, 197, 200, 201, 211
Alchian, Armen A., 45, 102
Alexander, John A., 30
Alexandersson, Gunnar, 30
Allaire Works, 159
Alleghenies, 147, 151
Anderson, H. Dewey, 21
Andreano, Ralph, 18
Andrews, Israel D., 163, 191
Andrews, Richard B., 30
Appalachians, 74
Appleton, Nathan, 172
Arnold, John P., 66
Artle, Roland, 30, 31
Atkinson, Edward, 49, 50
Aurousseau, M., 30

Baking, in New York City, 205–207
Baldwin Locomotive Works, 176
Baltimore, Md., 9, 74, 80, 110, 111, 116, 124, 125–127, 134, 143 ff.

Baltimore and Ohio Railroad, 153, 165, 191
Barger, Harold, 50
Beckmann, Martin J., 35
Belcher, Wyatt Winton, 55, 78
Berkeley, Calif., 57
Berry, Brian J. L., 4, 24
Berry, Thomas Senior, 147, 154, 155, 163
Bicycle industry, 40, 95
Birmingham, Ala., 123
Bishop, J. Leander, 160, 169, 198, 207
Blackstone Canal, 164
Boalt, Gunnar, 128, 129
Boot and shoe industry, 36, 95, 158, 159, 170, 207
Boston, Mass., 9, 13, 18, 74, 80, 111, 116, 143 ff.
Boston and Albany Railroad, 49
Braibanti, Ralph, 97
Brass foundries, 95, 201
Breckenbridge, R. M., 80
Brewing industry, *see* Malt liquors industry
Bridenbaugh, Carl, 2
British Iron and Steel Institute, 127
Brockton, Mass., 36
Brooklyn, N.Y., 58, 74, 186, 208
Brozen, Yale, 102, 120, 135
Bücher, Karl, 184
Buffalo, N.Y., 23, 163, 164
Burchard, John, 2, 14, 100, 158
Burns, Arthur F., 53
Business cycle(s), 38, 82, 134, 137

Cadillac Automobile Company, 40
Calef, Wesley, 181

217

California, 73, 74
Callender, G. S., 156
Canals, 59, 153, 163, 164, 186, 191, 194
Capital, availability of, 80–81, 90–91, 102, 103, 121, 122, 135, 141, 152–157, 158, 214
  foreign, 181
  industrial, 76
Carman, James, 211
Carol, Hans, 26
Carter, C. F., 100
Carter, H., 14
Catskill Mountains, 169
Central place theory, 4, 5, 14, 15, 205
Chaloner, W. H., 81
Chandler, Alfred D., 91
Charleston, S.C., 46, 49, 110, 111, 115, 116, 118, 120, 124, 125, 186, 193, 195
Charlestown, Mass., 174
Chesapeake Bay, 193
Chicago, Ill., 24, 27, 54–55, 57, 63, 65, 66, 70, 74, 78, 79, 80, 115
Chinitz, Benjamin, 13
Christaller, Walter, 14, 34
Cincinnati, Ohio, 24, 58, 147, 154, 155, 189
Circular and cumulative causation, models of; processes of; *see* Urban-size growth and urban growth processes
Civil War, 7, 18, 120
Clark, Colin, 21
Clark, Victor S., 16, 18, 19, 66, 67, 95, 144, 145, 152, 156, 157, 162, 164, 169
Cleveland, Ohio, 47, 63, 66, 74, 80, 91, 115, 191
Clothing and apparel industry, 18, 115, 159, 170–172
Coastal trade, 147–148, 150, 178, 182, 190–191
Cochran, Thomas C., 18, 105
Cole, Arthur H., 105
Columbia, Pa., 164
Commerce, 18, 19, 24, 146–147, 168, 178, 179, 182, 183
  see also Foreign trade, Wholesaling
Communication, interpersonal, *see* Information, circulation of

Connecticut, 10
Connecticut River Valley, 10, 165
Conrad, Alfred H., 61, 81, 195, 213
Construction, 27, 150, 154, 155, 175, 180, 190, 214
Coopery, 151, 173, 175, 208
Cootner, Paul H., 22, 29
Corporations, growth of, 76–77, 156
Cotton trade, 150, 172, 182, 194
Critical isodapane(s), 50, 67, 73
Cullom, Shelby M., 49, 53, 78
Czamanski, Stanislaw, 6

Dacey, Michael F., 34, 46, 99
Dahmen, Erik, 93
Danhof, Clarence H., 101, 122
Davidson, Percy E., 21
Davidson, S., 157
Davis, Lance E., 80, 122
Dean, William Henry, Jr., 53, 58, 164, 186, 190, 193
DeBow, James, 121
Delaware River, 193
Demerath, Nicholas J., 121
Denver, Colo., 25, 118
Depew, Chauncey M., 203
Des Moines, Iowa, 61, 67
Detroit, Mich., 40, 46, 47, 57, 61, 63, 74, 80, 111, 113, 115, 131, 164
Dickenson, Robert E., 3
Diseconomies, 26, 43, 55, 56, 71, 72, 136, 138, 163, 164, 202
Distilling, 172
Dix, John Adams, 146, 154, 168
Djakarta, Java, 128
Dodd, Stuart Carter, 117, 128, 129
Duesenberry, James S., 81, 97
Duncan, Otis Dudley, 35, 72
Dupriez, Leon H., 93, 103
Durkheim, Emile, 117

Eagle Works, 160
Easterbrook, W. T., 99
Easterlin, Richard A., 42, 50, 213
Easton, Pa., 162
East River, 197, 200, 201, 202
Economic base, 30–31, 181
Economic growth, 6, 13, 22, 26, 86, 87, 97, 144
Eldridge, Hope T., 38

Electrical machinery industry, 37, 77, 95
Electric light bulb industry, 88
Electric traction, 8, 55–57, 131
Elgie, Robert, 11
Emeryville, Calif., 57
Emigration, see Migration
Entrepreneurial behavior, 33, 45–46, 50, 67, 77, 79, 80, 81, 90–91, 98–101, 103, 105, 112, 122, 123, 135, 194, 214
Erickson, Charlotte, 38, 79, 132, 133
Erie Canal, 112, 150, 164, 165, 166, 172, 191, 194
Ernst, Robert, 200, 208
Evans, George Heberton, Jr., 122
Exports, see Foreign trade
External economies, see Agglomeration economies

Fabricant, Solomon, 59, 66
Factor immobility, 83
Fall River, Mass., 147
Fellner, William, 110
Fels, Rendigs, 87, 119
Fishlow, Albert, 22, 52, 148, 183
Fleisher, Aaron, 43
Fleming, Marcus, 104
Fletcher, Henry J., 61, 78
Florida, 174, 186
Flour milling, 172
Fogel, Robert W., 22
Foreign trade, 146–150, 153, 168, 178, 181, 182, 183
France, 19, 127
Freedley, Edwin T., 152, 176, 177
Freight rates, 44, 49, 51, 52, 53, 62, 77–78, 163–164, 191
 see also Canals; Railroads
Frickey, Edwin, 17, 18
Friedmann, John R. P., 13
Friedrich, Carl J., 6, 34
Fuchs, Victor R., 22

Gallatin, Albert, 143, 152
Gallman, Robert E., 16, 20, 21, 42, 60, 213
Garrison, William L., 24
General Electric Company, 77
Georgia, 174
Germany, 19, 127

Gerschenkron, Alexander, 14
Gestalt psychology, 91
Gilfillan, S. C., 88, 90, 91, 96, 108, 118
Ginsburg, Norton, 44
Glaab, Charles N., 2
Glasgow, Scotland, 154
Goodrich, Carter, 157
Gottmann, Jean, 146
Gould, Peter, 10, 58, 166, 186, 189, 190, 191
Grand Rapids, Mich., 61
Gras, N. S. B., 184
Great Britain, 19, 154, 157
Great Lakes, 183
Great Plains, 74
Green, Constance M., 2, 153
Guernsey, R. S., 205
Gunawardena, K. A., 33

Habakkuk, H. J., 103, 104, 127, 133, 134, 149, 157, 159
Hagen, Everett E., 51, 86, 105, 117, 118, 132, 145
Hägerstrand, Torsten, 5, 28, 39, 117, 128, 129, 135, 137, 139, 140, 141
Haggett, Peter, 33
Haig, Robert Murray, 30
Hale, Nathan, 177
Hall, Henry, 200
Handlin, Oscar, 1, 2, 14, 100, 147, 154, 158, 159, 207, 211
Hardy, Rollo, 10
Harper Brothers, 159
Harrington, Virginia D., 153, 168
Harris, Chauncy D., 72
Hart, John F., 39
Hauser, Philip M., 2
Hawley, Amos H., 57
Henderson, W. O., 81
Hendrick, Burton J., 127
Hirschman, Albert O., 14, 15, 26, 33, 104
Hoboken, N.J., 208
Hodgen, Margaret T., 105
Hoe, R. H., & Co., Inc., 203
Hoffman, W. G., 81
Hollidaysburg, Pa., 164
Holmes, Isaac, 146, 154, 155, 179
Hoover, Edgar M., 33, 36, 40, 203
Hoselitz, Bert F., 6, 96

Hoyt, Homer, 1, 55
Hudson River, 59, 130, 165, 193, 202
Hutchins, John G. B., 174

Imperfect knowledge, 5
Imports, *see* Foreign trade
Indiana, 57
Industrial location theory, 5, 6
Industries, *see* Manufacturing
Information, circulation of, 8, 28, 37, 40, 87, 92, 96, 99, 127–131, 132, 134, 137, 172
Initial advantage(s), 15, 16, 25, 37, 49, 52, 53, 59, 73, 78, 81, 83, 140, 145
Innovation(s), industrial, 8, 9, 28, 29, 37–41, 60, 61, 62, 86 ff., 179, 183, 202
  consumer tastes and, 127
  definition of, 89
  diffusion of, 8, 11, 28, 87–88, 89, 127, 132, 134–141
  growth rate of cities and, 117
  imitative behavior and, 101–102, 116, 117, 129
  location of in United States, 105 ff.
  size of cities and, 116–117, 129
  societal conditions and, 104–105, 119–120 ff.
  supply and demand conditions affecting, 102–104, 116, 140
  urban concentration of, 98–105
Interstate Commerce Commission, 77
Invention(s), industrial, 8, 9, 28, 37–41, 61, 86 ff., 152, 160, 179, 183, 202
  definition of, 88
  growth rate of cities and, 117
  location of in United States, 105 ff.
  per 10,000 capita rate of 109, 111 ff.
  problem awareness and, 91–92 ff., 119, 125, 132, 135, 139
  size of cities and, 112–116, 129
  societal conditions and, 96–98, 119–120 ff.
  solution awareness and, 94 ff.
  supply and demand conditions affecting, 90–91, 93, 112
  urban concentration of, 90–98, 111
Iowa, 54, 63

Iron and steel industry, 17, 44, 54, 63, 66–67, 69, 70, 94, 132, 140, 152
Irrational behavior, 5, 45, 76, 101, 136
  see also Entrepreneurial behavior
Isard, Walter, 6, 13, 26, 27, 30, 31, 61, 71, 83, 99, 100, 139, 184

Jackson, P. T., 172
James River, 193
Janson, Carl-Gunnar, 128, 129
Jefferson, Mark, 90
Jenks, Leland H., 22, 52, 105
Jerome, Harry, 38, 39
Jersey City, N.J., 208
Jewkes, John, 88, 107
Johnstown, Pa., 164
Jones, Chester Lloyd, 165
Jones, Fred Mitchell, 149
Journey-to-shop, 205
Journey-to-work, 56, 131
  in New York City, 207–213

Kain, John F., 6
Kahn, Richard F., 30
Kanawha River, 193
Kansas, 34
Kansas City, Mo., 25
Kansky, K. J., 72
Kant, Edgar, 58
Katz, Elihu, 96
Kaufman, Harold F., 121
Kensington, Pa., 161, 196
Keynes, John M., 30
King, Leslie J., 24
Kirkland, Edward Chase, 19, 27, 61
Knowles, L. C. A., 19
Kurtz, Paul, 10
Kuznets, Simon, 10, 11, 41, 42, 51, 88

Labor availability, 78–79, 144, 157–158, 214
Labor productivity, 19–20, 21, 104
Lake Erie, 191
Lambert, John, 200, 213
Lampard, Eric E., 2, 3, 12, 13, 14, 32, 41, 44
Land values, 55, 154, 155, 200, 203
Lebergott, Stanley, 42, 182
Lee, Everett S., 43
Lehigh Canal, 165
Lehigh Valley, 162

Leland, Faulconer and Norton Company, 40
Leven, Charles L., 30, 31
Liepmann, Kate K., 207
Linkages, 9, 26, 29, 31, 43, 61, 93, 103–104, 116, 118, 168, 197, 200–203, 214
Lippincott, Isaac, 59
Liverpool, England, 150, 154
Livingood, James Weston, 153, 163
Location theory, economic, 3, 4, 5, 6
Location theory, geographic, 3, 4, 7, 11
London, England, 128
Long, Clarence D., 20, 21, 42, 82
Los Angeles, Calif., 13, 23, 24, 31, 74, 78, 111, 113, 115
Lösch, August, 5, 14, 34, 43, 76, 184, 189
Louisiana, 165
Louisville, Ky., 24, 58, 111, 115, 116, 118, 124, 125, 191
Lövgren, Esse, 39
Lowell, Francis C., 172
Lowell, Mass., 147

Machinery and foundry product industry, 54, 160, 176
Machine tool industry, 40, 91, 116, 133, 144
McCormick, Cyrus, 54
McCormick Manufacturing Company, 65
McKelvey, Blake, 2, 19, 21, 76
McKenzie, R. D., 12, 21
McLane, Louis, 151, 156, 158, 159, 161, 163, 170, 172, 175
McLaughlin, Glenn E., 21
Maclaurin, W. Rupert, 89
McPherson, Logan, 77
Madden, Carl H., 48
Maine, 150, 174, 186, 191
Maizels, Alfred, 35
Malt liquors industry, 36–37, 39, 63, 65–66, 68, 70
Manchester, N.H., 36
Mandelbaum, Seymour J., 3, 130
Manhattan, *see* New York City
Mansfield, Edward, 102, 118, 135
Manufacturing, 18–19, 25, 26, 30, 31, 33, 43–44, 51, 53, 61, 78, 81, 90, 113–117, 118–119, 121, 141, 144 ff.
  commerce-serving, 173–175, 179, 214
  concentration of, 12, 13, 26, 59, 60–61, 63, 91, 100, 103, 139–140, 143, 158, 160–161
  employment, 19–20, 21, 24, 34, 54, 59, 62–63, 73, 113, 114, 115, 118, 132, 170
  entrepôt, 112, 168–173, 179, 180, 214
  "footloose," 40, 46, 60, 63, 138–140
  intraurban location of, 9, 56, 130–131, 145, 196–213
  "market-oriented," 14, 32, 35, 37, 44, 65, 73, 113, 136–138, 175–176, 179
  in mercantile city, 144 ff.
  output, 16, 19, 22, 59
  "raw-material oriented," 37, 60, 138, 140–141
  specialization, 14, 41, 52, 53, 74, 103, 118, 160
  wages, 42–43, 82, 125, 126, 157, 182, 211–213
Manufacturing Belt, 77
Marble, Duane F., 128
Marburg, Theodore F., 150
March, James G., 98, 99, 102
Maritime Provinces, 147, 191, 194
Market accessibility, 34–35, 44, 72–76, 166–167, 183, 190, 193, 214
Market area(s), 14, 29, 31, 32, 40, 50 ff., 60, 67, 71, 76, 78, 82, 126, 138, 163, 164, 166, 195
  competition, 25, 46, 118–119, 166, 177, 186, 189
  hierarchy of, 15, 34, 35
Market potential, *see* Market accessibility
Markham, Jesse W., 100
Marshall, Alfred, 13, 86
Mars Works, 160
Marx, Karl, 86
Massachusetts, 42, 61, 153
Massell, Benton, 86
Mayer, Harold M., 3
Medford, Mass., 173
Mease, James, 151, 159, 160
Megalopolis, 35
Meier, Richard L., 3, 28, 41, 100, 128
Memphis, Tenn., 123

INDEX

Mercantile city(ies), 24, 59, 113, 143 ff.
  economic functions of, 146–152
  internal structure of, 196–197
  manufacturing in, 144 ff.
Mergers, *see* Corporations, growth of
Merrimac Valley, 147
Merton, Robert K., 109
Meyer, John R., 61, 81, 195, 213
Miami, Fla., 12
Michigan, 53, 115
Migration, 33–39, 79, 104, 121, 127, 131–134, 144, 157, 158, 179
Mikesell, Marvin W., 135
Mill, John Stuart, 86
Miller, Ann Ratner, 42, 50
Milwaukee, Wis., 23
Mining machinery and equipment industry, 115
Mississippi, 165
Mississippi River, 74, 127, 147, 156
Mitchell, Harry A., 149, 165
Mobile, Ala., 49, 111, 113, 115, 116, 118, 120, 124, 125
Moes, John E., 195
Mohawk Valley, 59
Morrill, Richard L., 5, 14, 39, 58, 166, 186, 189, 190, 191
Morrison, John H., 200
Morrissett, Irving, 34
Moyamensing, Pa., 196
Multiplier effect(s), 25, 26, 27, 28, 29–32, 41, 44, 51, 54, 61, 78, 81, 82, 83, 89, 111, 118, 119, 126, 134, 149, 179–183, 190, 194, 214
Murphey, Rhoads, 96
Myrdal, Gunnar, 15, 26

National Road, 165
Nebraska, 54
Neidercorn, John H., 6
Nelson, Ralph L., 49, 50
Nelson, Richard L., 135
Neu, Irene D., 19, 22
New Bern, N.C., 193
New England, 10, 172
New Hampshire, 61
New Haven, Conn., 35, 46, 47
New Jersey, 111, 130, 191
New London, Conn., 186
New Orleans, La., 23, 36, 58, 111, 113, 115, 116, 118, 120, 124, 146, 147, 149, 150, 156, 162, 164, 165, 182, 215
New York and Harlem Railroad, 208, 211
New York Central and Hudson River Railroad, 49
New York City, 9, 10, 11, 18, 38, 42, 52, 59, 66, 70, 74, 80, 91, 95, 111, 115, 126, 128, 130, 143 ff.
Norborg, Knut, 4
Norfolk, Va., 186, 193, 195
Norris Locomotive Works, 176
North, Douglass C., 30, 183, 195
Northern Liberties, Pa., 196
Nystuen, John D., 128

Oakland, Calif., 57, 74
Ohio Canal, 191
Ocracoke Bar, 193
Ohlin, Bertil, 15, 83, 190
Olsson, Gunnar, 28, 38, 39, 73, 128, 135
Omaha, Neb., 25, 118
Opie, Redvers, 15
Osofsky, Gilbert, 2

Panschar, William G., 205, 207
Parsons, Talcott, 96
Passer, Harold C., 44, 56, 77, 82, 91, 95
Patapsco Falls, 161
Patent statistics, U.S., 8, 11, 37, 87, 106–109 ff.
  see also Invention(s), industrial
Paterson, N.J., 153, 161, 172, 201
Pemberton, H. Earl, 129
Penman, Frank, 66
Perloff, Harvey S., 10, 15, 30, 34, 78
Persson, Åke, 73
Pfouts, Ralph W., 31, 32
Philadelphia, Pa., 9, 18, 24, 74, 80, 91, 115, 126, 143 ff.
Phillips, Ulrich Bonnell, 193, 194
Piedmont, 193
Pitkin, Timothy, 143
Pittsburgh, Pa., 24, 39, 46–47, 58, 66–67, 70, 94, 162, 163, 164
Population increase, natural, 41–42
Portland, Me., 74, 80
Portsmouth, Ohio, 191

P_1P_2/D (interaction hypothesis), 137, 190
Pratt, Edward Ewing, 203
Pred, Allan, 4, 5, 6, 39, 50, 51, 71, 117, 139, 166, 190, 207
Printing and publishing, 173–175
  in New York City, 202–205
Private-information field(s), 128–130, 132
Providence, R.I., 80

Railroad equipment industry, 93, 95, 176
Railroads, 22, 49–55, 58, 72, 77–78, 112, 144, 153, 162, 163, 183, 191–192, 194
  see also Freight rates
Rapoport, Anatol, 129
Rashevsky, N., 102, 130
Ratajczak, Donald, 2, 13, 24, 30, 51, 58, 142, 184, 185, 189, 190
Ratzel, Friedrich, 117
Ravenstein, Ernest G., 137
Real estate speculation, 154, 155, 180, 190
Redfield, Robert, 96
Redlich, Fritz, 137
Rees, Albert, 42
Reizenstein, Milton, 191
Relative accessibility, *see* Market accessibility
Richmond, Calif., 57
Richmond, Va., 46
Riley, Elmer A., 54
Ritschl, Hans, 184
Rochester, N.Y., 189
Rodgers, Allan, 34, 35, 67
Rogers, Everett M., 28, 101, 120
Roscher, Wilhelm, 184
Rosenberg, Nathan, 40, 91, 93, 94, 95, 116
Ross, Edward A., 140
Rostow, W. W., 19, 145
Roterus, Victor, 181
Roth, Lawrence V., 58
Roxborough, Pa., 161
Rubin, Julius, 156, 164, 194
Rural-to-urban migration, *see* Migration

Sacramento, Calif., 74

Sacramento Valley, 73
St. Louis, Mo., 39, 58, 63, 74, 78, 80, 110, 111, 127, 147, 164
Salsbury, Stephen, 18
Salter, W. E. G., 88
Sanders, Barkev S., 109
San Diego, Calif., 51, 142
San Francisco, Calif., 47, 51, 52, 57, 73, 74, 78, 80, 113, 115, 124, 128
San Joaquin Valley, 73
San Leandro, Calif., 57
Santee Canal, 193
Savannah, Ga., 195
Sawers, David, 88, 107
Scale economies, 13, 50, 51, 52, 59, 61, 82, 100, 118, 125, 139, 163, 197
Schäffle, Albert, 184
Scharf, Thomas, 160
Schlesinger, Arthur Meier, 2
Schmoller, Gustav, 184
Schmookler, Jacob, 86, 91, 92, 93, 110
Schnore, Leo F., 2, 4, 7
Schumpeter, Joseph A., 15, 28, 86, 87, 89, 94, 103, 119, 120, 142, 145
Schuylkill Navigation, 165
Schuylkill River, 161
Scoville, Warren C., 95, 132
Secor, Theodosius F., & Co., 201
Segal, Martin, 79
Semple, Ellen Churchill, 193
Sewing machine, 95, 115
Shaler, Nathaniel Southgate, 49
Sheldon, G. W., 208
Shipbuilding, 173–174
  in New York City, 197–202, 208
Shubik, Martin, 98
Simmel, Georg, 129
Simon, Herbert A., 98, 99, 102
Singer, Milton, 96
Site and situation, 58, 192–193
Slaughtering and meat packing, 54
Smelser, Neil J., 33, 96
Smith, Adam, 86, 116
Smith, D. M., 5
Smith, J. Calvin, 199
Smolensky, Eugene, 2, 13, 24, 30, 51, 58, 142, 184, 185, 189, 190
Solow, Robert, 86
South Chicago, Ill., 57
Southern cities, class structure in, 120–121, 124

Southwark, Pa., 196
Southwark Foundry, 176
Sparks, Jared, 151, 160, 172
Spatial processes, 5, 6, 7, 12, 15, 141
Speirs, Frederic W., 211
Spengler, Joseph J., 97
Sprague, Frank J., 56
Springfield-Holyoke, Mass., 35
Spring Gardens, Pa., 161, 196
Stage of transportation, 6, 197, 201, 205, 207
Staten Island, N.Y., 208
Steam engines, 144, 160, 161–163, 169, 201, 202
Steam power, *see* Steam engines
Steiner, Robert L., 32
Stewart, John Q., 72, 75, 167
Stigler, George J., 21, 22, 44
Still, Bayrd, 197
Stillman, Richard, 88, 107
Stokes, I. N. Phelps, 197, 208, 211
Stolper, Wolfgang, 13, 37, 43
Strassmann, W. Paul, 94, 98, 102, 104
Sugar refining industry, 168–169, 208
Supply areas, 52–53, 195
Supreme Court, U.S., 109
Susquehanna River, 156, 163
Sutherland, Alister, 89
Sweden, 73

Taafe, Edward J., 58, 166, 186, 189, 190, 191
Tanning, 168–169, 202
Taussig, Frank W., 86, 152
Taylor, George Rogers, 19, 22
Taylor, Graham Romeyn, 57
"Technological convergence," 94–96, 102, 112, 113, 117, 119, 134
"Technological disequilibrium," 93–94, 102, 103, 104, 112, 116, 117, 119, 134, 139
Technological progress, *see* Innovation(s), industrial; Invention(s) industrial
Tehran, Iran, 128
Terminal and transshipment costs, 53, 58, 164, 168
Tertiary activities, 22, 27, 32, 33, 81, 82, 83
Tertiary sector, *see* Tertiary activities

Textile industries, 16, 115, 143, 144, 152, 153, 161, 172, 173
Thomas, Brinley, 38
Thomas, Dorothy Swaine, 38, 39
Thomas, William L., Jr., 190
Thompson, Wilbur R., 15, 83, 90, 131, 181, 185
Thorp, William L., 44, 49, 63
Thresholds, 14, 16, 26 ff., 116, 117, 136, 137, 138, 167, 179, 180, 183, 194, 205, 214
Thrupp, Sylvia L., 97
Tiebout, Charles M., 30, 31, 45
Tobacco processing, 169
Törnqvist, Gunnar, 74
Transportation improvements, 29, 72, 166, 186 ff., 214
 see also Canals; Electric traction; Railroads
Transport costs, *see* Freight rates
Trenton, N.J., 35
Troy, N.Y., 46
Tsuru, Shigeto, 43
Tucker, George, 192
Tung, Tze Hsiung, 99, 100, 139
Turnpikes, 153, 163–164, 191

Ullman, Edward L., 15, 34, 77, 190
Uncertainty, 89, 98–100, 103, 116, 117, 139, 140, 194
 see also Entrepreneurial behavior
Urban geography, 3, 4
Urban growth processes, *see* Urban-size growth
Urban hierarchy, 33–37, 46–48, 60–61, 66, 73, 74, 111, 115, 119, 136, 137, 138, 141, 186
Urban-size growth and urban growth processes, 3, 7, 8, 9, 14, 16, 19, 27, 29, 32, 43, 46, 48, 57, 58, 66, 78, 83–85, 116, 128, 142, 145, 184, 193
 model of, 21, 24–29, 37, 40, 41, 49, 81, 87, 89, 118, 127, 130, 177–185, 214
 selective, 46 ff., 145, 177, 186–196
Usher, Abbot Payson, 8, 91–93, 128
U.S. Treasury Department, 155

Vance, James E., Jr., 5, 56, 57, 197, 207

Vance, Rupert B., 121
Vernon, Raymond, 44, 203
Vining, Rutledge, 32

Wade, Richard C., 2, 120, 147
Wagner, Philip L., 135
Waltham, Mass., 161
War of 1812, 150, 153, 173, 182, 215
Ward, David, 56
Ward, Stillman, & Co. Novelty Works, 201
Warner, Sam B., Jr., 3, 56, 134, 158
Warntz, William, 75, 167
Washington, D. C., 12, 36
Water power, 161, 162, 163, 172, 214
Weber, Adna Ferrin, 1, 42, 61, 78, 169, 202
Weber, Alfred, 6, 13, 33, 34, 44, 50, 60, 72, 126, 163
Weber, Max, 129
Westcott, Thompson, 160
West Indies, 165
Westinghouse Electric Corporation, 77, 82

Westinghouse, George, 95
Wheeling, W.Va., 162
Wholesaling, 18, 26, 55, 148 ff., 172 ff.
Wilkinson, Thomas O., 12
Williams, B. R., 100
Williamson, Harold F., 153
Williamson, Jeffrey G., 2, 215
Wilson, L. S., 57
Wirth, Louis, 129
Woglom, William H., 43
Wolpert, Julian, 45, 99
Woodbury, Levi, 161, 162, 208
Worcester, Mass., 164
World War I, 7, 21, 43, 59
Wright, John S., and Company, 65
Wrigley, E. A., 26

York, Pa., 35
Young, Allyn, 41
Youngstown, Ohio, 61
Yuill, Robert S., 138

Zipf, George Kingsley, 79, 128, 137

HC
105
P9

DATE DUE	
OCT 2 2 1979	APR 2 6 2006
	MP 728